curse + berate in 69+ languages

ISBN-13: 978-1-933368-86-3

Cataloging-in-Publication Data available from the Library of Congress

Cover design by Renee Zmuda
Interior design by T. Warburton y Bajo & R. V. Branham
Printed in the United States of America

Soft Skull Press
New York, NY

softskull.com

curse + berate in 69+ languages

r. v. branham — editorial wrangler-in-chief

channing dodson — asst. editor + gaelicist + kanji wrangler

sarah barrett — italian consultant + cyrillicist

liz swados — cartoons
graham willoughby — illustrations

renee zmuda — cover design
samuel ward — tech support

gobshite quarterly interns + volunteers

who worked directly + indirectly on this enterprise:
heather akin + l. c. bobalova + melissa bobotek + lindsey boldt + alex cacciari + sabrina canfield + b.c. + johanna droubay + emma dupine + marisa feinstein + kevin friedman + ann haroun + rachel hart + kea krausse + david lansdowne + jeannette lehn + jeremy loomis-norris + jaden lowrey + julia mccallum + kerry meade + richard melo + toshi misu + mark nowak + kris penthel + mike rinaldo + kumar sichel + nora simmons + kerry skemp + paul smith + cecily swanson + steve tune + brian zierdt

additional illustrations credited

being a concise + cunting compendium + verbal pictionary + day-for-night-book + of salaams + salutations + greetings + schadenfreude + unblessings + invective + invidious comparisons + insults + sarcasms + snits + pouts + shit-fits + unkind words + anti-benedictions + obscenities, delicate + indelicate + blasphemies + verbal agggressssions + cris-de-coeur + merde-de-jour + esprit de l'escalier + sinister wisdoms + tantrums + thought-crimes + bigotries + dutch courage + tijuana bibles + german sense of humor + aneurysms-for-brunch + other cunt-offs + fucka-youze-allzes + sit-next-to-mezes in approx. 90 languages — give or take a dialectic or uncivil war ...

curse + berate in 69+ languages

Humani nihil alienum.
Nothing human is alien to me.
— Terrence (185 BC — 159 BC)

boom, Ka-,
— atrributed to John Lydon
& Afrika Bambaataa

Soft Skull Press
Brooklyn, NY
2008

this
one's
for

Andrea
&
Albert
&
Margaret
&
Jacqueline
&
Bob
&
Estelle

INTRODUCTION introduksie LAQ'DÎM patckerana'l AURKEZPEN ПРАДСТАУЛЕННЕ үанрмùn INTRODUCCIÓ upoznavanje PŘEDSTAVENÍ indføreelse INLEIDING sisse-juhatus MOARREFI esittely INTRODUCTION réamhrá ROIMH-RÀDH einleitung ΕΙΣΑΓΩΓΗ GABATARWA hakdam ĀBHĀS KATHĀ inngangur INTRODUZIONE 序文 noaum s'koa'ul SO-GAE præfatio IESNIEGŠANA pratarmė ПРЕДГОВОР pendahuluan INTODUZZJONI 引言 SŪCĪ tlaaquilitzl TLHAGIŠO innføring PREFÁCIO riqsichiy PREFAȚĂ ПРЕДИСЛОВИЕ *ПРЕДГОВОР* HORDHAC intro-ducción INTRODUKTION pauna UPAK KIRAMAN boht nahm AVATĀRIKA önsöz ПЕРЕДМОВА ĀBHĀS KATHĀ *МУКДДИМА* TIÊN-DÃN rhagymadrodd ÌFIHÀN isanduleliso *

r. v. branham

A guaranteed winner for bar bets is to ask someone if they know the opening line to "Last Tango in Paris" — & then ask them if they know what Nimrod's last words most probably were; then tell them that the opening line & last words are one & the same.

The movie's opening line and the probable last words of Nimrod are also a useful nuclear option to invoke when asked to give a Thanksgiving Prayer. [2] (In this volume you will find Nimrod, architect of the Tower of Babel, under WANKER.)

Three more bar bet questions: What insult has the most time zones, & what is the language of this insult? [3] (As a bonus, from what language did this loanword originate?) And what is the most common insult south of the Kush, in south Asia? [4] What was Vladimir Illyich Lenin's favorite word? [5]

A well-known travel writer wrote not long ago that the Finns have no swear words. Entries in this volume attest to the various ways that the Finns would beg to differ. Indeed, in the years since 1984, when a friend, Terry Boren, first planted the seed for this project, I have had enlightening conversations with the occasional French Canadian, ex-Peace Corps volunteer, or Iranian ex-pat wherein I was told that there were no swear words in French, Swahili, or in Farsi. "Merde," I replied, & then said something else ending in "con." And when an Iranian bookseller told me no Persian or Iranian ever swore I marveled how amazing it must be to stand in a meadow with your head so far up in the clouds, communing with the cosmos & advising God, that you could just ignore all the cow shit oozing between your toes.

Now the dials on the way-back machine spin further back, to an aggie town on the border between California & Baja California, where the sun spent the winter, & spring, summer, fall & winter. This was during the Korean & Vietnam wars, & as a reflection of the time our town had the highest per capita heroin overdose rate in the country.

On the plus side everyone had air conditioning, & you could cross the border for cheap Chinese food or pick any number of air conditioned movie palaces, where the movies, whether American, French, or Italian, were (mostly) dubbed into Spanish — *there was only one movie palace on the California side, & it had bilingual bingo every Friday night, no doubt in accordance with the Treaty of Guadalupe-Hidalgo.* (Still, it was unfair that the Mexican movies weren't dubbed into English, or Yiddish.) And this being California, the town was filled with children of the European and Asian W.W.-II diasporas. Spanish, or its proto-Spanglish dialects, tended to be the lingua franca. The various expat languages were ancilliary, English among them.

There were smatterings of Hungarian, Dutch, Yiddish, Hindi, German, Italian, French, Russian, Catalan, and Cantonese. Everybody knew a few profanities from their mother country. (Stronzo, merde, schtupp, yoni, lingam, kunti.)

Then there were summers with Aunt Barbara, who decided to teach me Russian and Greek. But who insisted that we begin with writing and reading lessons, not with anything conversational. I thought this perverse, and so it was a daily struggle with tears on both sides before noon. The odd thing is that the Russian Cyrillic has returned, a bit, allowing this project to continue even as a steady parade of Russian-speaking interns departed. (With the notable exception of Sarah Barrett, who during this last spring and summer helped us get our Cyrillic house in order, as well as providing us with current Italian expressions.)

when I first climbed through the library stacks at USC and UCLA in 1985 seeking anything on what the journal *Maledicta* called "Verbal Agression," & when I bought pitchers of beer for the staff at Greek restaurants or for polyglottal aerospace engineers or getting my friend Margaret to shake some smatterings of Nahuatl from her noggin', little did I know that twenty years later I would be translating Croatian poets into Spanish, & typesetting Bosnian, Croatian, Czech, Danish, French, Greek, Hungarian, Indonesian, Polish, Slovenian, & Spanish essays, poems & fiction. (Arabic, Japanese, & Bengali go to people who know those alphabets & who can typeset them in In-Design-compatible fonts.)

Why do people swear? This is asked by Puritans, prudes, & hall monitors. One would more reasonably ask why people don't swear more often. Mencken said that people are at their most interesting when they are at their worst, & Dorothy Parker asked of those with nothing nice to say that they sit next to her. That cheeky bastard Jesus tried to have it both ways. First he said love your enemies & turn the other cheek; then he was a sword to cleave father from son. And let's not even bring up Gautauma. It has take the intercession of Sta. Sofia & Quan Yin & La Virgen de Guadalupe to make good on religion's campaign promises of compassion & mercy. And don't even think of going into a bar in Eastern Europe or Latin America & saying something about the Virgin de Guadalupe or Sta. Sofia. Jesus you can probably get away with, but show one iota of disrespect to Sta. Sofia or La Virgen & you will get your ass/arse handed back to you or your executors or assigns.

There are many functions of language. One is to deny or combat reality, & another is to describe it with love or hate or some admixture of the two. Steven Pinker has made some tart & useful observations about language & evolutionary biology in relationship to swearing. And, from the late lamented *Maledicta* to such websites as Alt Language & Insultmonger, there are incubators where golems are being created to speak truth to bullshit.

Even though the language police are returning, their task is ever more evidently absurd, hypocritical & self-defeating. There is no pure language. English itself came to be from Anglo-Saxon invasions, French invasions, Viking invasions, Danish settlements, Shakespeare neologizing from Latin, & more recently from the cornershop with its tandoori take-out & bhangra soundtracks. Spanish, like French, is evolved from Latin, but also had to contend with 800 years of Moorish occupation. And those countries which faced the spectre of modernization through arranged marriage like Russia & Japan & Turkey in the 17th, 18th & 19th centuries, respectively, had to borrow the vocabularies they did not have to describe these new things they here-to-for had not seen. And a Creole language like Tagalog is vibrantly alive & cooking.

Attempts to police language or set it up in a citadel are doomed. On one hand there was Bahasa Indonesia with its edict that the new language contain no swearing, and immediately the loan-word smugglers set up shop. On the other hand, there is the odd and geeky case of Esperanto, which even went to the trouble of codifying & listing swear words. Yet even within Mensa you will find more speakers of Tolkien's Elvish or Paramount Star Trek™ Klingon than of Esperanto. (We cannot, alas, risk a single Klingon epithet; we would suffer a Paramount fatwah.)

Which brings us back to my Pilgrim's regress. After years, & years & years, of dealing with weekly & demi-monthly "independent" & "alt" newspapers & journals, I was warming up to yet another reasoned rant when a journalist friend told me to put up & shut up; he even offered to help me start a publication. I had been talking about how US culture in general, & publishers, & especially magazines & newspapers were *muerto en el culo*. The ideal magazine, I feel, should be like a multi-lingual *Harper's* on ecstasy or a *New Yorker* on an æther-absinthe bender, yet not be New York or Boston-based, & should treat the whole world as its borough. As I began to run a multilingual quarterly magazine, *Gobshite Quarterly*, with en-face translation, I began to work with interns, three to seven fresh faces every three to six months, & half of those bilingual. I would bring up my language researches & my folders & questionaires, & I would get a few words or phrases, or current dirty dozen expressions. (Half had just returned from Europe or Asia or Latin America.) And most of my contributors & their translators are multilingual. Some like Marilyn Hacker and Norma Comrada have been helpful in getting leads. Contributors like Christoph Keller, Frederic Raphael and his son Stephen Raphael, and Luisa Valenzuela have sent words and phrases, & answered queries. (A whole network of Northern Europeans & Brazilians have been extremely helpful, but due to the sort of work they do, have to be very off-the-record.) So the folders began to grow, with scraps of papers & lists. One intern volunteered to start organizing these materials and transcribing them into RTF and DOC format, and did so quietly, but so quietly he forgot to tell me what folder they were in. That folder narrowly escaped being flatlined along with the computer — but no matter, I was not aware he had done as much as he had. One day I spoke to a certain editor about this book you hold in your hands, & he asked for further details, & I sent him an outline, & some sample pages, & three years & six deaths later, here we are, wrestling with the motherfucking curling on the InDesign, dealing with MS Word crashing constantly (must hit Save). (Done.)

A word about the six deaths. From the summer of 2005 to early 2006, six of my closest friends died. One of them was also my sister. Each of these people was a raconteur par excellence and each in their own fashion a magesterial motherfucker. One was a contributor to the magazine, two of them (including my sister) had provided me with extensive Spanish & Portuguese entries through the years (and even some Nahuatl). Another, a retired Finnish-Montanan radiologist, was the most sarcastic & ha-ha funny motherfucker it has ever been my pleasure to know. Three others were well-established professional writers, one a McArthur-genius grantee. So hello again, Andrea, Albert, Margaret, Jacqueline, Bob, & Estelle. And goodbye, again. The planchette and ouija board await you.

Another word about language police. People have been getting ticketed lately, in the UK, at least, for wearing offensive t-shirts, cheeky t-shirts expressing some wit or sarcasm. Some local statutes deem these hate speech. What pray tell the fuck will they do when the see the 69+ language™ t-shirts? Then there is this kid, a victim of the Stockholm syndrome, a pawn or prawn in the culture wars. His parents have strapped good manners to his chest like a bomb & sent him forth to destroy free speech, to the extent of sending him to Pasadena city council meetings begging them to initiate stiff fines of several hundred dollars for crimes against the civil society. Fuck the civil society, what about a civic society. (We can't rebuild a city, but we can make everyone mind their fucking P's & Q's.) Those neo-cons are getting twitchy again, even talking about the City on the Hill. If what we have is any indication of their City, give me Nimrod's tower any day. Q

*) ENGLISH, [& IN ALPHABETICAL ORDER:] AFRIKAANS, ARABIC, ARMENIAN, BASQUE, БЕЛАРУС, CANTONESE, CATALAN, CROATIAN, CZECH, DANISH, DUTCH, ESTONIAN, FARSI, FINNISH, FRENCH, GAEILGE, GÀIDHLIG, GERMAN, ΕΛΛΗΝΑΣ, HAUSA, HEBREW, HINDI, ICELANDIC, ITALIAN, 日本語, KHMER, KOREAN, LATIN, LATVIAN, LITHUANIAN, MACEDONIAN, MALAYU, 中文, MARATHI, NAHUATL, N. SOTHO, NORWEGIAN, PORTUGUESE, QUECHUA, ROMANIAN, РУССКИЙ•ЯЗЫК, СРБИН, SOMALI, SPANISH, SWEDISH, TAGALOG, TAMIL, TELEGU, THAI, TURKISH, UKRAINIAN, URDU, ОЬЗЕКЧА, VIETNAMESE, WELSH, YORUBA, ZULU.

2 *"Fuck God!" This with much shaking of fisties at the heavens by both Brando & O'Toole.*

3 *Kurva. = she won't sleep with you, ergo, she is a whore, a bitch and a slut — as the situation demands. Probably a terrorist, too. The word is Russian, and spoken or immediately understood from the Italian-Slovenian border all the way east (understood everywhere north of the Kush to Vladivostok...even becoming a loan word in Mongolian (A loan word from Polish, just like vodka.)*

4 *Sister fucker.*

5 *Per* **Dermo! The Real Russian Tolstoy Never Used,** *Lenin's favorite word was: Говно govno (f.) / Говнюк govnyuk (m.) / "Shit-head.".*

"I am Gen. MacArthur's asshole," & other late night ponderings while listening to Joy Division...

channing dodson

Though its subject matter varies from culture to culture, no language is without profanity, despite assertions to the contrary. For children, learning profanity is often a special thrill—one of the first means of expressing something that you know to be frowned upon or even subversive. Over time, this thrill wears off for most people and we toss off curse words with little regard to their actual meaning, merely as intensifiers or space fillers in our spoken language. Learning profanity in a foreign language is often a good way of recapturing that sense of excitement from childhood. Profanity is perhaps the easiest thing to learn in a foreign language and the hardest to forget: long after the myriad of case endings, irregular verb conjugations, and rules for speech register leave your brain, those curse words learned from a classmate still reside happily there.

Sometimes errors made in a foreign language provide gateways to learning taboo speech. Perhaps one of the most famous examples of this occurred in Japan shortly after the end of WWII when an advisor to Gen. Douglas MacArthur who had been trained to speak Japanese introduced himself to his Japanese counterpart. He made himself perfectly understood; however, he did commit one crucial blunder by simply holding a vowel for too long: komon became kōmon and the intended statement "I am Gen. MacArthur's advisor" came out instead as "I am Gen. MacArthur's asshole."

Another good example of a Japanese blunder came from a friend, also an American, this time teaching English in Japan for fun & profit. Whilst teaching a class of middle-aged housewives, he was trying to explain that his interest in Japanese culture had been ignited by watching Speed Racer as a small child. Known originally in Japanese as Maha Go Go Go, its theme song was quite catchy & pleasant & my friend regaled his audience with a hearty rendition of the chorus. Unfortunately, he bungled the title and as he shouted "Manko go-go! Manko go-go! Manko go-go-goooo!!!," his students' faces turned pale. "Manko" means "pussy" in Japanese.

A thing I am quite pleased about regarding this collection is the breadth of languages represented. Many of the world's most commonly spoken languages are here, but there are also a variety of minority languages as well, many of them with rich aquifers of filth. Minority languages are often decried by uninformed, fascist zipperheads as being inferior or deficient in terms of their expansiveness of vocabulary: when I was a student at the University of Glasgow learning Scottish Gaelic I once read an op-ed piece in The Scotsman by a whinging, pathetic little worm of a man who styled himself a bit of a cultural maverick; he was complaining that any money spent on Gaelic was a waste because it was an inferior and outdated language. His evidence came from attending an outdoor Gaelic music festival, where he quickly elucidated that there was no word in Gaelic for "marquee." What he forgot to mention is that there is no word in English for marquee, either. We borrowed it from the French.

We live in an era where speakers of minority languages are working harder than ever before to assert their linguistic rights and cultural plurality. I am delighted that at the time of this writing, punk bands such as Mill a-h Uile Rud, Oi Polloi, and Là Luain, as well as more pop-oriented bands like Nad Aislingean and The Picturebooks are all writing quality songs in Scottish Gaelic, many spiced with judicious amounts of profanity. Mr. Op-Ed Writer from The Scotsman can go fuck himself 'na thòin le botal briste (in his arse with a broken bottle).

I sincerely hope that you, the reader of this book, will find its contents entertaining, educational, and (in)appropriately eye-opening. Just remember that we bear no responsibility for any injuries—physical or emotional—sustained while using it. Have fun. *Q*

I.)

TWO CURSES

... really ...

DRáPRúN /
A
KILLING
RUNE

Dreprún / Dráprún: Þessa stafi skal maður skrifa á blaði og kasta í hestfar hans, þá mun einhver gripur hans deyja ef hann styggir þig óforþént og byrg stafinn í hestfarinu.

A Killing Rune: This stave is to be written on a piece of paper and if a man has insulted you without reason, throw it where his horse has trodden and cover it. Some of his livestock will then die.

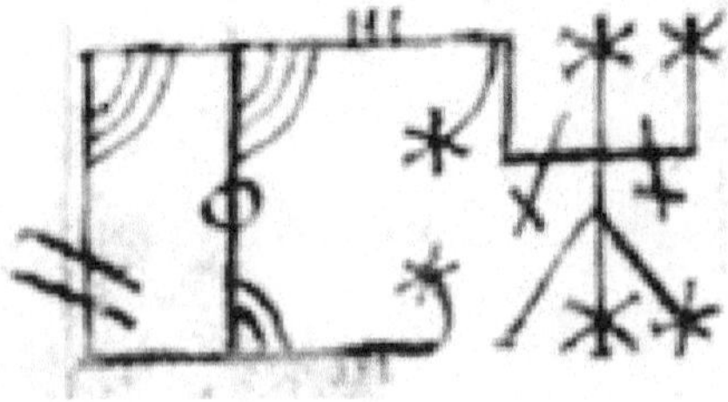

A
Fá
STúLKU/
TO
GET
A
GIRL:

Að fá stúlku: Þennan staf á að skrifa í lófann á hægri hendi með eigin blóði sem tekið er ofan af þumalfingri á vinstri hendi. Þá á að taka í hönd stúlkunnar og mæla þessi orð: „Legg ég lófa minn í þinn lófa, minn vilja í þinn vilja. Verði þér í beinum svo þú brennir öll nema þú unnir mér sem sjálfri þér. Svo heit verði þér þessi orð, svo megn og sterk sem eilífðin er. Allir töfrar og fjölkynngi fj..... villi vit þitt til ástar og elsku við mig; og allar þær vættir, sem í jörðu búa, séu mér liðsinnandi á þessa leið."

To Get a Girl: This sign should be written in the palm of your right hand with blood from the tip of the thumb on the left hand. Take the girl's hand and recite: "My hand I lay in yours, my will in yours. May your bones burn lest you love me as much as I love you. These words shall be as passionate and powerful as eternity. All magic and sorcery turn your mind towards love of me and may all those who inhabit subterranean abodes assist me in this."

— 17th. C. Icelandic grimoire
(Antikvarisk-Topografiska Arkivet, Stockholm)

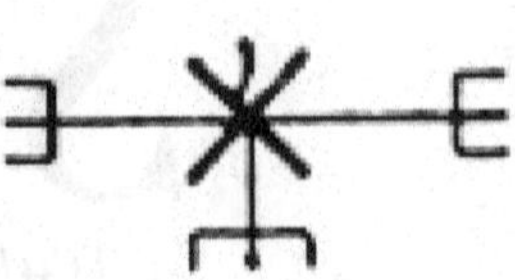

II.) WORDS

& a few phrases…

座頭市

ポン中

Јебо свој усрани панк бенд

Хуй моржовый!

сикељ

φολοβιριπτα

κεκάκι

ABNORMAL (& VARIATIONS) ЖЫНДЫ

AFRIKAANS onreëlmatig
ALBANIAN anormal
ARABIC śâzzîn / śawâz
BASQUE eznormal
BELARUSIAN ненармальны / nenarmal'ny
BENGALI asbabhābī
BOSNIAN nenormalan
BULGARIAN neobicʺaen
CANTONESE bintaai
CATALAN anormal
CREOLE/HAITIAN pa nèmal
CROATIAN/SERB nenormalan; ненормалан /nenormalan
CZECH abnormální
DANISH uregelmæssig
DUTCH abnormaal
ESTONIAN ebaloomulik
FARSI ajib *
FINNISH poikkeava
FRENCH anormal(e)
GAELIC, IRISH mínormálta
GAELIC, SCOTS neo-chumanta
GERMAN regelwidrig
GREEK, MOD. ανωμαλος/ anomalos
GUJARATI vicitra
HAUSA bako
HEBREW l'tkyn
HINDI asvabavika
HUNGARIAN abnormális
ICELANDIC óvanalegur
INDONESIAN aneh
ITALIAN anormale
JAPANESE 異常な ijō na
KANNADA vikruta
KAZAKH жынды / jındı
KHMER châmla-êk
KOREAN pyŏn-t'ae-jŏk
KURDISH nenormal
LATIN abnormis
LATVIAN nenormāls
LITHUANIAN keis'tas
MACEDONIAN ненормален / nenormalen
MALAYU luarbiasa
MALTESE stramb
MANDARIN 反常的 / fǎngcháng de
MARATHI acata
MONGOLIAN хачин / hačin *
NAHUATL tlahuehuetzqui **
NORWEGIAN unormal
POLISH nienormalny
PORTUGUESE anormal
ROMANIAN anormal
RUSSIAN ненорма́льный / nenormal'nyj
SLOVENIAN nenormanla
SOTHO, N sa tlwaelegago
SPANISH anormal
SWAHILI -geni *
SWEDISH avvikande
TAGALOG alangán
TAMIL anniyam
TELEGU anyamu
THAI bplàirk *
TURKISH doğal olmayan
UKRAINIAN ненормальний / nenormal'nyy
URDU ajib
UZBEK гайритабий / gayritabiy
VIETNAMESE kỳ *
WELSH anghynffredin
YIDDISH mod'neh *
YORUBA sàjèjì / sàjòjì
ZAPOTEC estrañu *
ZULU ngavamile

* *odd, strange;*
** *ridiculous, odd-ball.*

ABORTION (& VARIATIONS) ἐκτρωσέ

AFRIKAANS Jou misraam-kindje. [2]
ALBANIAN dështímmjek
ARABIC esqâţ *
BASQUE haurregoitze *
BELARUSIAN почвара / počvara
BENGALI garbhapat *
BOSNIAN abortus *
BULGARIAN аборт / abort *
CANTONESE Lohkjái! [3]
CATALAN avortament *
CROATIAN / SERB pobačaj *; побачај / pobačaj *
CZECH zakrněnì *
DANISH mislykket forsøg *;
DUTCH miskraam *; abortus *
ESTONIAN abort *
FARSI saqt´e janin *
FINNISH raskaudenkeskeytys *
FRENCH avortement *
GAELIC, IRISH ginmhilleadh *
GAELIC, SCOTS casg-breith *
GERMAN Fehlgebert *
GREEK, MOD. ἐκτρωσέ / éktrosé *
HAUSA zub da ciki *
HEBREW nepel *
HINDI garabhpāt *
HUNGARIAN Te abortusz! [3]
ICELANDIC fósterlát *
INDONESIAN aborsi *
ITALIAN / PORTUGUESE / SPANISH aborto *
JAPANESE 中絶 chūzetsu *
KANNADA / MARATHI garbhapāta *
KAZAKH аборт / abort *
KOREAN yu-san *
LATIN abortus *
LATVIAN aborts *
LITHUANIAN aborto *
MACEDONIAN пометнува / pometnuva **
MALAYU keguguran *
MANDARIN 流产 liúchăn *; 你是 流产 Nichi liúchăn! [3]
NEPALI garbhasrāv *
NAHUATL netlatlaxililiztli *
NORWEGIAN bomskudd *
POLISH (sztuczne) poronienie *
QUECHUA sullusqa *
ROMANIAN avort *
RUSSIAN абортa /aborta *
SLOVENIAN abortus *
SOTHO, N pholotšo *
SWAHILI kutoa mimba *
SWEDISH Dit misfoster! [3]
TAGALOG pagpapalaglág *
TAMIL azikaru *
TELEGU garbhapaatam *
THAI gahb tam táang *
TURKISH düşük *
UKRAINIAN / UZBEK аборт / abort *
VIETNAMESE danh tù' *
WELSH erthyliad *
YIDDISH abort *
YORUBA ìsénú *
ZULU ukuphuphuma kwesisu *

* *abortion/miscarriage;*
** *miscarry;*
2 *"You abortion baby!"*
3 *"You abortion!" / "You're an abortion!"*

流产

ADULTERER/ ADULTERESS, CUCKHOLD (& VARIATIONS) ЗИНО

AFRIKAANS egbreker *
ALBANIAN tradhëti bashkëshortore *
ARABIC zāni *(m)* / zān'ya *(f)* *
BASQUE adulteriogile ; gizon *(m)* / emakume *(f)*
BENGALI upasēbaka *
BOSNIAN preljubnic *
BULGARIAN прелюбодеец / prelyubodeets *
CANTONESE gàanfù *(m)* / yàhm fúh *(f)* *
CATALAN adúlter *(m)* / adúltera *(f)* *
CROATIAN preljubnic *(m)* / preljubnica *(f)* *; прељубниц/ preljubnic *(m)* / прељубница / preljubnica *(f)*
CZECH cizoložník *(m)* /cizoložnice *(f)* ; parohá [2]
DANISH ægteskabsbrud **; hanrej [2]
DUTCH echtbreker *(m)* / echtbreekster *(f)* *
FARSI marde zenâ kâr *(m)* / zane' zenâ kâr *(f)* *
FINNISH avionrikkoka *
FRENCH adultère **; porter de cornes [3]
GAELIC, IRISH adhaltramas **
GAELIC, SCOTS adhaltraiche **
GERMAN bescheißen [4]
GREEK, MOD. κερατα / kerata **
HAUSA zina **
HEBREW minaep *
HINDI / URDU zani *
ICELANDIC hórkarl *(m)* / hórkona *(f)* * ; kokkáll [2]
INDONESIAN pezina
ITALIAN adultero *(m)* / adultera *(f)* *; cornuto [2]
JAPANESE 間男 maotoko *
KANNADA jārini *
KOREAN kan-t'ong **
LATIN adulter *(m)* / adultera *(f)* *
MACEDONIAN браколомник / brakolomnik *
MANDARIN 通奸人 tōngjiān rén *; 你有漂亮的绿帽子。Nǐ yǒu piāo liàngde lü mào zi. [5]
MARATHI bahilvyasani *
NAHUATL tlaxintli [2]
NORWEGIAN hanrei [2]
POLISH romans [6]
PORTUGUESE chifrudo *(m)* / chifruda *(f)* [2] ; pôr chifre em alguém [7]
ROMANIAN adulter *(m)* / adulteră *(f)* *
RUSSIAN невѐрный муж / nevernyi muž *(m)*; невѐрная жена / nevernaya žena *(f)* *
SOTHO, N seotswa *
SPANISH poner los cuernos [7]
SWAHILI zinaa **
SWEDISH bedragen ätka man [2]
TAGALOG torótot [2]
TAMIL carastiri *(f)* *
THAI gàan nôk jai **
TURKISH zâni *(m)* / zâniye *(f)* *; boynuslanan erkek [2]
UKRAINIAN перелюбник / perelyubnik *
UZBEK зино / zino **
VIETNAMESE gian-phu̲ *(m)* / dâm-phu̲ *(f)* *
WELSH godinebwr *(m)* /godinbwraig *(f)* *
YORUBA agbèrè *(f)* *
ZULU isifebe *(m)* /isiphingi *(f)* *

* *adulterer /adulteress;*
** *adultery;*
2 *"cuckhold";*
3 *"wearing [cuckhold's] horns";*
4 *"Shitting on" = cheating on;*
5 *"You wear a pretty green [cuckhold] cap";*
6 *love affair, infidelity;*
7 *"putting the [cuckhold's] horns on someone."*

間男

ANARCHIST, PINKO COMMIE (& VARIATIONS) агитпунк

AFRIKAANS kommunis [2]
ALBANIAN komuníst *(s.)* /komuníste *(pl.)* [2]
ARABIC fawda'wi *
BASQUE gori [3]
BELARUSIAN / BULGARIAN / MACEDONIAN / RUSSIAN анархист / анархи́ст / anarkhist *
BENGALI rajadrohi / ainer birodhi [4]
BOSNIAN / CROATIAN / SERB anarhista *; анархиста / anarhista *
CATALAN / PORTUGUESE / SPANISH anarquista *
CANTONESE gunhgcháa ndóngyùhn [2]
FARSI jenāh e chap [3]
FINNISH Kommari! [3]
FRENCH Communiste gauchisant! [3]; Situationiste de merde! / Connard de Situationist! [21]; J'emcule ton premier mai! [18] Catho coco [11]
GAELIC, IRISH cumannaí [2]
GAELIC, SCOTS co-mhaoineach [2]
GERMAN roter Kommunist [4]
GREEK, MOD. αναρχικός / anarhikós *
HAUSA mulkin rud´u *
HEBREW / NORWEGIAN / SWEDISH anarkist *
HINDI / URDU Naxalite [5]; Marx-wadi [6]; Lal-salām! [7]
HUNGARIAN zöld [8]
ICELANDIC sófa kommi [10]
INDONESIAN anarkis *
ITALIAN anarchico *(m)* /anarchica *(f)* *; sinistroide [4]; cattocommunista [11]
JAPANESE 共産党者 kyōsantōsha [2]; 赤軍者 sekigunsha [20]
KOREAN kong-san chu-ŭi-ja [2]
MALAYU penganut faham anarki *
MANDARIN 你妈了操尝毛主席! Nǐ māle cào cháng mao zhǔ xí! [12]
MARATHI anayaka *
MONGOLIAN анархи / anarhi *;
NEPALI sambidhān *
POLISH komunistyczny [2]; solidarność [13]
PORTUGUESE comunista cor de rosa [4]
SOMALI shūci [3]
SOTHO, N. mokominisi [3]
SPANISH ¡Pinchi Comunista! [14]; ¡Pinchi Sendaro Luminoso! [15]
SWAHILI mokoministi [2]; wanachamba [16]; mjamā [9]; mchochezi [17]
TAGALOG daga-bundok komunista [4]; rebelde [17]
TELEGU arājakam *
THAI kormunit [2]
TURKISH anarcişt *; komünist [2]
UKRAINIAN комуніст / komunist [2]
UZBEK соьлчи / so'lchi [3]; агитпунк / agitpunk [19]
VIETNAMESE công-sản [2]
WELSH comiwnydd [2]
YORUBA àìlóba *
ZAPOTEC anarquia *
ZULU isiphekulankuni *

* *anarchist; NEPALI/TELEGU/ZAPOTEC: "anarchy";*
2 *"Communist";*
3 *"Commie!"; SWAHILI/UZBEK: "Left winger";*
4 *"Pinko Commie" / "Pinko Commie!";*
5 *Violent neo-Maoist Indian sub-continent faction;*
6 *"Marxist";*
7 *"Red salute," to greet or mock Fellow Travelers;*
8 *"Greenie" / "Green";*
9 *"Socialist";*
10 *"Armchair radical" / "Sofa Commie";*
11 *"Catholic Communist";*
12 *"Yr mother fucked Chairman Mao."*
13 *"trade union anarcho-syndicalists"/badge of honor;*
14 *"Fucking Communist!"*
15 *"Fucking Shining Path!"*
16 *"Party member" = fellow traveler;*
17 *"Agitator"; TAGALOG: "Rebel," lit. or fig.;*
18 *"Fuck yr May Day!";*
19 *"Political agitation centre," Russian loan word;*
20 *"Japanese Red Army Faction member";*
21 *"Situationist wanker."*

ASS/ ARSE, BUTT/ BUTTOCKS (& VARIATIONS) κολο

AFRIKAANS aars * ;
Koekstamp en giggel? / Koekstamp en lag? [2] ;
Ada [3]
ALBANIAN bythë *
ARABIC chalf *
ARMENIAN vor *
BASQUE mokor *
BELARUSIAN / RUSSIAN зопа / zopa * ;
жопа / žopa *
BENGALI / GUJARATI / HINDI / URDU gānd *
BOSNIAN šupak **
BULGARIAN гyз / guz *
BURMESE chu *
CANTONESE peigú *
CATALAN culdolla [4]
CHABACANO pu'it *
CREOLE/HAITIAN dèyè *
CROATIAN / SERB dupe * ;
дупе / dupe *
CZECH prdel *
DANISH God røv! [5] ;
Min bare røv! [6]
DUTCH reet *
FARSI bâsan *
FINNISH persikapylly [7]
FRENCH cul *
FRENCH (VERLAN) luc
GAELIC, IRISH / GAELIC, SCOTS tóin * ; tòin *
GERMAN analfixient [8] ;
Arsch mit Ohren [9]
GREEK, MOD. κολο / kolo *
HAUSA dāuwawa
HEBREW tahat
HUNGARIAN A béka segge allatt. [10]
ICELANDIC rass *
INDONESIAN / MALAYU pantat *
ITALIAN / SPANISH culo *
JAPANESE ケツ ketsu *
KANNADA dodda thikā [4]
KAZAKH / UZBEK кот / kot *
KHMER ka'kōt *
KOREAN hŭng-mun **
LATIN clunis *
LATVIAN pakalja *
LITHUANIAN shikna *
MACEDONIAN Убав газ / Ubav gaz! [5]
MALTESE tirma *
MANDARIN 屁股 pìgu *
MARATHI phodrya *
NAHUATL tzintlantin *
NORWEGIAN ræv *
POLISH dupa *
PORTUGUESE cuzão [4]
QUECHUA siki papan *
ROMANIAN cur *
SLOVENIAN rit *(m)* /rito *(f)* *
SOTHO, N punya [11]
SWAHILI tako *
SWEDISH arsle *
TAGALOG wepáks *
TAMIL kundi
TELEGU guddha *
THAI dàak *
TURKISH göt *
UKRAINIAN дупа / dupa *
VIETNAMESE mông di´t *
WELSH twllt din **
YIDDISH tuchis *
YAQUI/YOEME chove *
YORUBA ìdí *
ZAPOTEC xa´na´ *
ZULU isinqe *

* *ass/arse, butt;* ** *ass/arsehole, rectum;*
2 *"Bump asses/arses together & giggle" / "Bump asses/arses together & laugh";*
3 *"Perfect ass/arse" / "Kraut queer";*
4 *"big ass/arse";*
5 *"Nice ass/arse!";*
6 *"My bare ass/arse!" = yeah right;*
7 *"Peach fuzz ass/arse";*
8 *"Anal retentive";*
9 *"An ass/arse with ears";*
10 *"Under the frog's ass/arse";*
11 *S. African township gay ass/arse-fuckery.*

ASSHOLE / ARSEHOLE (& VARIATIONS) гамен

AFRIKAANS poephol *
ALBANIAN bythë *
ARABIC / TUNIS. mēboun **
ARMENIAN sirpan *
BASQUE Alu hori! **
BELARUSIAN / RUSSIAN / UKRAINIAN срака / sráka [2]
BENGALI / GUJARATI / HINDI / URDU gānd *
BOSNIAN / CROATIAN / SERB šupcino *; шупцино / šupcino *
BULGARIAN гамен / gamen **
BURMESE chu *
CANTONESE peigú *; fú yuht [3]
CATALAN el forat de cul *
CHABACANO pu'it *
CZECH řiť *; zmrd **
DANISH røvhul **
DUTCH klootzak *
ESTONIAN perse auk *
FARSI kûn *
FINNISH Vittun perseenreikä! [4]
FRENCH picassul **
FRENCH (VERLAN) luc *
GAELIC, IRISH áthán *
GAELIC, SCOTS toll-tòine *
GERMAN Blödes Arschloch! [5]
GREEK, MOD. κολο / kolo *
HAUSA dubura *
HEBREW tahat *
HUNGARIAN fenék **
ICELANDIC rassbora *
INDONESIAN lobang pantat *
ITALIAN / SPANISH culo *
ITALIAN / TUSC. budiùlo **
JAPANESE ケツの穴 ketsu no ana *
KANNADA thikā *
KAZAKH / UZBEK кот / kot *
KHMER ka'kōt *
KOREAN net hŭng-mun [6]
LATIN culus *
LATVIAN dirsa *
LITHUANIAN shiknaskyle *
MACEDONIAN дупе / dupe *
MALTESE ja condom mc'arrat [7]
MANDARIN 屁股 pìgu *
NAHUATL tzintli *
NORWEGIAN brunøyet **
POLISH fagas *
PORTUGUESE O seu olho do cú é tão imenso que até um porta-aviões cabe lá dentro. [8]
QUECHUA / BOLIV. oqoti *
ROMANIAN găoază *
SLOVENIAN rit *(m)* / rito *(f)* *
SOTHO, N motete *
SWAHILI mkundu *
SWEDISH rövhål *
TAGALOG buldét *
TAMIL kundi *
THAI Kòon nan yàae! **
TURKISH şerç *
VIETNAMESE lo dĭt *
WELSH Twll din pop Saes! [9]
YIDDISH tuchis *
YAQUI / YOEME chomim *
YORUBA ìdí *
ZAPOTEC xa'na' *
ZULU ingquza *

* *ass/arsehole, rectum;*
** *rude ass/arsehole, jerk, idiot, wanker; BASQUE: "Such an ass/arsehole!"; THAI: "You ass/arsehole!"*
2 *"shit-chute" ("broke 'em? nearly wrecked 'em!");*
3 *"tiger's cavern";*
4 *"(You) Fucking ass/arsehole!";*
5 *"(You) Stupid ass/arsehole!";*
6 *"internet ass/arsehole";*
7 *"Ambulatory torn condom" = ass/arsehole, idiot, jerk;*
8 *"Yr ass/arsehole's so huge an aircraft carrier would fit right in";*
9 *"Ass/arseholes to all Englishmen!"*

images: GobQ/T. Warburton y Bajo

ASS/ARSE, DIRTY, BLOODY ASS/ARSE (& VARIATIONS)

AFRIKAANS bloed aars **
ALBANIAN bythë e papastër *
ARABIC Tā'la shim tēzy. [11]
ARMENIAN vor makrogh [2]
BASQUE anburu **
BELARUSIAN бздзеч / bzdzeć [6]
BENGALI pedo gangaram [11]
BOSNIAN hemeroide **
BULGARIAN mirizlivia guz *
BURMESE wùng shàw [5]
CANTONESE chow peigú [3]
CATALAN merde al cul [5]
CHABACANO yede puwit *
CREOLE/MAURIT. fesser casser [4]
CROATIAN / SERB usrano dupe [5]; усрано дупе/usrano dupe [5]
CZECH zlatá žila *
DANISH smudsig røv [6]
DUTCH kontmoeras [7]
ESTONIAN must perse *
FARSI kûn nashhûr *
FINNISH kuraperse [8]
FRENCH cul sale *
GAELIC, IRISH tóin salach *
GAELIC, SCOTS tòin salach *
GERMAN scmutziger Arsch *
GREEK, MOD. σκατο κολε /skato kole [5]
HEBREW tahat meluchlechet *
HINDI / URDU gandi gānd *
HUNGARIAN drisko [5]; Menj a büdös picsába. [9]
ICELANDIC óhreinn rass *
INDONESIAN bokong bau *
ITALIAN culo sporco *
JAPANESE 汚いケツ kitanai ketsu *
KAZAKH сазды кот / sazdy kot *
KOREAN sŏl-sa [5]
LATIN clunis immunda *
LATVIAN zemes dirsa *
LITHUANIAN purvinas shikna *
MACEDONIAN валка газ / valka gaz *
MALAYU memburan [5]
MALTESE sormi mahmug *
MANDARIN 赃的屁股 zāng de pìgu *
MONGOLIAN чатсаг алдсан / chatsag aldsan [5]
NAHUATL apitzallitl [5]
NORWEGIAN skam bakende *
POLISH brudny dupa *
PORTUGUESE cu sujo *
ROMANIAN găoază murdără *
RUSSIAN мудак / mudak *
SINHALA killi puka *
SLOVENIAN drisko [5]
SOTHO, N matšala **
SPANISH peste a culo [3]
SWAHILI bawasiri **
SWEDISH slarvpotta *
TAGALOG álmos **
TAMIL hotah kundi [6]
TELEGU kampu guddha [6]
THAI thàang ruàang [5]
TURKISH basur **
UKRAINIAN брудний жопа / brudnyy žopa *
UZBEK тирраҳила / tirraqila [5]
VIETNAMESE bêm tri **
WELSH gotsan drewllyd *
YORUBA abìdí rírùm [6]
ZAPOTEC xa´na´ nabiidi´ *; yuba ndaani´ [5]
ZULU bheka **

* *"dirty ass/arse";*
** *"bloody/bleeding ass/arse", piles;*
2 *"ass/arse wiper";*
3 *"smelly ass/arse";*
4 *"broken ass/arse";*
5 *"shitty ass/arse," flaming shits/diarrhea;*
6 *"filthy stinking ass/arse";*
7 *"ass/arse-swamp";*
8 *"muddy ass/arse";*
9 *"Go up a smelly ass/arse."*
10 *"Dude, come & sniff my ass/arse!"*
11 *"farty ass/arse."*

ASS-FUCKER / ARSE-FUCKER / BUTT-FUCKER, PEDERAST (& VARIATIONS) жопойеб

AFRIKAANS betty boems *; kak naii [2]
ALBANIAN bythëqirë *
ARABIC / TUNIS. hsān [3]
BASQUE atzelari *(m)* / atzelara *(f)* *
BELARUSIAN підарасіч / pidarasić *
CATALAN donar pel cul / donar pel sac *; Hullo, fogó! [4]
CHABACANO Ching´a na buli. [5]
CROATIAN pederčine *
CZECH Oustat mi prdel. [7]
DANISH røvpuller *; bæskubber [6]; Op i røven med det. [7]
DUTCH naad cosmonaut [8]; aarsridder [9]
ESTONIAN pepuvend [10]
FARSI bachchazboz [11]
FINNISH homoperse [12]; ruskean reiän ritari [13]; vitun tyynynpurija [14]
FRENCH baiseur de bout *; tante [15]; enculé [16]
GAELIC, IRISH Suas do thóin le buideal briste. [17]
GAELIC, SCOTS Suas do thòin le botal briste. [17]
GERMAN Arschficker *; Arschkriecher, der [18]; Arschgeiger, der [19]
GREEK, MOD. κριστόφορος / khristóforos [20]; κεκάκι / kekáki [21]; ψυκοτραγόπουρος / psykhotraghópouros [22]
GUJARATI gandh mareh *
HEBREW Mizdayen ba tusik *
HINDI / URDU londay baz *
ICELANDIC þrjótur *; rassríðari *; Hoppadu uppi rassgatid a ter. [23]
ITALIAN inculare *; cullatone [24]; il giochetto dei frati [25]
JAPANESE ケツでやる人 ketsu de yaru hito [26]
KAZAKH жопойеб / zhopoyeb *
KHMER Choy k'det anh. [7]
LATIN are pedico *
MACEDONIAN педериште / pederishte *
MALAYU main sembrit *
MALTESE F´oxx dawq il pufti apostli! [27]
MANDARIN 干你屁股。Gàn nǐ pìgu. [26]
MARATHI battebaja *; pascadadvaragami *
NORWEGIAN rompepuler *; rumpeknul-ler *; bærsjølpuler [6]; baksethumper [28]
POLISH Chuj ci w dupe! [29]
PORTUGUESE / BRAZ. arrombado [16]; queima-rosca [30]
RUSSIAN жопник / žópnik *; Арбуз на солнце зреть, Армяська в жопу любит еть. / Arbúz na sólnce lyúbit zret', Armyáška v žopu lyúbit et´. [31]
SERBIAN педе / pede *
SOTHO, N punya [32]
SPANISH culear *; ¡Jodete y aprieta el culo! [27]; buscar petroleo [33]; por Detroit [34]; Ir por el camino de tierra / Ir por el camino de grava [35]
SWAHILI basher *; unafirwa *
SWEDISH rövknullare *; röv-knytkävs-knullare [36]
TAGALOG érbum *; kantutero sa p´wet *
TURKISH oğlancı *
UKRAINIAN педераст / pederast *
UZBEK ака'си / aka'si [37]

WELSH Twll din pop Saes! [38]
YIDDISH Tsu tillas gescheften! [39]
ZULU umenzi wenkoshana * ;
ayina **

* *ass/arse-fucker, pederast;*
** *ass/arse-fuckery, pederasty;*
2 *"shitfuck" = accident;*
3 *"horse";*
4 *"Hi there, ass/arse-fucking bottom faggot!"*
5 *"Fuck the ass/arse."*
6 *"shit-fucker/ shit-pusher";*
7 *"Up the ass/arse with that."*
8 *"Butt-crack Cosmonaut";*
9 *"ass/arse rider";*
10 *"ass/arse-pal, Ass/arse-fuck buddy";*
11 *"Collector of dancing toy-boys";*
12 *"ass/arse-puppet";*
13 *"Faggot Knight of the Bung-hole";*
14 *"Fucking pillow-biter";*
15 *"Auntie";*
16 *"ass/arse fucked";*
17 *"Up yr ass/arse with a broken bottle";*
18 *"ass/arse crawler";*
19 *"ass/arse strummer";*
20 *"Christopher," pederast;*
21 *pederast's virgin jail-bait;*
22 *"priest's soul";*
23 *"Climb up yr ass/arse";*
24 *gay ass/arse bandit;*
25 *"friar's 'little game'...";*
26 *"Fuck you up the ass/arse";*
SPANISH: "Fuck yrself up the ass/arse!," Cub.
27 *"Fuck those poofter faggot Apostles!"*
28 *"back-seat humper";*
29 *"Dick/cock up yr ass/arse!"/"Bugger you!";*
30 *"ass/arse-burn";*
31 *"Watermelons love the sun, Armenians love being ass/arsefucked." — Russ. proverb;*
32 *"ass/arse-fucking. /S. African Township gay term;*
33 *"Drill for oil";*
34 *"like Detroit," rear-end/from behind;*
35 *"Take the dirt road. / Take the gravel road.", Chil.;*
36 *ass/arse-fist-fucking;*
37 *"older brother";*
38 *"Ass/arseholes to all Englishmen!";*
39 *"Shove it!"*

Κριστόφορος

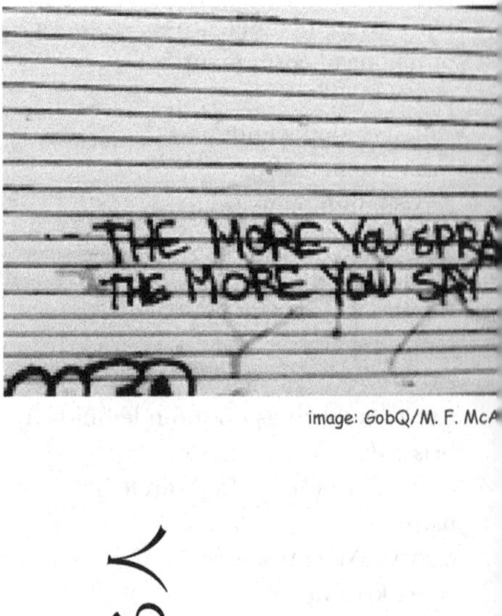

image: GobQ/M. F. McA

ケツでやる人

ASS KISSER / ARSE KISSER (& VARIATIONS) 胡麻すり

ARMENIAN vor lzogh **
BURMESE Bec mon chu. **
CROATIAN / SERB ljubî dupe ;
љубî дупе / ljubî dupe **
DANISH røvslikker ** ;
stjerneslikker [9]
DUTCH bruinwerker [2]
ESTONIAN suudlema kakker **
FINNISH perseen nuolija *
FRENCH Va te faire foutre! **
GAELIC, IRISH Póg mo thóin. **
GAELIC, SCOTS Pòg mo thòin. **
GERMAN Leck´ mich. **
GREEK, MOD. Φιλεσε το κολο σου. /
Filese to kolo sou. **
ITALIAN Baciami il culo. **
JAPANESE 胡麻すり gomasuri [2]
LATIN Potes meos suaviari clunes. [3]
LATVIAN dirsaaliideejs [4]
MALTESE Busli sormi à la francisa. [8]
MANDARIN 亲我的屁。Qīn wǒde pìgu. **
PORTUGUESE puxa saco [2]
ROMANIAN Pupa-ma´n cur. **
RUSSIAN Иди в жопу. / Idí v žopu. **
SLOVENIAN Zaleti se v´rit. **
SPANISH Besa mi culo. **
SWAHILI barakala [5]
SWEDISH rövslickare * ;
kyss mig i arslet. **
TAGALOG C.I.A. [6] ;
sip-sip *
UKRAINIAN Узни мене. / Uzny mene. [7]
YIDDISH tuchis leker [2]

* *"ass/arse-kisser";*
** *"Kiss my ass/arse." / "Go kiss ass/arse."*
2 *"ass/arse-kissing brown-noser";*
3 *"You may kiss my ass/arse."*
4 *"ass/arse crawler," ass/arse-kisser;*
5 *"Yes-Man," ass/arse-kisser.*
6 *"Certified Imelda Acolyte," ass/arse-kissing fascist;*
7 *"Kiss my ass/arsehole."*
8 *"French kiss my ass/arse!"*
9 *"starsucker."*

ケツをなめる人

ASS-LICKER / ARSE-LICKER (& VARIATIONS)

ケツをなめる人

AFRIKAANS Siug aan my aambeie en wag.... **
ARABIC / TUNIS. qaffaf *
ARMENIAN vor lzogh *
BENGALI pa chato *
CANTONESE jyun lūng *
CATALAN petó negre [2]
DANISH Stjerneslikker [11]
DUTCH reetkever [4]
FRENCH lèche cul *
GERMAN Arschlecker *
GUJARATI chatio *
HEBREW ohel batahat [5]
HINDI / URDU gānd chatna *
ICELANDIC rasssasleikja *
INDONESIAN isep pantak [3]
ITALIAN Leccaculo! *
JAPANESE ケツをなめる人 / ketsu wo nameru hito *
KOREAN hŭng-mŭnuro [9]
LITHUANIAN subinlaizhis *
MALAYU cari muka [10]
NORWEGIAN Rompesuger [3]
PORTUGUESE cheira o cú [13]
RUSSIAN жополиз / žopolíz *
SPANISH El beso negro. [2]
SWAHILI barakala [12]
SWEDISH rövslickare *
TAGALOG sipsip *
TURKISH göt yaliçiyi *
WELSH Cer i sychu fy penol fi. [12]

* *ass/arse licker, lick-ass/arse;*
** *Suck on my hemorrhoids & wait...*
2 *"black kiss," rim job;*
3 *suck ass/arse; ass/arse sucker;*
4 *"ass/arse-beetle";*
5 *ass/arse eater;*
7 *How'd I find you up my ass/arse?*
8 *ass/arse face.*
9 *rim job.*
10 *suck-up;*
11 *"Star-sucker";*
12 *Suck my ass/arse;*
13 *sniff ass/arse.*

ЖОПОЛИЗ

image: GobQ/T. Warburton y Bajo

BALLS/ BOLLOCKS (& VARIATIONS) □ 丸

AFRIKAANS belia *; goons *
ALBANIAN loqe *
ARABIC/LIBY. Dlawez! *
ARMENIAN ander **
BASQUE potro [2]
BOSNIAN/SLOVENIAN jaja *
BULGARIAN ташаки / tashaki *
CANTONESE bō jí *;
CATALAN boles *; Collons! *
CHABACANO guevoz *
CROATIAN/SERB jaja ; jaja /jaja *
CZECH koule *
DANISH nosser *
DUTCH kloten *
ESTONIAN kotte *
FARSI tokhman *
FINNISH kivekset *
FRENCH couilles, les *; joyeuses [3]
GAELIC, IRISH magairlí *
GAELIC, SCOTS tiadhan *
GERMAN Eier, die *
GREEK, MOD. Αρηίδα! /Arhídia! *
HINDI/URDU lora *; gote *
ICELANDIC Eistu! *; þvættingur! *
INDONESIAN biji *
ITALIAN coglioni *; con de palle [6]
JAPANESE 金玉 kintama *
KAZAKH жумуртка / zhumurtka *
LATIN coleus, i *
LATVIAN pauti *; kule [4]
LITHUANIAN Pautai! *
MACEDONIAN мадиња / madinja *
MALAYU telur *
MALTESE bajd *
MANDARIN □丸 gaowán *
MARATHI gotya *;
MONGOLIAN төмсөг/ tömsög *
NAHUATL atexicolli *; oquichnacayotl **
NEPALI geda *
NORWEGIAN baller *
POLISH jaja *
PORTUGUESE Bolas! *
ROMANIAN coaie *
RUSSIAN мудьа/mud´a *; Яйца!/Yaytsa! *
SINHALA eta deka *
SOTHO, N lerete [2]
SPANISH cojones *; pelotas *; huevos [5]
SWAHILI mapumbu *; makenbe *
SWEDISH Fan! *; Skit! *
TAGALOG burát *; yágbols *; bétlog **
TAMIL kotai *
TELEGU an<u>d</u>akōśam [4]
THAI Rai sàa ra! *; nàa [6]
TURKISH taşiack *
UKRAINIAN яєчко / yayechko *
UZBEK уругъдон / urug´don [2]
VIETNAMESE bỉu dái [4]
WELSH carreg [2]
YORUBA kóró <u>e</u>p<u>o</u>n [2]
ZULU masende *; bheka [2]

* *balls/bollocks.; Balls!/Bollocks!*
** *cock-&-balls/bollocks;*
2 *ball/bollock;*
3 *"bringers of joy";*
4 *scrote', ballsack,*
5 *"eggs," balls/bollocks;*
6 *brass balls/bollocks, chutzpah; ITAL: "ballsy."*

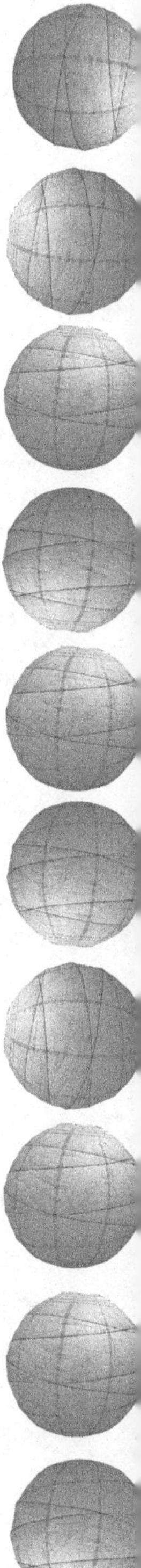

BALLS, BLUE / BOLLOCKS, BLUE
(& VARIATIONS)

BOSNIAN Bole me jaja! [2]
CATALAN frontó pelota [3]
DANISH nossesaft [4]
DUTCH gekke kloten/klootzak **
FRENCH les deux orphelines [5]
GERMAN dicke Eier haben *
ITALIAN allupato [6]
MARATHI andya *
SPANISH pelotas michinados *; ¡Porque me pica el huevo! [7]
YORUBA asópa [8]
ZULU masende bakontshana [9]

* *Blue/swollen balls/bollocks, horny;*
** *crazy balls/bollocks;*
2 *"My balls/bollocks are aching!"*
3 *balls-slamming-between-thighs-just-below-pussy sex game;*
4 *balls/bollocks-sweat;*
5 *"The 2 orphans," wanker's balls/bollocks;*
6 *"starved as a wolf," horny male;*
7 *"Because my balls/bollocks itch!"*
8 *"elephant balls/bollocks;*
9 *sex toy strapped to the balls/bollocks.*

BALL-BREAKER / BOLLOCK-BREAKER, BALL-BUSTER / BOLLOCK-BUSTER
(& VARIATIONS)

Яйца разбит

ARABIC / LIBY. Ma tunfukhhumlish. *
BULGARIAN ташак копеле / tashak kopele [2]
CATALAN No em toquis els collons. *
FRENCH Tu me casses les couilles. *
ITALIAN rompiballe / rompipalle **; scassapalle **; Non romperemi le palle. *
KAZAKH Сенде жумуртка жок! / Sende zhumurtka zhok! [4]
MALTESE Bla bajd! [3]
RUSSIAN У тебя нет яйцав. / U tebya net yaytsav. [4]; Яйца разбит. / Yaitsa razbit. [5]
SPANISH ¡Ahuevado! [3]
TELEGU Box paguluddi. [6]
THAI Set gùu nàae meung! [7]
YIDDISH nudz [8]
YORUBA kóró epon

* *"Don't bust/break my balls/bollocks."*
** *balls/bollocks-breaker/buster;*
2 *"balls/bollocks bastard,"*
3 *"No balls/bollocks!"*
4 *"You've got no balls/bollocks,"*
5 *Break your balls/bollocks;*
6 *I'll break your balls/bollocks.*
7 *"I've got you by the balls/bollocks, you bastard!"*
8 *ball/bollock-breaking/busting.*

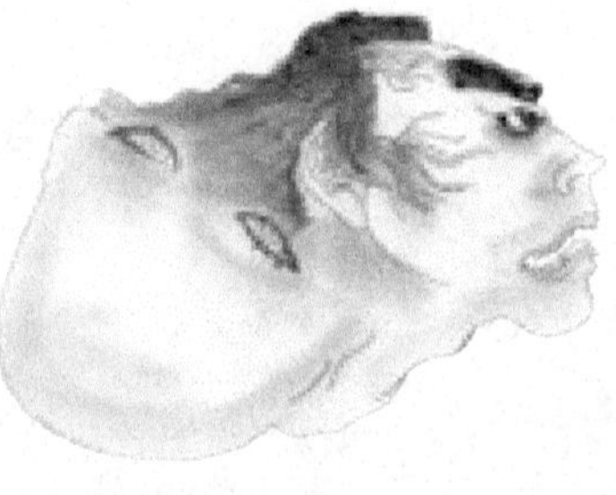

illustr., © 2008, Graham Willoughby

BALLS-FOR-BRAINS
(& VARIATIONS) МУДОЗВОН

ALBANIAN loque kandari *
BULGARIAN ташак / tashak [2]
CATALAN torracollons *; caracollons [3]
DANISH nosserøv [4]; nossefår **
FINNISH pallinaama [3]
FRENCH couilles-pour-cerveau *
GAELIC, IRISH magairí in ionad eagna chinn *
GAELIC, SCOTS tiadhan airson ean-chainn *
GERMAN / SW. Du bisch en Schofsekel. [5]
HINDI Gote mu mein ā gaye. [6]
ICELANDIC heimskingi *
INDONESIAN biji *
ITALIAN stronzo [7]; coglione [8]
MARATHI gotya kapalat [9]
NORWEGIAN pøngle [3]
PORTUGUESE bolas-pra-cérebros *
RUSSIAN мудозвон / mudozvon [10]
SPANISH huevada *; mermelada de huevas [11]; huevón [12]

* *balls/bollocks-for-brains;*
** *sheep balls/bollocks, balls/bollocks for brains;*
2 *one-ball/bollock dumb-ass/arse wanker;*
3 *balls/bollocks-face;*
4 *"Ball-ass/arse," balls-for-brains, fuck-up;*
5 *"You sheep's bollocks ass/arsehole!"*
6 *"He's got his balls/bollocks in his mouth." = He's in for some major-league serious shit.*
7 *Balls/ bollocks-for-brains shit-head rotten bastard;*
8 *Balls/bollocks stupid.*
9 *balls/bollocks on your forehead;*
10 *plays with his balls/bollocks & talks total & complete bullshit;*
11 *balls/bollocks jam;*
12 *lazy-ass/arse big balls/bollocks balls/bollocks-for-brains.*

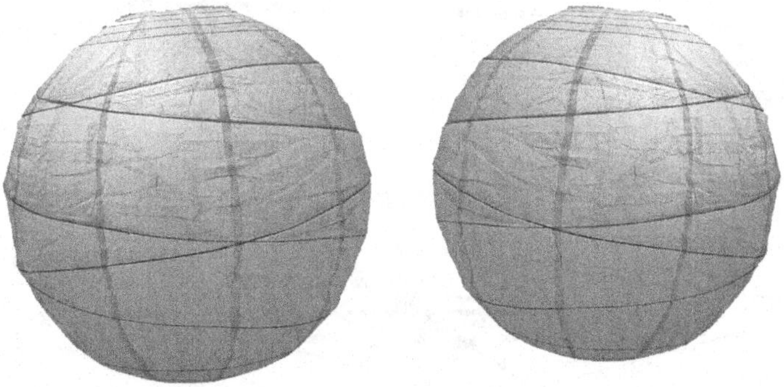

BALLS, KISS MY / LICK MY (& VARIATIONS)

Полижи ми jaja.

AFRIKAANS Jy suig goons/balle/belia. **
BOSNIAN Ma poljubiti mi jaja.[2]
CROATIAN / SERB Poliži mi jaja.[3]; Полижи ми jaja. / Poliži mi jaja.[3]
DANISH Sut mine behårede løg.[4]
ESTONIAN Ime kotte. *
GAELIC, SCOTS Pòg mo thiadhan. *
HINDI / URDU Bahen ke takke![5]
ITALIAN Leccami le palle.[3]
LATIN palas meos / meas lambe[3]
LATVIAN Laizī olas.[3]
MALAYU Sedut telur. *;
MALTESE Bewsli l´ bajd.[2]
PORTUGUESE Chupa as minhas bolas. *; Lambe-me os colhões.[3]; Chera os meus ovos.[6]
SLOVENIAN Jajca mi poli i. *
SPANISH Chupa mis grandes huevos.[7]
TURKISH Taşackimi ye. *

* *Suck my balls/bollocks;*
** *You suck balls/bollocks;*
2 *Kiss my balls/bollocks;*
3 *Lick my balls/bollocks;*
4 *Suck my hairy onions;*
5 *Suck your sister's balls/bollocks;*
6 *Sniff my balls/bollocks;*
7 *Suck my great big balls/bollocks.*

BALLS / BOLLOCKS, DIVINE (& VARIATIONS)

CATALAN Collons de deu! *; Plogués tant que l'aigua arribés al cel i els pei-xos piquessin els collons de Sant Pere, pensant-se que són molles de pa. **
SPANISH ¡Me cago en los veinticuatro co-jones de los apóstoles putos de Jesús![2]

* *"God's Balls!/God's Bollocks!"*
** *I wish it rained so much that the waters flooded heaven & the fish bit St. Peter's balls/bollocks, thinking they're bread crumbs.*
2 *"I shit on the 24 balls/bollocks of the faggot Apostles of Christ!"*

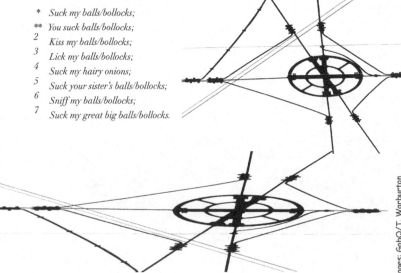

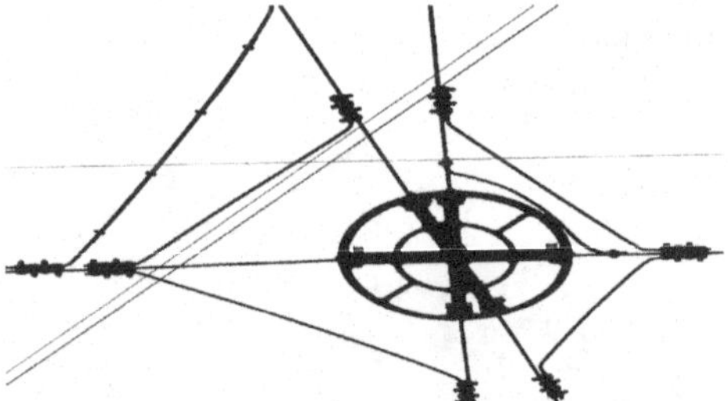

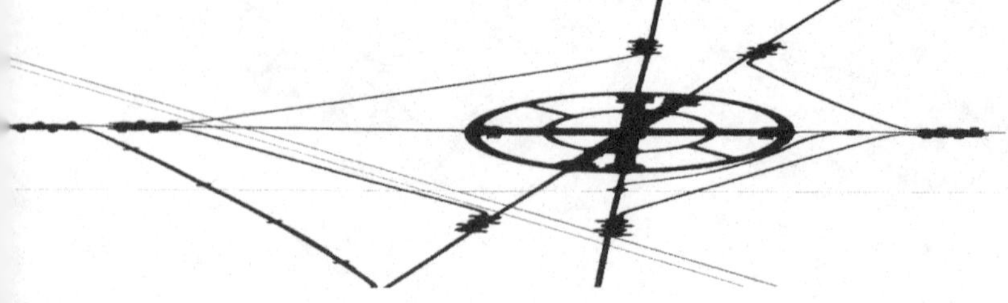

images: GobQ/T. Warburton y Bajo

BASTARD
(& VARIATIONS)

AFRIKAANS So'n helsem! **
ALBANIAN kopil *
ARABIC sharmute *
ARMENIAN khartakh *
BASQUE sasikume *
BELARUSIAN баиструк / bajstruk *
BENGALI haramjada *
BOSNIAN glupan *
BULGARIAN ташак копеле / tashak kopele [2]
CANTONESE kai daih *; pūk gāai fo *
CATALAN caganer [2]
CHABACANO cabron [12]
CREOLE/HAIT. bata *
CROATIAN / SERB kopile *; копиле / kopile *
CZECH levoboček *
DANISH narrøv *
DUTCH luie rotzak [5]
ESTONIAN tibla *; värdjas *
FARSI harâmzâdeh *; zinda [6]
FINNISH Äpärä! *
FRENCH salop *; salaud *
GAELIC, IRISH tuilí *; bastún *
GAELIC, SCOTS dìolain *
GERMAN Du fauler Sack! [5]; Drecksack [7]
GREEK, MOD. μουλε / moule *
GUJARATI tunpa *
HAUSA d'an iksa *
HEBREW Tamut ja zevel. [8]
HINDI / NEPALI / URDU harami *
HUNGARIAN Ő egy rohadék! **
ICELANDIC óþokki *; þrjótur *; bastarður *
INDONESIAN bangsat *; Keparat! *
ITALIAN / PORTUGUESE bastardo *
JAPANESE 野郎 yarō *
KHMER xusxñat *
KOREAN sŏ-ch'ul *
LATIN filius nolius [9]
LATVIAN padirsensis *
LITHUANIAN mergvaikis *
MACEDONIAN копиле / kopile *
MALAYU anak haram [10]
MANDARIN 王八蛋 wáng bā dàn *
MARATHI codica [16]
MONGOLIAN бутач / butač *
NAHUATL tepalconetl *
NORWEGIAN Jaevel! *
POLISH nieślubne diecko *
ROMANIAN nelegitim *
RUSSIAN говнюк / govnyuk *
SINHALA kariya *
SLOVENIAN pizdonterje *
SOMALI we´el *
SOTHO, N sehwirihwiri [19]
SPANISH coño [11]; cabron [12]
SWAHILI Yehe ni mshenzi. **
SWEDISH Jävla idiot! [13]
TAGALOG anak sa labas *; bató [14]
TAMIL bādu *
TELEGU sigguleni lamdikoduku [15]
THAI kŏw le´ou! **
TURKISH piç *
UKRAINIAN позашлюбний / pozashlyub-nyý *
UZBEK баччаталоқ / bachchataloq [16]
VIETNAMESE con tu·-sinh *
WELSH uffar gwirion [17]
YIDDISH Momzer! *
YORUBA omáàlè [18]
ZAPOTEC xiñi gui´xhi´ *
ZULU i(li)nyela *; umlanjwana *

* *bastard/Bastard!*
** *What a bastard!/He's a real bastard!*

2 *ball/bollock-bastard;*
3 *shitty bastard;*
4 *fucking bastard;*
5 *lazy bastard/You lazy bastard!;*
6 *bastard, punk;*
7 *dirty dirt-bag bastard;*
8 *Die, you bastard.*
9 *foundling bastard /motherless fuck;*
10 *rotten bastard;*
11 *cunting bastard;*
12 *stubborn obstinate cocksucker bastard;*
13 *Fucking idiot!/Bastard!*
14 *cold-hearted stingy bastard;*
15 *brazen bastard;*
16 *bastard, S.O.B.—Farsi loan word;*
17 *silly-ass/arse bastard;*
18 *bastard/concubine's son;*
19 *bastard, scoundrel, cur.*

野郎

BESTIALITY,
SEE:
DOG/HORSE/GOAT/CAT FUCKER,
SHEEP SHAGGER

бутач

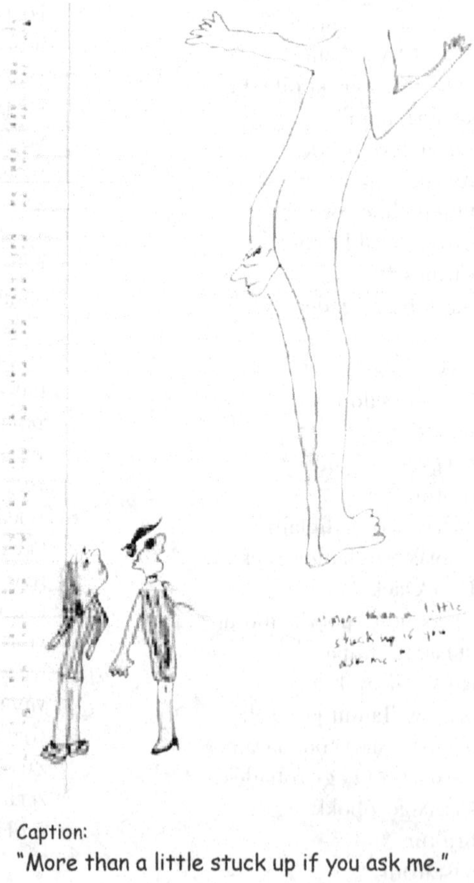

Caption:
"More than a little stuck up if you ask me."

Liz Swado

BITCH
(& VARIATIONS) 臭三八

AFRIKAANS teef *;
Jou teef! **;
Betty [2]
ALBANIAN busht *;
kurve *;
putane *;
ARABIC sharmuta *
ARMENIAN kaz´ *;
poz [4]
BASQUE txacurreme *;
urdanga *
BELARUSIAN бліадз / bliadz [4]
BENGALI khanki *
BOSNIAN kurvo *
BULGARIAN кьчка / kučka *;
мастия / mastiya [4]
CANTONESE baat pòh *;
dohngfúh *
CATALAN meuca *;
mala pècora *;
gossa *
CHABACANO cabrona *;
puta [4]
CREOLE/HAITIAN femèl chen *;
CROATIAN / SERB kuka *;
кука / kuka *
CZECH čubka *;
nemravny´ [12]
DANISH tøjte *;
grimme kælling [8]
DUTCH kaffer *;
vingerwijf [14]
ESTONIAN lits *;
emane koer *
FARSI lakâteh *;
jedeh sefat [12]
FINNISH narttu *;
pirullinen [12]
FRENCH garce [12];
poufiasse *;
conasse *;
FRENCH (VERLAN) Tassepé! [4]

GAELIC, IRISH bitseach *
GAELIC, SCOTS baobh *
GERMAN Gertrud [4];
Bißgurrn [5];
Funzen [15];
Kratzbüschtn [16]
GREEK, MOD. σκιλα / skila *
GUJARATI rhannd [4]
HEBREW kalba *;
frescha [17];
Lo mafhi-dim kalba im zain. [18]
HINDI / URDU kutiya *;
sali kutti [17]
HUNGARIAN kurva *
ICELANDIC gribba *;
heimska belja [17]
INDONESIAN lonte *
ITALIAN baldracca *;
bagascia [4]
JAPANESE アマ ama *
KANNADA bhosdi *
KAZAKH сука / suka *;
куган / kugan [6]
KHMER gurta *
KOREAN mi chin nyon *;
shibal nyon [4]
LATIN matris prolapsus *
LATVIAN kuce *;
mauka *
LITHUANIAN kale *
MACEDONIAN батти / batti *;
сачхма / sachma [8]
MALAYU anging betina *;
Cingkak! [6]
MALTESE qahba *;
Qahba f xalata. [7]
MANDARIN 臭三八 chòu sān bā [13]
MARATHI s´vānī *;
kutrī *
MONGOLIAN жингэр / žinger *
NEPALI kukurni *
NORWEGIAN tøs *;
Jævla hore! [10];
ondskapfull [12]

POLISH suka *;
crowa *
PORTUGUESE baranga [8];
cabra vadia [4]
ROMANIAN căţea *;
târfa [4]
RUSSIAN / UKRAINIAN сука / súka *;
Цучка дерганая / Tsučka derganaya. [6]
SINHALA balli *;
vesa balli [4]
SLOVENIAN kurba *;
Ti pofukana pizda! [10]
SOMALI kumayo *
SOTHO, N mpša e tshadi *
SPANISH cabrona *;
maldita puta [10];
jamona [11]
SWAHILI mbwa *;
Jahili—nakala tatu! [9]
SWEDISH slyna *;
Jävlahora! [9]
TAGALOG hindót *;
chákakhan [8];
tunggák [17]
TAMIL šunī *
TELEGU munda [4]
THAI săm sòrn *;
yai bâh [6]
TURKISH orospu *;
cadı kadın *;
fahişe *
UZBEK жалйаб / djalyab *;
қанжиб / qanjib [4]
VIETNAMESE chó cái *
WELSH ast *;
ast salw [8]
YAQUI / YOEMI chu hamut *
YIDDISH farbisener [12]
YORUBA abo kòokò *;
ajá [4]
ZULU isindindwa *;
injakazi *

* *bitch, cow;*
** *You bitch!*
2 *bitch. /Afrikaans gay slang;*
3 *annoying cow/bitch;*
4 *bitch / whore / slut;*
5 *"nasty bitch," Bavarian dial.;*
6 *"crazy psycho bitch";*
7 *"bitch-at-work/ on-the-clock";*
8 *ugly bitch/harridan;*
9 *"Bitch—in triplicate!"*
10 *"Fucking bitch!" / "Fucking whore!"*
11 *fat bitch;*
12 *sour & bitchy;*
13 *"Smelly 3/8 Bitch!" = "3/8" being World Women's Day.*
14 *wanking bitch;*
15 *"Ugly bitch," Vien.;*
16 *quick-tempered bitch;*
17 *stupid bimbo bitch/cow;*
18 *"You won't scare a bitch with a cock/dick!"*

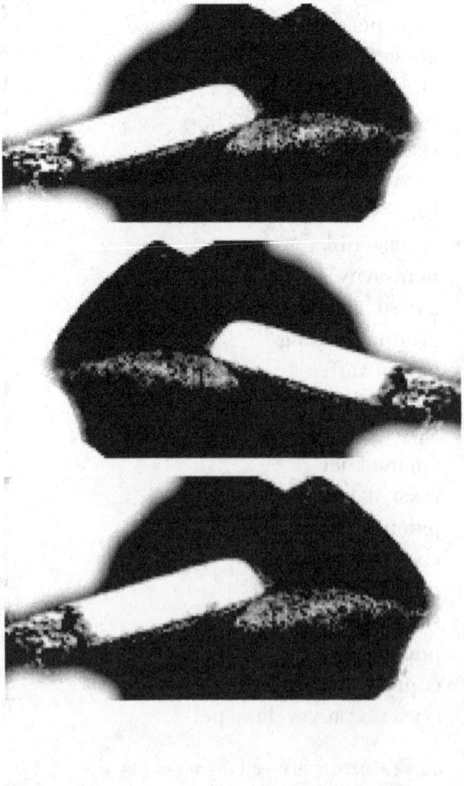
image: GobQ/T. Warburton y Bajo

BLOW-JOB (& VARIATIONS) минет

AFRIKAANS penelingus * ;
slangpark [2]
ARMENIAN Kunem berand. [3]
BELARUSIAN Храц на дудцы-валасіанцы / Hrac’ na dudcy-valasiancy [4]
BULGARIAN духане / duhane *
CANTONESE háu baau [5]
CATALAN mamada * ;
francès *
CROATIAN / SERB Napuši se kurčine. ;
Напуши се курчине. / Napuši se kurčine. [6]
CZECH kouit ptáka [7]
DANISH guldvask [8]
DUTCH Je moeder pijpt goed. [9]
ESTONIAN Võta suhu. [10]
FRENCH turlute [12] ;
fair une pipe [15]
GAELIC, SCOTS obair-shèididh*;
ceann-là*
GERMAN blasen *;
Flöten [12];
Soll ich dir ene blasen? [18]
GREEK, MOD. Παρε μυ ενα τσιβυκι. / Pare mu ena tsivuki. [10]
GUJARATI mukh maithun *
HINDI / URDU lora chusna [6]
HUNGARIAN gecinyaló **
ICELANDIC munnmök *;
munngæler *;
Tottadu mig. [10]
ITALIAN pompa / pompino *;
bocchino *;
l’arte bolognese [19]
JAPANESE おフェラ ofera *
KOREAN panta *;
emu *
LATIN irrumare [13];
fellare [14]
LITHUANIAN Chiulp byby. [10]
MACEDONIAN не го дрибʌај в уста. / Ne go driblaj v usta. [20]
MANDARIN 吃蕉 chī jiāo [16]
NORWEGIAN sædgurgler [21]
POLISH laska *;
robić loda [17];
Zrobisz mi laske/loda? [21]
PORTUGUESE boquete *;
facer um bico [13]
ROMANIAN muie *
RUSSIAN минет / minet *
SLOVENIAN Pofafi mi ga. [10]
SPANISH / PAN. cromao *
TAGALOG lólipop *
TELEGU Chēka bey. [10]
UZBEK оғизга олиш / oghizga olish *

* *Blow-job;*
** *jism/cum-licker;*
2 *“Snake park,” public ‘loos;*
3 *“Fuck your mouth,”*
4 *“play a hairy horn,”*
5 *“mouth bomb,”*
6 *“Blow my dick/cock,”*
7 *“smoke a bird”;*
8 *“goldwash”;*
9 *“Yr mother gives splendid blowjobs.”*
10 *“Blow me;”*
11 *“whistle/ toot,”*
12 *“Play the skin flute,”*
13 *give/do blowjob;*
14 *receive/get blowjob,*
15 *“Give a pipe,” blowjob;*
16 *“eat banana,” blowjob;*
17 *“Do an ice cream”;*
18 *“Would you like a blowjob?”*
19 *“Bolognese Art,” Bolognia, Emilia-Romagna dial.;*
20 *“Quit sucking on it.”*
21 *“spunk/semen-gurgler”;*
21 *“Could you blow me?”*

BOOBS,
SEE:
TIT/TITTY,
TITS/TITTIES,
BOOBS

吃蕉

BOSSY / NOSEY (& VARIATIONS)

мијешати

AFRIKAANS baasspelerig *
bemoeisiek [2]
ALBANIAN dominúes (m) / dominúese (f) [3]
ARABIC hi´śariyîn (m) / hi´śari´ya (f) [2]
BASQUE lepaluze ** ;
muturluze *
BENGALI parasri katar **
CATALAN maniare **
CROATIAN / SERB miješati [2];
мијешати / miješati [2]
CZECH pánovitý *
DANISH diktatorisk *;
domirende *;
nysgerrig **
FARSI tēlēt **
FINNISH hössöttävä [2]
FRENCH fouineur **
GAELIC, IRISH fiosrach **
GERMAN herrisch *
GREEK, MOD. αθιακριτος / athiakritos **
HINDI / URDU har chēz me nāk dālnā ** ;
robdār *
ICELANDIC ráðríkur *;
forvitinn ** ;
hnýsinn **
ITALIAN prepotente **
JAPANESE お節介な osekkai na *
KOREAN kan-sŏp ha-da **
MANDARIN 霸道的 bàdào de *
NORWEGIAN nysgjerrig **
POLISH apodyktyczny *;
wścibski **
PORTUGUESE mandão(dona) *
RUSSIAN вла́ный / vlányy *
SPANISH mandón * ;
mocoso **
SWEDISH nyfiken ** ;
vigtig-petter *
TAGALOG palautós *
TURKISH ârminrane *
UKRAINIAN опуклий / opukliy *
UZBEK буйруқбоз / buyruqboz *
VIETNAMESE tò-mò **
WELSH ymyrrwr [2]
YORUBA aládási [2]
ZULU shushisayo *

* *bossy;*
** *nosey/rude;*
2 *meddlesome/meddler/meddling;*
3 *overbearing;*

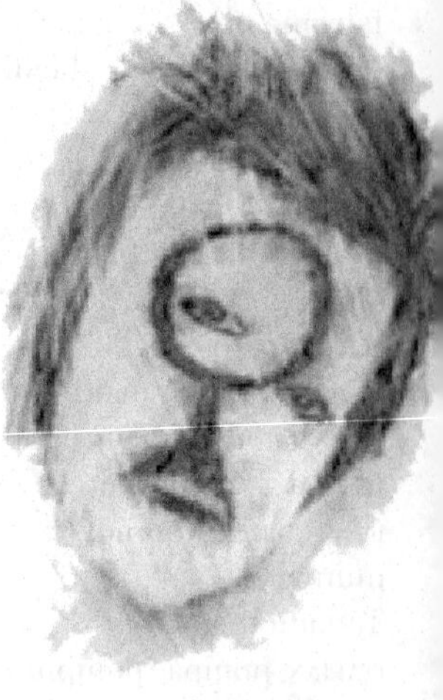

illustr., © 2008, Graham Willoughby

お節介な

BULLSHIT
(& VARIATIONS)

Γιοματος σκατά!

AFRIKAANS Kate Kakpraat [2]
ALBANIAN Them dokrra. **
ARMENIAN eshō kak [3]
BASQUE Kakazaharra! *
BELARUSIAN пиздзеч / pizdzeć **
BENGALI baje/mithye katha *
BOSNIAN seronja [4]
BULGARIAN Глъпости! / Gluposti! *
CANTONESE gwái wáa *
CATALAN torracollons [4]
CROATIAN / SLOVENIAN / SERBIAN sve sranje ; све срање / sve sranje *
CZECH hovno *
DANISH Fuld af lort! [5]
DUTCH lullekoek *; lullepraat *
FARSI kosseh sher *
FINNISH paskapuhetta / hevonpaska * ; Paskanmarjat! [6]
FRENCH conneries * ; C'est conneries / C'est merde! [7]
GAELIC, IRISH Cac capaill! [8]
GAELIC, SCOTS 'S e tòrr cac a th'ann. [9]
GERMAN Hundeschiss [10]; scheißdreck *
GREEK, MOD. Γιοματος σκατά! / Giomatos skatá! *
HEBREW Faltzan. [12]
HINDI / URDU Bakchodiyān!
ICELANDIC lygalaupur [5]; hommaskítur [13]
INDONESIAN Tai lu! [14]
ITALIAN stronzata *; spara cazzate [4]
JAPANESE バカバカしい bakabakashii *
KAZAKH Б'ок жеме. / Bhok zheme [15]
KOREAN Jokkă ji mă! *
LATIN Bovis stercus/Spucatum tauri! *
LATVIAN buljlja sūds * ; kakja spiras [16]
MALAYU karung kosong [4]
MANDARIN 狗屎 gŏu shĭ [10]; 屁话 pì huà *
MONGOLIAN Хуцаад баи / Hutsaad bai. [19]
POLISH pierdolić **
PORTUGUESE merda de vaca *; Você tá zoando! [16]
ROMANIAN cacat de pisică [16]
RUSSIAN мудозмон / mudozmon [17]
SPANISH la mierda del toro *
SWEDISH skitsnak * ; dumheter *
TAGALOG pang-loco * ; echoséro *(m)* / echoséra *(f)* [4]
THAI kêe móh [4]; farang kèenók [18]
UKRAINIAN Йак в сіцку сраты. / Yak v sicku sraty. **
WELSH Malu cachu. *; Paid a malu chau. [19]
ZULU inganckwane [20]

* *"bullshit" / "Bullshit"!*
** *"Talking bullshit" / "Talks bullshit";*
2 *"Katie Bullshitter";*
3 *"donkey shit";*
4 *"bullshitter";*
5 *"Total bullshit!" / "Full of shit!"*
6 *"shit-berries";*
7 *That's bullshit!*
8 *"Horse shit!"*
9 *"It's a load of bullshit";*
10 *"dog shit";*
11 *"Why do you talk such bullshit?"*
12 *"speaks in farts";*
13 *"gay shit";*
14 *"You bullshitter";*
15 *"Don't talk shit if you don't eat shit";*
16 *"cat shit";*
17 *"talks shit & plays w/his balls";*
18 *"Birdshit foreigner";*
19 *"Don't bullshit me";*
20 *"cock-&-bull tale, bull-shit."*

BULLSHIT, NOMINKLÁTURA-STYLE
(& VARIATIONS)

RUSSIAN Пиздёт как Ленин / Pizdet kak Lenin. *

RUSSIAN Пиздёт как Троцкий. / Pizdet kak Trotskiy. **

RUSSIAN Пиздёт как Сталин / Pizdet kak Stalin. [2]

RUSSIAN Пиздёт как Ҳрушчев. / Pizdet kak Khruščev. [3]

RUSSIAN Пиздёт как БрешҲрушчев. / Pizdet kak Brešnev. [4]

RUSSIAN Пиздёт как Горбачёв. / Pizdet kak Gorbačöv. [5]

RUSSIAN Пиздёт как Ыелтзен. / Pizdet kak Yeltzin. [6]

RUSSIAN Пиздёт как Путин. / Pizdet kak Putin. [7]

* *Bullshits like Lenin;*
** *.... Trotsky;*
2 *.... Stalin;*
3 *.... Khruschev;*
4 *.... Brezhnev;*
5 *.... Gorbachev;*
6 *.... Yeltzin;*
7 *.... Putin .*

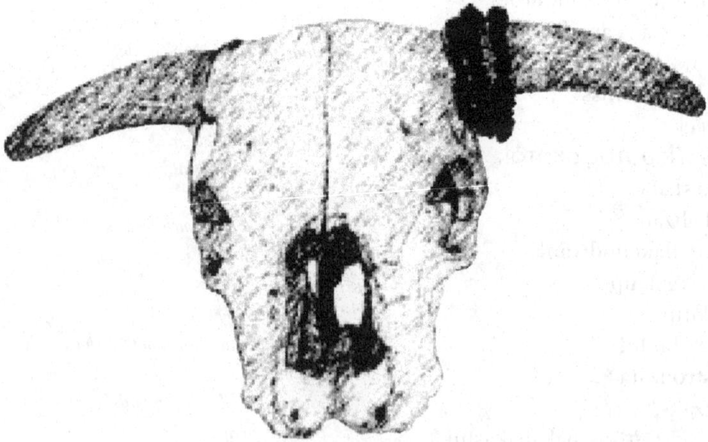

image: GobQ/T. Warburton y Bajo

BULLY / TYRANT (& VARIATIONS) いじめっ子

AFRIKAANS afknouer *(pl.)* *
ALBANIAN tyrán **
ARABIC balta´gi / baltági-´ya *
BASQUE mokokari *
CANTONESE ngokba *
CATALAN abusananos [2]
CROATIAN tiranin *
CZECH násilnik *
DANISH bølle *
ESTONIAN riiukukk *
FARSI tēlēt **
FINNISH kiusaaja *
FRENCH fouineur ** ; péte sec [3]
GAELIC, IRISH maistín *
GERMAN Raufbold *
GREEK, MOD. α πρόσωπο που χρησψοποίεί βια / a prósopo poi hrepsopoíeí via *
HEBREW ba ʻal *
HINDI / URDU bānkā *
ICELANDIC hrekkjusvín [3]
ITALIAN bullo *(m)* / bulla *(f)* [3]
JAPANESE いじめっ子 ijimekko **
MALAYU zalim *
MARATHI agadhaṯa *
NAHUATL tlacamixpoloc *
NORWEGIAN bolle [3]
POLISH tyran **
PORTUGUESE valentão *
ROMANIAN gălăgios *
RUSSIAN зади́ра / zadíra *
SERBIAN насилник / nasilnik *
SOTHO, N ngnwete *
SPANISH / TAGALOG matón [4]
SWEDISH uoversittare *
TAMIL cilami *
TELEGU udāsi *
THAI kón phàan *
TURKISH zorba *
UKRAINIAN залыакуватй / zalyakuvaty *
UZBEK буйруқбоз / buyruqboz *
VIETNAMESE du-côn *
WELSH erlidiwr *
YORUBA adánilóró *
ZULU ingqweie *

* *bully;*
** *"tyrant";*
2 *bully, child abuser;*
3 *one who cuts dry farts, grumpy bully.*
4 *"killer," bad-ass/arse, thug, bully.*

зади́ра

image: GobQ/Marisa Feinstein

BUSY BODY, NOSEY, GOSSIP (& VARIATIONS) чақимч

AFRIKAANS Agat´a / Agatha [2]
ARABIC qīl wa qāl *
BASQUE esamesa *; usnakari **
BELARUSIAN плётка / plëtka *
BENGALI pete katha thake na **
BOSNIAN treč *
CANTONESE sihfei *
CATALAN xafarderia *
CREOLE/HAITIAN tripotay *
CROATIAN / SERB torokanje ; торокање / torokanje *
CZECH babská huba * ; toura **
DANISH bagtalelse *
DUTCH geroddel *
ESTONIAN klatš / klatšija **
FARSI dari vari *
FINNISH juoru *; juoraja *
FRENCH bavardage *; Mes affaires font mal au cul. [3]
GAELIC, IRISH cardáil *
GAELIC, SCOTS bruinnein *
GERMAN / BAV. Ratschkathl *
GREEK, MOD. κουτσομπολης / koytsompolis**
HAUSA jìta jìta *
HEBREW rekheelot *
HINDI / URDU afwah *
ICELANDIC þvadur * ; slettireka **
ITALIAN chiacchierone *(m)* /chiacchierona *(f)* *
JAPANESE ゴシップ好きな人 goshippu suki na hito *
KOREAN chap-dam *
LATIN gerrarum *
LATVIAN tenkas *
LITHUANIAN liĕuvau´ti *
MACEDONIAN гласина / glasina [4]
MALAYU berbual [4]
MANDARIN 爱飞短流长的人 àifēi duăn liú-cháng de rén **
MARATHI davandāla [5]
MONGOLIAN хөөрөө / hööröö *
NAHUATL tlatenehualoni *
NEPALI gaph *
NORWEGIAN folkesnakk *
POLISH plotkarz *(m)* / plotkarka *(f)* *
PORTUGUESE fofocas * ; Se liga na porra da sua vida, caralho. [6]
ROMANIAN fleoncánire *
RUSSIAN сплéтня / splétnya [4]
SOTHO, N mosebi *
SPANISH chismoso * ; entremetido **
SWAHILI uzushi **
SWEDISH tompt prat * ; skvallerkärring **
TAGALOG chú-chu [5] ; escoopéra [7]
TAMIL akkappōr *
TELEGU uusu *
THAI gàan sòop sip *
TURKISH dedıkodu *
UKRAINIAN плітки / plitky *
UZBEK чақимч / chaqimch [8]
VIETNAMESE chuyên ngôi lê dôi mách *
WELSH clonc *
YIDDISH r'cheelus *
YORUBA aládásí *
ZULU i(li)cevucevu *

* *gossip;*
** *busy-body, gossip;*
2 *gay gossip;*
3 *"My affairs will hurt yr ass/arse"—m.y.o.f.b.;*
4 *rumours, gossip;*
5 *gossip, tattler;*
6 *"Mind yr own fucking business, you prick!," Braz.;*
7 *manipulative gossip;*
8 *sneak/slanderer.*

CHAUVINIST PIG, MALE/ SEXIST PIG (& VARIATIONS)

大男子主义口

AFRIKAANS seksis vark **
CANTONESE daaih nàamyán jyúyih [2]
CROATIAN / SERB seksistički ; сексистички / seksistički **
CZECH šovinista *
DUTCH een seksist **
FRENCH un phallocrate *
GERMAN Chauvi *
GREEK, MOD. ενας σουυινιστις / enas souvinistis *
ICELANDIC karlremba *
ITALIAN schifoso maschilista *
MANDARIN 大男子主义口 dànánzǐzhǔyìzhě *
PORTUGUESE um machista *
RUSSIAN Пошлая свеня / pošlaya svenya *
SPANISH chauvinista cabrón [4]
SWEDISH mansgris *
VIETNAMESE dàn ông chống chuyên nam nũ´ b inh` quyê`n *
ZULU azeyise ezinye izizwe *

* *chauvinist pig/male chauvinist pig;*
** *sexist/sexist pig;*
2 *male chauvinism;*
3 *male chauvinist bastard.*

illustr., © 2008, Graham Willoughby

Пошлая свеня

ενας σουυινιστις

сексистички

CHICKEN SHIT, COWARD (& VARIATIONS) 孱

AFRIKAANS bangbroek *
ALBANIAN burracák/ burracáku *
ARABIC / MOROC. maroud *
ARMENIAN vakhi´god *
BASQUE oilo *
BELARUSIAN засранiеч / zasranieč **
BENGALI neka[2]
BOSNIAN / CROATIAN plāšljivac *
BULGARIAN страхливец / strakhlivets *;
прислио / prislio[4]
CANTONESE móuhdáamge yàhn *
CATALAN cagueta[5];
cagacalces[6]
CREOLE/HAITIAN kapon *
CZECH srác[4];
zbabělec * ;
DANISH feje hund * ;
tøsedreng[8]
DUTCH bagger schijten[4]
ESTONIAN Situ püksi.[9]
FARSI nâmard *
FINNISH paskavatsa[3]
FRENCH lâche *;
péteur *(m)* / péteuse *(f)*[10]
GAELIC, IRISH / GAELIC, SCOTS cladhaire[3]
GERMAN feigling *
GREEK, MOD. διλος γαριολι / dilos garioli[3]
HAUSA matsoraci *
HEBREW pakhdan *
HINDI / URDU Phat ke hāt me āna.[4]
ICELANDIC skítseiði[3];
brennivínskjarkur[11]
ITALIAN cacasotto[3]
JAPANESE ひきょう者 hikyōsha *
KOREAN kŏp-jaeng-i *
LATIN muricidus * ; mortuo leoni et lepores insultant[12]
LATVIAN glēvilus *
LITHUANIAN bailys *
MACEDONIAN мрсулко / mrsulko[3]
MALAYU penakut *
MANDARIN 孱 chán *
MARATHI bhibhista *
NAHUATL yollamicqui *
NEPALI derrpok *
NORWEGIAN feigning *
POLISH tchórz *
PORTUGUESE cagalhão[3];
borra-botas[13]
QUECHUA llaqlla *
ROMANIAN poltron *
RUSSIAN дристат / dristát **
SERBIAN кукавица / kukavica *;
пика / pika[14]
SOTHO, N lefšega *
SPANISH cagón[4];
¡Eres un/una cagado/cagada![15]
SWAHILI mwoga *
SWEDISH tönt[2];
fegis[2]
TAGALOG kákak[2];
tarkók[2];
dagá[16]
TAMIL cakita *;
kottai-cettavan *
TELEGU kāpurusudu[8]
THAI kêe klàt[3]
TURKISH korkak *
UKRAINIAN боягуз/boyaguz *
URDU Phat ke hāt me āna.[4]
UZBEK макиёон / makiyon[18]
VIETNAMESE nhút-nhát *
WELSH llwfrddyn *
YIDDISH shvuntz[3]
YORUBA ojo èǹìyàn *
ZAPOTEC namuxé *
ZULU i(il)gwala *

* *coward/cowardly;*
** *"Shits his pants!"*
2 *coward, wuss, scaredy-cat;*
3 *chicken-shit coward;*
4 *pants-shitter/scared shitless/shits mud;*
5 *shitty coward;*
6 *shits candy;*
7 *cowardly dog;*

8 *"girly-boy," effeminite coward;*
9 *"Go shit yourself/yr pants";*
10 *farty coward;*
11 *"Dutch Courage";*
12 *"Even rabbits attack a dead lion;"*
13 *shits-in-his-boots;*
14 *cowardly cunt of a man;*
15 *"You're a shitty coward!"*
16 *scared shitless & struck stupid by love;*
17 *emasculated coward—no balls/bollocks;*
18 *"chicken," coward—Farsi loan word.*

Liz Swados

διλος γαριολι

CHILD MOLESTER, PÆDOPHILE (& VARIATIONS)

ロリコン

AFRIKAANS Werf eter. [8]
CANTONESE hāai yáu [4]
CATALAN abusananos [6]
CZECH / RUSSIAN pedofil *; педофил / pedofil *
FARSI motejâvez [5]
FRENCH pédophile *
GAELIC, IRISH mís-úsáid ghnéis ar pháistí [2]
GERMAN Kindbelästiger [5]
GREEK, MOD. κεκάκι / kekáki [9]
ICELANDIC barnaníðingur **
ITALIAN pedofilo *; pedoporno [7]
JAPANESE ロリコン rorikon [3]
MANDARIN 恋童癖者 liàntóngpǐzhě *
NORWEGIAN barneknuller [10]; barne-bæsjsniffer [11]
PORTUGUESE molester dia criança **
SPANISH molestador **
SWAHILI kujamiiana kwa maharimu [12]
SWEDISH barnknullarre [10]
UKRAINIAN педофілія / pedofiliya *
YORUBA asenilori [13]

* *pædophile;*
** *child molester;*
2 *child sexual abuse;*
3 *Lolita complex;*
4 *molester of females;*
5 *molester;*
6 *child abuser;*
7 *child porn;*
8 *old bastard child molester in the bk.-yard;*
9 *"jailbait," virgin adolescent or pre-adolesc. enticed by pederast;*
10 *"baby-fucker";*
11 *"baby-shit sniffer";*
12 *incest;*
13 *"Sugar-daddy," fucks young girls & pimps them out.*

κεκάκι

CLIT, CLITORIS (& VARIATIONS)

τριψε το μυνι

AFRIKAANS snor mossel *
BASQUE emazakil *
BENGALI sut-marawni **
CATALAN la perla[2];
la caputxeta vermella[3];
el punt-G [4];
jugar al Parxís [5]
CROATIAN "Grickao si klitoris, Lepi Mario" [6]
CZECH ztopořit se [7]
DANISH kilderen [8]
DUTCH beffen [9]
ESTONIAN häykieli *
FINNISH häykieli *
FRENCH clito *;
Léche mon clito. [10]
GAELIC, IRISH brillín *;
Breall! [12]
GAELIC, SCOTS brillean *
GERMAN Kitzler, der *
GREEK, MOD. τριψε το μυνι / tripse to muni [11]
HEBREW Lakeki li et hadgdegan. [10]
HINDI / URDU chunni *;
Mera chunni chōs. [10];
chhola phudakna [13]
ICELANDIC snípur *
ITALIAN grilletto [14];
fare un ditalino [11]
JAPANESE あそこ asoko *
MALAYU bijik *
MALTESE zibjah *
MANDARIN 阴蒂 yīn dì *
NAHUATL zacapilli *
NORWEGIAN klit *;
onanere [11]
PORTUGUESE grelo *
ROMANIAN lindic *;
degetica [11]
RUSSIAN сикель / síkel' *
SINHALA huthey bijja *
SLOVENIAN ščegija *
SPANISH clíto *;
pipote *
SWAHILI kisimi *
SWEDISH klitorist *
TAGALOG maní' *;
ngatngát [11]
THAI tob bed [11]
TURKISH bızır *
ZULU umsunu *

* *clit;*
** *clit-rubbing wanker;*
2 *"pearl";*
3 *"little red hood";*
4 *G-spot;*
5 *"Play parchisi," clit-finger;*
6 *"You bit the clit, pretty boy Mario" — cult Croat. punk rock song, "Pannonian Satan";*
7 *erect clit;*
8 *"tickler";*
9 *clit-licking;*
10 *"Lick my clit";*
11 *clit wank;*
12 *"You fool/dumb clit!"*
13 *erect clit;*
14 *"gun trigger"*

сикель

あそこ

COCKSUCKER/ DICK SUCKER (& VARIATIONS) Сорши

AFRIKAANS Delphiniums soek. [2]
ALBANIAN Hanksh karin tim! [3]
ARABIC/TUNIS. Ardā il asba. **
ARMENIAN galert´zotogh * ;
Gleer ger. **
BELARUSIAN чуясос / čujasos *
BOSNIAN Pusi kurac! **
BULGARIAN свиркажиа / svirkazhia *
BURMESE Nga l̲èe s̲oat. [3]
CANTONESE hām lán ** ;
wáan luhk gáu [4]
CATALAN mamar la [5] ;
xuclar la [5]
CHABACANO chuparol *
CREOLE/HAITIAN souse´ zozo **
CROATIAN / SERB puči kurac*;
пучи курац / puči kurac*
CZECH vikoui [6]
DANISH piksluger * ;
Sut djævlepik din bøsseludende. [7]
DUTCH Ga een pik zuigen! * ;
Ga je moeder pijpen. [8]
ESTONIAN türaimeja *;
Laku ennast. [9]
FARSI keerlees *
FINNISH kullin lutkuttaja *;
Ime mun muna. [3]
FRENCH enfoiré *;
Avaler la fumée. [10]
GAELIC, IRISH Diúl mo bhod. [3]
GERMAN Schwanzlutscher, der * ;
Saugen mein shwanse. [3]
GREEK, MOD. ψολογλιφι / psologlifi * ;
Ρουφα ελλινικο καβλι. / Roufa elliniko kavli. [11]
HEBREW Lech timzoz. **
HINDI / URDU lund chōsō / lund chusu *
HUNGARIAN faszszopó *
ICELANDIC typpasjúgari * ;
fífl *

ITALIAN ciuccia cazzi *;
leccacazzi [13]
la boccharina (f)
JAPANESE おフェラする人 ofera suru hito *
KAZAKH Сорши. / Sorši. **
KOREAN Ko-chu pal-uh. [3]
LATIN irrumator *
LATVIAN penjalaizha / pipeljlaizha *
LITHUANIAN bybciulpys *
MACEDONIAN Дами го пушиш калешио. / Dami go pušiš kalešio. [15]
MALAYU Isap/Hisap kote. **
MALTESE Busli garrretta ala francisa. [16]
MANDARIN 哈棒 hā bàng **;
哈屌 hā diǎo **
MONGOLIAN Боовеиг мин хо. / Booveig min kho. [3]
NORWEGIAN kuksuger * ;
Sug kuk. **
POLISH Zjedz moj chuj. [3]
PORTUGUESE lambe-pissas * ;
Vai chupá uma piça. **
QUECHUA Pichiku mikhuy. [3]
ROMANIAN muist * ;
sugi pula **;
poponar [7]
RUSSIAN хуесос / khuesós * ;
хуеплет / khueplet [13]
SPANISH Chúpe me. / Chupame la verga! / Mama la pinga. [3] ;
mamon [17] ;
soplapichas / soplapitos [18] ;
¡Chupame el loly! [19] ;
!Chupa la que cuelga! [20] ;
¡Mamavergas! [21] ;
SWAHILI Nyonya boe. **
SWEDISH kuksugare. * ;
Sug min kuk. [3] ;
Din mama suger norsk svan pitt. [22]
TAGALOG chupador *
TAMIL Ūmpu. **
THAI chai ɓpàak [23]

TURKISH Çukummu yala. [3]
UKRAINIAN Сосы мене. / Sosy mene. [3]
UZBEK Кутагимний е. / Kutagimny ye. [3]
VIETNAMESE An cac tao nè. [3]
WELSH Mae dy fam yn llyfu cociau Saes. [24]

* *cock/dick-sucker;*
** *"(Go) Suck cock/dick";*
2 *"Cruise for delpheniums";*
3 *"Eat/suck my dick/cock";*
4 *"69";*
5 *"suck it/lick it";*
6 *"smoke up";*
7 *"Go suck devil-dick/cock you hunchbacked faggot."*
8 *"Go suck yr mother's dick/cock";*
9 *"Go suck yourself off";*
10 *"Swallow cigar smoke;"*
11 *"Eat Greek dick/cock";*
12 *dick/cock-sucker; cock-tease;*
13 *male dick/cocksucking faggot;*
14 *"little mouth vendor";*
15 *"Suck my huge dick/cock";*
16 *"French-kiss my foreskin";*
17 *"Cock/dick-licker," C. Ric.;*
18 *"Cock/dick-blower," C. Ric.;*
19 *"Suck the lollypop!, " Chil.;*
20 *"Suck what hangs!" / "Suck what dangles!"; Chil.;*
21 *"cock/dick suckler,";*
22 *"Yr mother sucks Norwegian swan cock/dick";*
23 *oral sex, eating cock or pussy;*
24 *"Yr mother licks Englishmen's cocks/dicks..."*

哈屌

COCK-TEASE / PRICK-TEASE, FLIRT
(& VARIATIONS)

男誑し

AFRIKAANS flerrie poes [2]
ARABIC neǵśa / neǵśîn **
BASQUE maitajotkatzaile **
CATALAN escalfapolles *; escalfabraguetes [3]
CHABACANO caraballa [4]
CROATIAN / SERB ra kurka *; ра курка / ra kurka *
CZECH koketovat [5]
DANISH narrefisse [6]
DUTCH flirten *
FINNISH härnättä *; pitää peliä **
FRENCH bandeuse * ; te coquet **
GAELIC, IRISH cliúsaí **
GAELIC, SCOTS leodag *
GERMAN Schwanznecken *
GREEK, MOD. ψολοβιρητα / psolovirihta*
HEBREW rodef *
HINDI / URDU lund sehlana *
HUNGARIAN fapicsa [8]
ICELANDIC daðurdrós *
ITALIAN donna che ama provocare gli uomini senza però concedersi *; ficona [8]
JAPANESE 男誑し otokotarashi *
MANDARIN 狐狸精 hú li jīng [7]
NAHUATL winyan skatesa **
POLISH draz nić **
PORTUGUESE mulher fresca *
RUSSIAN дрочила / dročíla *
SOTHO, N seaka *; goketša banna [9]
SPANISH / CUB. caliente pigna *
SWEDISH ribbträff *
TAGALOG alémbong [9]
THAI nàa maw *

* *cock/prick-tease;*
** *flirt;*
2 *cunty flirt/flirty cunt;*
3 *crotch heater / cock or pussy teaser;*
4 *ball-busting cock-tease/bitch;*
5 *coquet," gorgeous flirt;*
6 *"joker cunt," cock/prick-tease;*
7 *"spirit of fox," slutty & bitchy cock/prick-tease.*
8 *prick-teasing cunt;*
9 *slutty flirt & cock/prick-tease;*

illustr., © 2008, Graham Willoughby

CONCEITED / SNOTTY (& VARIATIONS)

Москаль

AFRIKAANS eiewys *
ALBANIAN karderr *(m)* 2
ARABIC mutakkabbir *
ARMENIAN hampag 3
BASQUE mokoti **
BELARUSIAN самалубивы / samalubivy 4
BENGALI nak ūnchu **
CANTONESE jihkwàge *
CATALAN vanitós *
CREOLE/HAITIAN grosye *
CROATIAN / SERB uvašen **; увашен / uvašen **
CZECH basibozuk **
DANISH storsnudet **
DUTCH snotterneus **
ESTONIAN ebaviisakas **
FARSI baland *
FINNISH räkänokka *
FRENCH pisse-froid 5
GAELIC, IRISH leitheadach *
GAELIC, SCOTS balganta *
GERMAN / BAV. Gschwoikopf **
GREEK, MOD. ψηλομιτι / psilomiti **
HEBREW bazooy **
HINDI/ URDU Sir Chada *; burā **
ICELANDIC hégómlegur *; hortugur **
ITALIAN borioso *; moccioso **
JAPANESE うぬぼれの強い unubore no tsuyoi *
KOREAN mu-re han **
LATIN malus pudor 6
MACEDONIAN мрсулко / mrsulko **
MALAYU biadab **
MANDARIN 狂 kuáng *
MARATHI ahaṅkārī *
MONGOLIAN нусс / nuss **
NAHUATL moneconi **
NORWEGIAN innsbilsk *; snørret **
POLISH zarozumiały *
PORTUGUESE ranhoso **; altivo **; patricinha 7
ROMANIAN înfumarat *
RUSSIAN мудак / mudak **; Москаль / Moskál´ 8; Своё говно не воняет. / Svoe govnó ne vonyáet. 9
SOMALI edebdaran **
SOTHO, N ikganšhago *
SPANISH mocoso **
SWAHILI fidhuli **
SWEDISH översittare **
TAGALOG ungás **
THAI keùuang **; khràan 10
TURKISH kendini beğenmiş *
UKRAINIAN зарозумілий / zarozumilyý *
UZBEK мақтанчоқ / maqtanchoq *
VIETNAMESE tĩnh tu-phu *
WELSH balch *
YIDDISH chutzpah 11
YORUBA láfojúdi **
ZAPOTEC nayá´ 10
ZULU i´qhoshela / i´li´qhoshela 12

* *conceited, arrogant;*
** *snotty, stuck-up, rude;*
2 *cocky;*
3 *snob;*
4 *vain;*
5 *"pisses cold/cold fish," snotty;*
6 *false modesty;*
7 *rich snotty bitch;*
8 *"Snotty Muskovite";*
9 *"[He] thinks his own shit doesn't stink";*
10 *aloof, indifferent, snotty;*
11 *per Harlan Ellison, "gall, brazen nerve, audacity, shamelessness, presumption-plus-arrogance, such as no other word, and no other language, can do justice";*
12 *conceited ass/arsehole.*

CONDOM, CONDOMS / RUBBER / RUBBERS (& VARIATIONS) ГОЛОШИ

AFRIKAANS connie *;
kondoom *;
femidom **;
sokkie [2]
ARABIC al-wāqī adhdhakarï *
ARMENIAN gandon *
BENGALI kandohm *
BULGARIAN презерватиф / prezervatif *;
презерватиф капут / prezervatif kaput [6];
BURMESE kung dung *
CANTONESE beiyahndói *
CATALAN paraigües *;
condó *;
Tinc condó. / Tinc paraigües. [7]
BOSNIAN / CROATIAN / SERB prezervativ *;
презерватив / prezervativ *
CZECH prezervatv *;
kondom *
DANISH præservativ *;
Nej, jeg har ikke en præservativ, har du? [8]
DUTCH condoom, een *;
Ga een condoom zuigen! [9]
FARSI kâput [6];
Kâputam pareh shod. [10]
FRENCH capote anglais [4];
capote [5]
GAELIC, IRISH coiscín *
GERMAN Kondom *;
Gummi *
GREEK, MOD. προφυλακτικό / profilaktiko *
GUJARATI nirod *
HAUSA roba hana d'aukar ciki *
HEBREW gumy *
HINDI / URDU kāndam *;
nirod *
HUNGARIAN óvszer *
ICELANDIC smokkur *
INDONESIAN kondom *
ITALIAN preservativo, il *;
guanto, il [3];
goldone *
JAPANESE 座頭市 zatōichi [14]
KAZAKH тасак кап / tasak kap *;
презерватив / prezervativ *
KHMER s'raom un-nā-mai *
MALTESE ja condom mc'arrat
POLISH prezerwatywa *;
guma *
PORTUGUESE preservativo, um *
RUSSIAN Гандон! / Gandon! [11];
голоши / galóši [12];
нахуйник / naxújnik
SLOVENIAN kondom *
SPANISH / MEX el sin mangas *
SWAHILI kondomu *
TAGALOG goma *;
amóg *
THAI tŭng yahng à'nah'mai *;
tŭng yahng *
UZBEK презерватив / prezervativ *
VIETNAMESE bao cao su *

* *"condom" / "a condom" / "rubber"; BURMESE: "Condoms"*
** *"female condom";*
2 *"Little Sock";*
3 *"glove, the";*
4 *"English hood";*
5 *"hood";*
6 *"broken/torn condom";*
7 *"I have a condom";*
8 *"I don't have a condom—do you?";*
9 *"Go suck a condom;*
10 *"My 'hood' ripped."*
11 *"You condom!"*
12 *"galoshes";*
13 *"ambulatory torn condom" = asshole/jerk/idiot;*
14 *"unsheathed blade," condomless cock/dick, after cinema's blind Japanese swordsman.*

座頭市

CRAZY / INSANE / DELUSIONAL / FUCKED UP (& VARIATIONS) 神经病

AFRIKAANS kanksinnig *;
"Milly" [2]
ARABIC jin *;
jini [5]
ARMENIAN Ton xivirnes... [6]
BASQUE zoro *;
ero *
BELARUSIAN варьят / var´yat *
BENGALI matha kharap *;
dumukho sap [7]
BULGARIAN келеш / keleš [8]
CANTONESE song *;
díu gāu kui [4]
CATALAN boig *;
Estan lluitant al teu tarro. [9]
CHABACANO / TAGALOG loco-loco *
CREOLE/HAITIAN fou *;
CROATIAN / SERB lud *;
луд / lud *
CZECH blázív *;
dvoupólov [7]
DANISH skør *;
sindssyg *
DUTCH aso [11]
ESTONIAN hull *;
ogar *
FARSI divune *;
shaydoi [8]
FINNISH järjëton *;
hullu *
FRENCH fou *;
cheulou [10];
baisé vers le haut [4];
T es fou!? [12]
FRENCH (VERLAN) ouf *
GAELIC, IRISH craiceáilte *;
Tá tú glan as do mheabhair! [13]
GAELIC, SCOTS craicte *;
dòdach [14]

GERMAN verrückt *;
Du has wohl ´n Arsch offen. [15]
GREEK, MOD. τρελος / trelos *
GUJARATI gando *
HEBREW meturaf *;
meshuga [3];
ya muzar [10]
HINDI pāgal *;
sankī [10]
HUNGARIAN örlüt *
ICELANDIC geðveikur *;
vitlaus [2]
INDONESIAN sinting *
ITALIAN matto *;
pazzo *;
folle *
JAPANESE クルクル・パー kuru-kuru paaaa *
KAZAKH сорли / sorli [4];
куган / kugan [16]
KOREAN mi-ch'ĭn *;
byung shin [3]
LATIN demensentis *
LITHUANIAN psichas [3]
MACEDONIAN залуден / zaluden *;
занесен / zanesen *
MALAYU gila *;
gila bahasa [10]
MANDARIN 神经病 shén jīng bìng **
MARATHI pisanvalli *;
pisāṯa [5]
MONGOLIAN галзуу / galzuu *
NAHUATL ahmimati *
NEPALI pagal *
NORWEGIAN galning *;
Et virus herpa harddisken min. [17]
POLISH szalony *;
obłąkany *;
stukięty [2];
pojebany [4]
PORTUGUESE louco *;
fodido acima [4];
Vou ficar puto! [18]
QUECHUA waq´a *

ROMANIAN nebun *
RUSSIAN е-анашка / ebanaška *;
пиздоватый / pizdovátyy [4];
мудозвон / mudozvon [10];
Цучка дерганаја. / Tsučka derganaya. [16]
SLOVENIAN zmešan *
SOMALI Wād walantahay. [13]
SOTHO, N gafago *
SPANISH loco/loca * ;
loco pinga
SWAHILI enye wazumi * ;
wazumi **
SWEDISH tokig *;
galen **;
vansinnig [4]
THAI kón tington [4];
d´tit [5];
yai bâh [16]
TURKISH çılgın *
UKRAINIAN божевильний / boževil´nyy *
UZBEK ессиз / essiz *;
жинни /jinni [5]
VIETNAMESE diên *;
do khùng *
WELSH ynfyd *
YIDDISH farblondjet [2];
meshungina [10] ;
meshungina cunt [10] ;
YORUBA áfri * ;
asiwèrè **
ZAPOTEC ique ribí / ique ridxé **
ZULU ikhanda * ;
Uyahlanya yini? [12]

* *crazy, insane;*
** *delusional, lunatic;*
2 *"ditzy, daft, mad, lost";*
3 *psycho, psychotic;*
4 *fucked-up/weirdo, delusional;*
5 *"amour fou"*
= crazy/mad love or infatuation;
6 *"You're a nut case/fruitcake";*
7 *"bi-polar";*
8 *"mental, nut-case";*
9 *"They're fighting in yr head";*
10 *"weirdo/nuts/crazy";*
11 *sociopath/anti-social;*
12 *"Are you crazy?!";*
13 *"You're totally out of your mind!"*
14 *"Out of yr box";*
15 *"You've got your ass/arse open!"*
= You're crazy!
16 *"psycho bitch";*
17 *"A virus damaged my hard drive...";*
18 *"I'm going nuts/crazy!"*
19 *"crazy dick/cock";*
20 *"crazy cunt," atrributed to Woody Allen.*

τρελος

クルクル・パー

illustr., © 2008, Graham Willoughby

CRIPPLE/ CRIP, GIMP, LAME изрод
(& VARIATIONS)

AFRIKAANS kreuppele *
ALBANIAN topáll **
BASQUE txanket **
BELARUS./RUSSIAN/UKRAIN. калека/kaleka *
BENGALI langda **
BOSNIAN sakata *
BULGARIAN изрод/izrod [2]
CANTONESE bàige yàhn *
CATALAN malparit [2]
CREOLE/HAITIAN estropye *
CROATIAN osakatiti *
CZECH mrzák *
DANISH crackbarn [3];
rottebarn [4]
ESTONIAN sant *
FARSI cholagh *
FINNISH raajarikko *
FRENCH boiteux *(m)* / boiteuse *(f)* *
GAELIC, IRISH sreang [2]
GAELIC, SCOTS crùbach *
GERMAN Krüppel *
GREEK, MOD. αναπιρος / anapiros *
HEBREW yoste´ [2]
HINDI / URDU lunjā **
ICELANDIC bæklaður maður *
ITALIAN zoppo *(m.)* / zoppa *(f.)* *
JAPANESE 不自由者 fujiyūsha
KOREAN byungshin *
MALAYU orang kakat [2]
MANDARIN 使变跛 shǐ biànbǒ *
MARATHI apārā [5]
NAHUATL huelatzin *
NORWEGIAN infall [2]
POLISH kaleka *
PORTUGUESE aleijado *(m)* / aleijada *(f)* *
ROMANIAN schilod *
SPANISH lisiado *;
cojo *;
fenómeno [2]
SWEDISH krympling *;
hugskott [2]
TAGALOG taong kakatuwá [2]
THAI bàawt *
TURKISH kötürüm *
WELSH effryd *
YIDDISH kalikeh *
ZULU isidalwa *

* *cripple;*
** *gimp/lame/unable to use hands &/or feet;*
2 *lame/crippled/malformed freak;*
3 *crack baby/crack child;*
4 *rat-child;*
5 *deformed ugly freakish idiot. "Born feet first."*

images: GobQ/T.Warburton y Bajo

CROOK, GONIF, SHYSTER
(& VARIATIONS)

AFRIKAANS skurk *;
kroek *;
verneuker **
ALBANIAN tinzár *
ARABIC ganav *;
qallob **
ARMENIAN kunel **
BASQUE iruzurtzaile *
BENGALI jocchor **
CANTONESE jeuifáan *
CATALAN malfaçtor *
CREOLE/HAITIAN vòlè *
CROATIAN propalìca *;
beda od čovjeką [2]
CZECH zloinec * ;
cikan [2];
apac [3]
DANISH forbryder *
DUTCH hufter [4]
ESTONIAN roimar *
FARSI kolâh bardâri **
FINNISH kouku * ;
kaarre *
FRENCH escroc *(m)* * ; houlette *(f)* *
FRENCH (VERLAN) Ce mec est chelou. [5]
GAELIC, IRISH gadaí *
GAELIC, SCOTS gadaiche *
GERMAN Schnorrer *
GREEK, MOD. απανδεονα /apandeona *
HEBREW ramay **
HINDI / NEPALI / URDU chōr *
HUNGARIAN roma [2]
ICELANDIC krimmi *;
svikari **
INDONESIAN penipu **
ITALIAN imbroglione *(m)* / imbrogliona *(f)* *;
JAPANESE 犯罪者 hanzaisha *
KHMER jao *
KOREAN pŏm-choe-ŭe *
LATIN flur *
LITHUANIAN kablys´ *

MACEDONIAN крадетс / kradets *
MALAYU curaang *
MALTESE halliel *(m)* / halleal *(f)* *
MANDARIN 罪犯 zuìfàn *
MARATHI cora *
NAHUATL malinqi *
NORWEGIAN forbryter *
POLISH zgięcie *
PORTUGUESE chaveca *
RUSSIAN зюлик / zyulik **
SERBIAN пропалица / propalìca *
SLOVENIAN tat *
SOMALI dambīle *
SPANISH caga-sala [6] / caga-cosina [6] /
caga-bañera [6] / caga-balcon [6]
SWAHILI mhalifu *
SWEDISH tjuv **
TAGALOG matinggéra *
TELEGU doganakoduku **
THAI kêe góng [7]
TURKISH değneğ *;
kanca *
UKRAINIAN крюк / kriuk *
URDU xuligan [8]
UZBEK қалб / qalb [2]
VIETNAMESE tô̲l-pha̲m *
WELSH drygwr *
YIDDISH gonif **
YORUBA bòlójú *
ZAPOTEC gubaana´ *
ZULU iselelesi *

罪
犯

* *crook, gonif, thief;*
** *shyster, con-man, cheat;*
2 *"gypsey," cheat, liar, crook, thief;*
3 *"Apache," robber, crook;*
4 *"rip-off artist";*
5 *"That guy is louche/criminal/crooked/rough trade";*
6 *burglar who ritually shits in yr living rm./ shits in yr kitchen/ shits in yr bathtub/ shits on yr balcony;*
7 *"shitty crook."*

CUNT, PUSSY (& VARIATIONS) (お) まんこ

AFRIKAANS poes *;
slymsloot *;
suikerbus [2]
ALBANIAN piçkë *
ARABIC kus / kūz *;
zabour *
ARMENIAN bōuts *;
pouts *;
iqap´ogh *
BASQUE alu(a) * ;
potorro *;
ematutu *
BELARUSIAN / UKRAINIAN пизда / pizda *
BENGALI gud / gude *
BOSNIAN / POLISH / ROMANIAN pizda *
BULGARIAN коте / kote *;
катеритча / kateritchka *;
пеперудка / peperudka *
BURMESE sòot`baht
CANTONESE hāi *;
yàmdouh *;
bāau yùh [4]
CATALAN cony *;
conill *;
paparrús *;
fufa *;
patata *;
pera [5];
El cony de deu! [6]
CHABACANO coño * ;
puki *
CREOLE/HAITIAN coco *
CROATIAN / SERB pička *;
пичка / pička *
CZECH kunda *;
pia *;
pochva *
DANISH mis *;
fisse *;
drivhuset [7];
revne [8]

DUTCH kut * ;
flamoes * ;
vleesroos [9]
ESTONIAN vit * ;
tuss / tussu *
FARSI kos * ;
faraj *
FINNISH pillu *;
pimppi *;
tuhero *;
Vittujen kevät! [10]
FRENCH con *;
cromouille [8];
la chatte [11]
GAELIC, IRISH báltái *;
pís *
GAELIC, SCOTS pitean *;
faighean ** ;
truiteag *;
piseag [11]
GERMAN Fotze, die **;
Muschi, die [11] ;
Puderdose, die *
GREEK, MOD. μουνί / muní *
GUJARATI / HINDI / URDU chōt *
HEBREW kus *
HUNGARIAN picsa * ;
pina *
ICELANDIC kunta *;
pussa *;
píka *;
tussa *;
skithæl *;
kvensköp;
drullosokkur *
INDONESIAN memek / pepek*;
puki *
ITALIAN brinca *;
fica *;
figa *;
finca *
JAPANESE (お) まんこ (o-)manko *
KANNADA tullu / thulla *
KAZAKH / UZBEK ам / am *

KHMER pom pēt *
KOREAN bojii / pojii *
LATIN cunnus *
LATVIAN pezha *
LITHUANIAN pyzda *
MACEDONIAN пичка / pička *;
пичкина клисура / pičkina klisura [12]
MALAYU pantnat *;
puki *;
pepek *
MANDARIN 阴道 yīndào *
MARATHI pucchi *
MONGOLIAN пизда / pizdá *
NAUATL maxactli *
NEPALI puti *
NORWEGIAN møs *;
bollemus [13];
fitte *
PORTUGUESE braguilha *;
cona *;
pita *
QUECHUA / BOLIV. chupilla *
RUSSIAN пизда / pizdá *;
манда / mandá *;
пиздобратия / pizdobrátiya [14]
SINHALA kimba *;
huttha *
SLOVENIAN pička *;
pižda *
SOMALI seel *
SPANISH coño *;
chocho *;
toto *;
La crica *;
almeja [15];
La cosita [16]
SWAHILI kuma *;
uke *
SWEDISH fitta *;
mus *;
slita [8];
mutta [17]
TAGALOG bilát *;
bwáka *;
choque *;
pudáy *;
kiki *;
kepias *
TAMIL punda / pundai *;
kōdhi *
TELEGU pōku *;
kutta *
THAI hêe *;
gaʻbpi *;
ai sat [17]
TURKISH şiftali *;
amçuk *;
amina *;
um **
VIETNAMESE lo`n *;
âm-da̲o *;
âm-môn *
WELSH cont tew [18];
gont hoyw [19];
cont *
YIDDISH k´nish *
YORUBA òbò *
ZULU golo *

阴道

* *cunt/pussy;*
** *cunt;*
2 *"sugarbush," pubes;*
3 *"Good pussy/cunt," Tunis.;*
4 *"abalone";*
5 *"fem. dog";*
6 *"God's cunt!"*
7 *"greenhouse";*
8 *"slit";*
9 *"flesh rose";*
10 *"Pussy Springs!"*
11 *"fem. cat";*
12 *"cunt canyon;*
13 *"mouse-bowl";*
14 *"Brothership/Fellowship of the cunt";*
15 *"clam";*
16 *"The little thing;"*
17 *"Twat";*
18 *"Fat cunt;"*
19 *"gay cunt."*

CUNT/ PUSSY, BLOODY (& VARIATIONS) течка

CATALAN sang a la figa [2]
FARSI periyod **;
ādat e māhāne **
FRENCH Les Anglais [3]
GERMAN/SW. Si hätt dä Schniider. [4]
GREEK, MOD. Φαε το μυνι με τιν περιοδο. / Fae to muni me tin periodo. [5]
PORTUGUESE O seu lambedor das xotas menstruadas. [6]
RUSSIAN течка / tečka ** ;
К ней го́сти пришли́. / K n´ey gósti prišlí. [7] ;
Тётка пришла́. / T´ótkă prišlá. [8]
SPANISH mala semana [9];
El beso del payaso [10]
SWAHILI hedhi **
TAGALOG kumain ng may regla [5]

* *Bloody cunt/pussy;*
** *"monthly";*
2 *"Blood in the pussy/cunt";*
3 *"Redcoats, the" / "English, the";*
4 *"She's got her days";*
5 *"Eat bloody pussy/cunt";*
6 *"You eat menstruating cunt/pussy."*
7 *"She has [her monthly] guests";*
8 *"Her aunt's visiting."*
9 *"bad week";*
10 *"the clown's kiss."*

Φαε
το
μυνι
με
τιν
περιοδο.

CUNT/ PUSSY, DIRTY (& VARIATIONS)

βρομομυνο

AFRIKAANS snerig poes *;
snoek poes [2]
ARABIC/MOROC. El hatchoune deyemak khanez. [3]
BULGARIAN пътка миризлива / putka mirizliva **
CANTONESE wùjòu hāi * ;
sēng hāi ** ;
jyù hāi [4]
CATALAN merda a la figa [5]
CROATIAN/SERB prljava pička * ;
прљава пичка / prljava pička *
DANISH snavset fisse * ;
Du lugter af gammel havmåge fisse. [6]
DUTCH vuil kut *
FARSI kos kasife *
FINNISH limavittu [7];
loskavittu [8];
kurapillu [9]
FRENCH Ma tante Rose a débarqué. [10]
GERMAN Mösensaft, der [11] ;
Fotzenatem, der [12]
GAELIC, IRISH báltaí salach *
GAELIC, SCOTS faighean salach *
GREEK, MOD. βρομομυνο / vromomuno *
HUNGARIAN A büdös picsába! [13]
ICELANDIC skítug píka *;
drulla kunta [5];
lyktar af píku [12]
ITALIAN fregna de vacca [14]
JAPANESE 汚いまんこ kitanai manko * ;
マンコっぽい息 manko-ppoi iki [12]
MACEDONIAN пучина канал / pičina kanal [15]
MALAYU pupek daki *
MANDARIN 烂屄 làn bī [16]
NORWEGIAN muggfitte [17]
PORTUGUESE buceta fedida ** ;
respiração da buceta [12]
A sua buceta cheira do peixe. [18]
RUSSIAN пиздá вонйучая / pizdá vonyúčaya ** ;
ебальник / ebál'nik [12]
SPANISH coñocagado [5] ;
alito de coño [12]
TAGALOG kiking mabaho **
THAI hèe men **
URDU bum bhonsda [19]
WELSH Mae gen ti cont mawr drewllyd. [20]
YIDDISH schmegma [21]
ZULU ngquza enukayo **

* *dirty cunt/pussy;*
** *"stinky pussy/cunt";*
2 *"fish cunt/pussy";*
3 *"Your mother's filthy pussy/cunt";*
4 *"pig cunt/pussy";*
5 *"shit in the cunt/pussy"/"shitty cunt";*
6 *"You stink like a herring gull's pussy/cunt";*
7 *"slimy pussy/cunt";*
8 *"slurpie-pussy/cunt";*
9 *"muddy pussy/cunt";*
10 *"Aunt Rosie's arrived";*
11 *"cunt juice";*
12 *"cunt breath" / "pussy breath)";*
13 *"Go to the stinking pussy/cunt!";*
14 *"cow's cunt";*
15 *"cunt canal";*
16 *"rotting cunt";*
17 *"moldy pussy/cunt";*
18 *"Your pussy stinks like fish";*
19 *highly, overly-fucked cunt;*
20 *"You've a big stinky cunt";*
21 *"yeast infection/discharge."*

汚いまんこ

CUNT-BRAIN / PUSSY-BRAIN, CUNT-FACE, CUNT HEAD
(& VARIATIONS)

носа
путка

AFRIKAANS poes gessig [2];
poesdom [3]
BELARUSIAN Пізда нам! / Pizda nam! [4]
BULGARIAN носа путка / nosa putka [5]
CANTONESE hāi yéung [2]
CATALAN caracony [2]
CROATIAN pičkin mozak **;
pička lice [2]
DUTCH neuskut [5]
FARSI kos-xumori [6]
FINNISH vittupaa *;
vittunaama [2];
Vedä vittu päähän. [13]
FRENCH cerveau de chat / cerveau de con **;
souffle de chat/con [7]
GAELIC, IRISH Do bháltaí don diabhal. [8]
GERMAN Fotzengehirn, das **;
Fotzen-
esicht, das [2];
Fotzenatem, der [7]
GREEK, MOD. μυνο μιαλο / muno mialo **
HINDI/URDU chut jaisi shakal [2];
chutiya **
ICELANDIC lyktar af píku [7]
INDONESIAN hidung memek [5]
ITALIAN testa de fregna *
JAPANESE マンコっぽい顔 manko-ppoi kao [2]
MACEDONIAN пичкина плуска/pičkina pluska [9]
MANDARIN 烂屄脸 làn bī liǎn [2]
NORWEGIAN fittesnute [5]
PORTUGUESE cérebro da buceta **;
cara da buceta [2]
RUSSIAN пиздогаловий / pizdógaloviy *;
ебальник / ebál´nik [10]
SERBIAN пичкио мозак / pičkino mozak **
SLOVENIAN Pičkin dim! [11]
SPANISH cabeza de coño *;
cerebro de coño **;
cara de coño [2]
TAGALOG utak kiki **
THAI na'hèe [2]
VIETNAMESE mac laón [2]
WELSH cont hyll [12]

* *cunt-head;*
** *cunt/pussy-brain;*
2 *pussy-gsvr/cunt-face;*
3 *dumb cunt;*
4 *"We're cunting done for!";*
5 *"pussy nose";*
6 *"pussy addict/pussy junkie";*
7 *"cunt/pussy-breath;*
8 *"Yr cunt to the devil!";*
9 *"cunt blister";*
10 *"pussy/cunt-mouth";*
11 *"Smokin' pussy!"*
12 *"ugly cunt;"*
13 *"Draw a cunt on yr forehead."*

пичкио
мозак

CUNT, YOUR MOTHER'S (& VARIATIONS)

Путката майна.

AFRIKAANS Jou moeder se poes! *
ARABIC Kūz umak! *
BOSNIAN Pižda ti materina! *
BULGARIAN Путката майна. / Putkata ti majna. *
CROATIAN / SERB Odi u pičku materine!; Оди у пичку материне! / Odi u pičku materine! **
FARSI Kos naneh. *; Kos khār. [8]
GREEK, MOD. Το μυνι τισ μανας σου. / To muni tis manas sou. [2]
HEBREW Kuz ima selcha. / Kuz umek. *
HINDI / URDU Teri mā ki ānkh. * ; Tere bāp ki chut mai teri maǍ ka lānd. [2]
HUNGARIAN Menj az anyad picsiajaba! **
ICELANDIC Sleiktu píkuna á mömmu þinni. [4]
INDONESIAN Pukima lu. / Puki mak lu. *
ITALIAN Cunn´e mama tua! / La frenga di mammeta! *
KAZAKH Шешенгинг амй. / Shesheng-ning amy. *
MACEDONIAN Мрш у пижду матер. / Mrsh u piždu mater! **
MALAYU Sebelum awak mati, saya nak kau tahu, mak kau ada kotek! [5]
MALTESE F´oxx dik it żukkini/bringiela ommok. [9]
PORTUGUESE Puceta da sua mãe. *
ROMANIAN Pizdă matii. *; Fututi pizdă matii! [6]
SLOVENIAN Pička ti materina! *; Pičkin sin. [7]
SPANISH Concha de tu madre! / Panoch-a de tu madre! *; Concha de tu herm-ana! [8]
SWAHILI Kuma mayo. *
TAGALOG Puki nam. / Puki iná. *
TELEGU Nē amma pāsu / parri. *
VIETNAMESE Cai lon ma mày. *
YORUBA Obo ìyá rè. *

* *"Yr mother's cunt/pussy!"*
** *"Go up your mother's cunt/pussy!"*
2 *"Fuck your mother's cunt!"*
3 *"Yr mother's cock in yr father's cunt!/ Yr mother's dick in yr father's pussy!"*
4 *"Go suck on yr mother's cunt/pussy!"*
5 *"Before you die, I want you to know that yr mother has a cock/dick!"*
6 *"Fuck yr mother's pussy/cunt!"*
7 *"Son of a cunt!"*
8 *"Yr sister's cunt!"*
9 *"Up yr mother's cunt/pussy with zuchini/egg-plant!"*

CUNT, DIVINE (& VARIATIONS)

CATALAN El cony de deu! *; Mecàgum el cony beinet! / Mecàgum el cony sagrat! **
FINNISH Kristuksen vittu! [2]

* *"God's cunt!"*
** *"I shit on the blessed cunt!" / "I shit on the sacred cunt!"*
2 *"Jesus Christ's cunt!"*

Мрш у пиџу матер.

DICK/ COCK/ PRICK (& VARIATIONS) 男根

AFRIKAANS trill *;
snot samboek *;
slang [2]
ALBANIAN kari *
ARABIC ayir *;
zib [3];
zeb [4]; atlā [4]
ARMENIAN ander *;
galēr *;
klir *;
juij *
BASQUE zakila *;
sastada *;
sastako *
BELARUSIAN чуй / čuj *
BENGALI bārā *; boga *
BOSNIAN / CROATIAN / SERB kurač *;
курач / kurač *
BULGARIAN буба / buba *;
хуй / khuj *;
чеп / čep *;
кур / kur *
BURMESE lèe *
CANTONESE làn *;
gāu *;
yàmging *;
lok chaht *; gwán *
CATALAN minga *;
cigala *;
membre *;
mànega *;
melindro *;
pui *;
tripode *
CREOLE/HAITIAN zozo *
CZECH pindour *;
urák *;
pero **;
pták *
DANISH snade *;
lem *;
spyd [6];
søslange [6]
DUTCH lul *;
pik *
ESTONIAN türa *
FARSI ālat *;
kir *
FINNISH kyrpaä *;
palli *;
slerssi *;
siitin *
FRENCH bitte *;
cigre *;
chauve roi henri [8];
chinois [9]
GAELIC, IRISH bod *
GAELIC, SCOTS bod *;
bigealais *;
crann [10]
GERMAN Pimmel, der *;
Schwanz, der *
GREEK, MOD. ψολί / psolí *;
καβλι / kavli *
GUJARATI loda *
HEBREW zayin *
HINDI / URDU lund *;
ling *;
kēr *
HUNGARIAN fasz [11]
ICELANDIC böller *;
reður *;
lókur *;
skaufi *;
typpi *;
limur *;
göndull *
INDONESIAN koltol *;
peler *
ITALIAN belino *;
cazzo *;
cacchio *;
uchello [5];
manico [12];

pesce [13]
JAPANESE ポコチン pokochin *;
男根 dankon [14]
KANNADA tunne *
KAZAKH тасак / kasak *;
котак / kotak *
KOREAN cha-ji *;
kochu *
KOREAN cha-ji *;
LATIN i capulus *;
ae falcula *;
i gladius *
LATVIAN pipele *;
pimpis *
LITHUANIAN bybis *;
byrka *
MACEDONIAN кур / kur *;
куреч / kureč *;
тофиљ / tofilj *
MALAYU konek *;
peler *
MALTESE pesisa *;
zobb *
MANDARIN 男根 nángēn [14]
MARATHI bulla *;
lavdya / lavda *;
kata / kanta [15]
MONGOLIAN бомбу / bombu *;
був / buv *
NAHUATL tepolli *;
tepulli *
NEPALI lado *;
kong *
NORWEGIAN kølle *;
pikk *;
kødd *;
snabel *;
kuk *
POLISH chuj *;
kon´ *;
fiut *;
kutas *;
praçie *
PORTUGUESE pila *;
cacete *;
pichota *;
caralho *;
piroca *;
piça [16];
pingola [16]
QUECHUA pisqu *;
pichiku *
ROMANIAN pula *
RUSSIAN елдак / eldák *;
мудо / mudó *;
хуй / khúy *;
SINHALA polla *;
paka *
SLOVENIAN kura *
SOMALI gōs *
SOTHO, N. lepele *
SPANISH verga *;
picha *;
pitón *;
falo *;
Chino tuerto [17]
SWAHILI uume *;
mboo *
SWEDISH kuk *;
pitt *
TAGALOG tóro *;
titi *;
nóta *;
dong *; batúta´ *
TAMIL pōlu *
TELEGU madda *
THAI leung *;
kòon jàawan *;
hám *;
TURKISH dallama *;
yarrak *;
tarraam *
UKRAINIAN хуй / khuy *;
член / člen *
UZBEK қотоқ / qotoq *; куток / kutok *
VIETNAMESE dai´ *;
buoi *;
ngọc-hành *

WELSH pydin *
YIDDISH putz [11]
YORUBA okó *
ZULU umphambili *

* *dick/cock/prick;*
** *"feather";*
2 *"snake";*
3 *"dick/cock/prick," Palest., Syr., Leb. dials.;*
4 *"dick/cock/prick," Tunes.;*
5 *"bird";*
6 *"spear";*
7 *"Sea snake";*
8 *"Bald king Henry";*
9 *"Chinaman";*
10 *"Tree";*
11 *prick, dick, cock; fool;*
12 *"handle";*
13 *"fish;*
14 *"man root";*
15 *annoying prick/bastard;*
16 *Braz.;*
17 *"One-eyed Chinaman."*

illustr., © 2008, Graham Willoughby

DICK, BIG/ COCK, BIG/ PRICK, BIG (& VARIATIONS) 大屌

AFRIKAANS weleda **;
Spier van pesier [2]
ALBANIAN kollodok [3]
ARMENIAN metz jugík *
BELARUSIAN стайакі / stajaki [4]
CANTONESE lok chaht chèuhng [5]
CATALAN trempera [4]
CZECH ztopořitse [6]
DANISH Fede pik! [7]
DUTCH grote slappe pik [8]
FINNISH mela [14]
GUJARATI lund che *
ITALIAN minchiazza **;
Ti metto il cazzo in bocca e te lo faccio uscire dalla culo. [9]
MALAYU kote besar *
MANDARIN 大屌 dà diǎo *
NORWEGIAN hestkuk [10]
ROMANIAN pula calului [10]
RUSSIAN кишка / kišká *;
хуйщче / khúyšče *
SPANISH Monstruo [11]
TAGALOG dakó´ *
TURKISH Eşein siki! [12]
ZULU elikhulu [13]

* *Big prick/dick/cock;*
** *"big basket";*
2 *"Pleasure muscle";*
3 *"crank-shaft";*
4 *"big cock/hard cock";*
5 *"long dick/cock";*
6 *"Big or hard cock/big or erect clit";*
7 *"Fat dick/cock/prick!";*
8 *"big floppy prick/dick/cock";*
9 *"If I stick my prick/dick/cock in yr mouth, it'll come out yr ass/arse!"*
10 *"Horse cock/dick";*
11 *"Monster";*

12 *"Donkey dick/prick/cock!";*
13 *"big lion;*
14 *"boater's pole, oar."*

DICK, TINY / COCK, TINY / PRICK, TINY (& VARIATIONS) — ХУЖ МОЛИВ

AFRIKAANS Chihuahua [14]
BOSNIAN mali kurač *
BULGARIAN хуж молив / khuj moliv [2]
CANTONESE lán hósai *
CATALAN txinorri minga *
CROATIAN pena * ;
penůtina *
FRENCH petit noeud *;
quéquette [17]
GAELIC, IRISH / GAELIC, SCOTS bod beag *
GERMAN Bierficker [3]
GREEK, MOD. μίκρι ψολί / mikri psolí **
GUJARATI bhose pupu [4]
HINDI / URDU chota lund *;
bandā [5]
ICELANDIC lítið typpi *;
smátyppi *
INDONESIAN knotol kecil **
ITALIAN Il tuo cazzo è un brufolo / Il tuo cazzo è minuscolo. [6]
JAPANESE 小さいチンチン chiisai chin-chin *
KOREAN go-ja **
LITHUANIAN pympis *
MACEDONIAN курле / kurle *
MALAYU konek gajus [7]
MANDARIN 你没有男根! Nĭ méiyŏu nán-gēn! [8]
NORWEGIAN barne-kuk [9];
dvergpikk [10]
POLISH pishiórek [11]
PORTUGUESE piça miniscula / pichota miniscula [12]
RUSSIAN хуек / khuék *;
З гу́лькин хуй. / Z gúlʹkin khúy. [13]
SERBIAN мали курач / mali kurač *
SPANISH chilito *;
Pinche pito de Pikachu! [14]
SWEDISH liten kuk *
TAGALOG dyútay [15];
jútay [15]
TURKISH Sennin sik goçuk. [16]
UKRAINIAN мініатюрний член / miniati-urnyý člen **
WELSH pygin bach *

* *tiny prick/dick/cock;*
** *micro-prick/dick/cock;*
2 *"pencil dick/prick/cock";*
3 *"tiny beer-bottle-neck dick/prick;*
4 *"clit prick";*
5 *"semi-prick/dick";*
6 *"Yr dick's a pimple/miniscule";*
7 *"cashew dick/prick";*
8 *"You've got no dick/cock!"*
9 *"Baby dick/cock";*
10 *"dwarf-dick/cock";*
11 *shriveled prick/dick/cock;*
12 *"miniscule prick/dick/cock";*
13 *"About as big as a pigeon's prick/dick..."*
14 *"Fucking Pikachu prick!"*
15 *"tiny dick/prick/cock" /gay term;*
16 *"Yr prick's/dick's/cock's small."*
17 *"Little tail."*

μίκρι ψολί

DICK/ COCK/ PRICK, CUT/ UN-CUT (& VARIATIONS)

Пососи залупу!

AFRIKAANS boerepiel [2];
brenda bris [3];
Jou pielvel! [4]
BASQUE zilmutur **
DANISH forhud **
FARSI katneh pust **
FRENCH chauve à col roulé [4]
GERMAN beschnitten *;
Flöte, die [6]
ICELANDIC forhúð **
INDONESIAN palaji **
ITALIAN prepuzio **
LATVIAN pipeljaada **
MALAYU kulup **
MALTESE garretta **;
Busli garretta a la francisa. [8]
NORWEGIAN förhud **
RUSSIAN Пососи залупу! / Păsasí zalúpu! [9]
SPANISH prepucio **
TAGALOG jupót [10];
pisót [7]
YORUBA atoto **
ZULU i(li)jawabu **

* *cut prick/dick/cock, circumcised;*
** *foreskin;*
2 *"Farmer's dick/cock," big & uncut;*
3 *"cut/circumcised cock/dick," gay term;*
4 *"You foreskin!"*
5 *"Dick/cock with a turtleneck";*
6 *"skin flute";*
7 *"firehose"/Cebuano loan word;*
8 *"French-kiss my foreskin!";*
9 *"Go suck a foreskin!"*
10 *"firehose, uncut."*

DICK FACE
(& VARIATIONS)

CANTONESE lán yéung *
CROATIAN / SERB kurac u lice *;
курац у лице / kurac u lice *
FARSI kira *
FRENCH cyclope **
GERMAN Schwanzgesicht *
GREEK, MOD. ψολο μυρι / psolo muri *
HUNGARIAN fazkalap [2]
ICELANDIC skaufafés *
INDONESIAN muka peler / muka koltol *
ITALIAN faccia di cazzo *
JAPANESE チンチンっぽい顔 chinchin-ppoi kao *
MANDARIN 屌脸 diǎo liǎn *
PORTUGUESE cara da piça / cara da pichota *
SPANISH cara de pito *;
careverga / cara de verga *
SWEDISH kukhuvud *
TAGALOG mukhang titi *

* *dick-face;*
** *"Cyclops";*
2 *"Dick/prick hat."*

ψολο μυρι

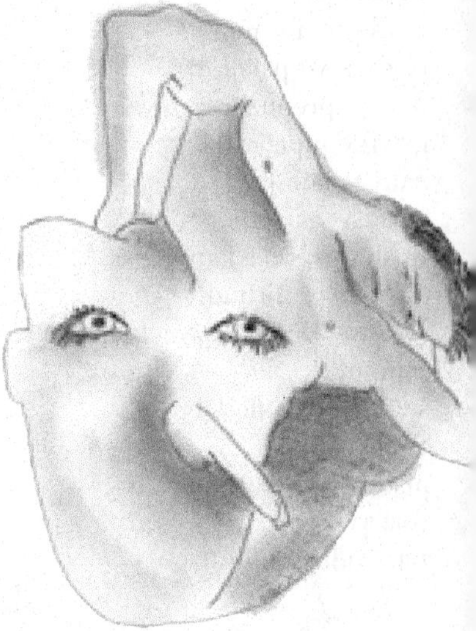

illustr., © 2008, Graham Willoughby

チンチンっぽい顔

DICK-HEAD / DICK BRAIN
(& VARIATIONS)

залупа

AFRIKAANS pielkop / trilkop *;
Jou pielkop [2]
ALBANIAN kokëkar *
ARABIC / TUNIS. m´nayyaq *
ARMENIAN kliris/klēris glukh *
BELARUSIAN залупа / zalupa *
BENGALI laewra aga *
BOSNIAN kurcoglavac *;
kurcorazum **
BULGARIAN курова глава / kurova glavá *;
Чичо хуй / Číčo khuj [3];
Вуичо хуй / Vúicho khuj [4]
CANTONESE lán tàuh *
CATALAN caparró *;
capullo **
CROATIAN / SERB kurac-mozak;
курац мозак / kurac-mozak **
CZECH Debil! / Debile! [5]
DANISH pikhoved *
DUTCH eikel *;
klootoog *;
paardelul [6]
GERMAN Schwanzkopf, der *;
Schwanz-gehirn, das **
GREEK, MOD. ψολομιαλε / psolomiale **
GUJARATI lund nu mathu *
HEBREW zayan sechel *
HINDI land ka bheja *
HUNGARIAN faszfej *
ICELANDIC fáviti *
ITALIAN testa di cazzo *;
picio *;
pirla *
JAPANESE チンチンっぽい脳 chinchin-ppoi nō **
KAZAKH котакпас / kotakpas *
KOREAN jot dae ga ri *
LITHUANIAN yibio galva *
MACEDONIAN куратс глава / kurats glava *
MALAYU kepala butoh *
MANDARIN 屌 头 dio tóu *
POLISH palançie *
PORTUGUESE monga *
RUSSIAN залупа / zalúpa *
SPANISH gillipolas *;
capullo *
SWEDISH kukhuvud *
TAGALOG utén *;
utak titi **
THAI hua kuay *
TURKISH sik kafal *
URDU lundōra [7]
UZBEK куток бош / kutok bosh *
WELSH pen pygen *;
cock oen [8]

* *"dick-head";*
** *"dick-brain";*
2 *"You dick-head!";*
3 *"Uncle Dick [Patern.]";*
4 *"Uncle Dick [Matern.]";*
5 *"You dick-head/dickwad/moron!";*
6 *"Horse's dick";*
7 *dick-head, ass/ arsehole, idiot;*
8 *"lamb's dick/cock."*

Вуичо Хуй!

DICK/ COCK/ PRICK IN YOUR EYE (& VARIATIONS)

Πυστσος στο ματι.

BOSNIAN Jebem ti oko! *

CROATIAN / SERB Kurac u oko! *; курац у око! / Kurac u oko! *

FARSI Kiram to tokme chesm! **

FRENCH Un bitte dans ton oiel. *

GERMAN Ein Schwanz in Ihrem Auge. *

GREEK, MOD. Πυστσος στο ματι. / Putsos sto mati. *

HEBREW Zayin b´ain! *

HINDI / URDU Teri mā ki ānkh. [3]

ITALIAN Mille cazzi nel tuo occhio. [4]

KAZAKH Козинэ котак кирсин. / Kozine kotak kirsin. *

LITHUANIAN Bybi tau i kilpe´. *

MACEDONIAN Сакам до клам буцо у фојто око. / Sakam do klam butso u fojto oko. [5]

PORTUGUESE Um piça no seu olho. *

ROMANIAN Futute n a privì! [2]

RUSSIAN Хуй тебе в глаз! / Khuy tebé v glaz! *

SWEDISH Stick i ögat. *

* *"A prick/dick/cock in your eye!"*

** *"My prick/dick/cock in yr eyeball!"*

2 *"Fuck you in the eye!"*

3 *"Fuck yr mother in the eye!"*

4 *A thousand pricks/dicks/cocks in yr eye!"*

5 *"I'll shove my prick/dick/cock in yr eye!"*

Козинэ котак кирсин.

images: GobQ/T. Warburton y Bajo//caryatid , M. F. McAuliffe

DICK/ COCK/ PRICK IN YOUR EAR/ FACE/ NOSE (& VARIATIONS)

Πουσος σκαβυλος

FINNISH slerssisorbettii / kyrpäsorbettii [5]

GREEK, MOD. Πουσος σκαβυλος / Pousos skavulos. [3]

HUNGARIAN Hogy a fasz üsse fel a szád-at! [4]

LITHUANIAN Bybi tau i vei'/vei'da. *

MACEDONIAN Сакам до кλам бцсо у фојто ушето / уво. / Sakam do klam butso u fojto usheto/uvo. **

PORTUGUESE Um piça / pichota no seu nariz. [2]

RUSSIAN Хуй тебе в глаз! / Khuy tebé v glaz! *;

Хуй тебе в рот! / Khuy tebé v rot! [6]

SPANISH Metete el pito por los oidos. / Metete la verga por los oidos. [7]

TAGALOG Titi sa tainga. [7]

* *"A prick/dick/cock in yr face";*

** *"I'll shove my prick/dick/cock in yr ear!"*

2 *"A prick/dick/cock in yr nose!"*

3 *"Slap my dick/prick/cock on yr face!"*

4 *"May a prick/dick/cock punch yr mouth!"*

5 *"dick sorbet;*

6 *"A prick/dick/cock in yr mouth!"*

7 *"Stick yr dick/cock in yr ear!"*

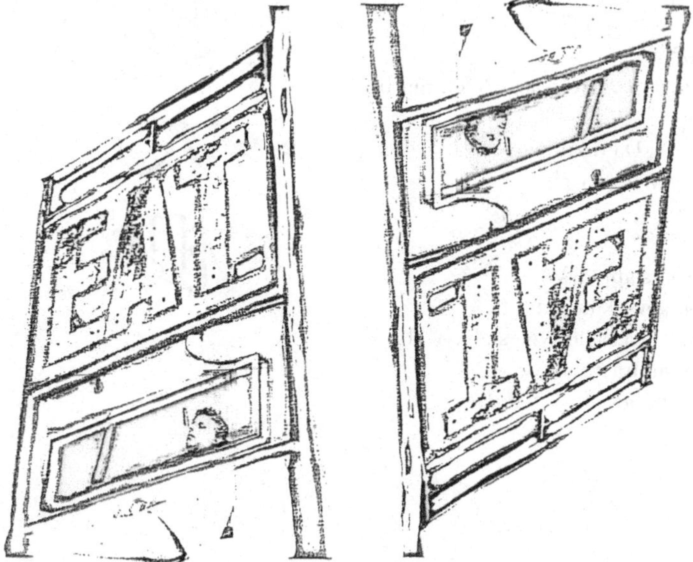

images: GobQ/T. Warburton y Bajo

DICK/ COCK/ PRICK, LIMP (& VARIATIONS)

хуй спексан

BASQUE ahalgabe *
BELARUSIAN нiестайак / niestajak **
BULGARIAN хуй спексан / khuj speksan [2]
CANTONESE singmòuhnàhng *
DANISH Bananen er vissen. [3]
FINNISH tuhkamuna [4]
FRENCH bitte mou *
GAELIC, IRISH bod bacach *
GAELIC, SCOTS bod bacaiche *
GERMAN schwacher Schwanz *
GREEK, MOD. μαλα κογαβλι / mala kogavli *
HINDI / URDU dhēla lund *
ICELANDIC slappur *
INDONESIAN kontol peluh *;
peler lunak **
ITALIAN E´duro averlo duro che duri. [5]
JAPANESE ひ ね 大 根 hine daikon [6]
KOREAN go-ja [7]
MANDARIN 阳萎 yángwěi *
NAHUATL totomicqui *
POLISH pishiórek [8]
PORTUGUESE piça frouxo / pichota frouxo *
RUSSIAN член маринований / člen marin-ovaniy [9]
SLOVENIAN Da ti kurac crkne. [10]
SPANISH malpalo [11];
malaoha [12];
mula [13]
SWEDISH slapptask *
TURKISH gevşek tarraam *
UKRAINIAN слабкий хуй / slabkyy khuy *
YORUBA akúra *;
baba bangbesi *

* *"Limp prick/dick/cock";*
** *"Soft prick/dick/cock";*
2 *"Crushed prick/dick/cock";*
3 *"The banana's whithered...";*
4 *"shooting blanks";*
5 *"It's hard to have a lasting hard-on";*
6 *"shriveled radish";*
7 *"dick-less";*
8 *"shriveled dick";*
9 *"marinaded prick/dick/cock";*
10 *"May yr prick/dick/cock die!"*
11 *"Sick stick/pole," Cub. dial.;*
12 *"Lousy lay" (m.), Cub.;*
13 *"female mule" (dir. at limp-dick males), Mex.*

ひね大根

DIRTY OLD MAN (OR WOMAN) / OLD PERV', LECH' / LECHER (& VARIATIONS)

μουδαρις

ALBANIAN cjap [2]
ARMENIAN ligdi **
BASQUE okerrazle [3]
CANTONESE hàahm sāp lóu *
CATALAN lasciu *
CROATIAN / SERB bezobrazan starač *; безобразан старач / bezobrazan starač *
CZECH smilník **
DANISH gammel knark [4]; gammel gris [5]
FARSI shavat parast **
FRENCH vieux perverti *
GAELIC, IRISH drúisiúil [6]
GAELIC, SCOTS sean-dhruisire *
GERMAN Ein geiler Wicht *
GREEK, MOD. μουδαρις / moudaris *
HINDI / URDU tharki budhdha *
ICELANDIC klámkarl *; öfuguggi *
ITALIAN vecchio sporcaccione *; vecchio schifoso [7]
JAPANESE スケベイ sukebē *
MALAYU jalang [6]
MARATHI andela *(m.)* / andila *(f.)* [6]
NAHUATL ahuilnenqui [6]
NORWEGIAN lidderlig [6]
POLISH stary wypaczać *(m.)* / stary wypaczyć *(f.)* *; stary deprawować [8]
PORTUGUESE pervertido velho sujo *
RUSSIAN Хуй моржовый! / Khuy moržóvyy! [9]
SLOVENIAN Koza! [10]
SPANISH viejo / ruco bellaco *; viejo / ruco pervertido *
SWEDISH snuskgubbe *
TAGALOG askuaríra de pápa [11]
TURKISH zampara *
WELSH trythillweh [12]
YORUBA as̱enilori [11]

* *dirty old man/old pervert;*
** *"lech'" / "old lecher";*
2 *"He-goat";*
3 *"perverter" / "corrupter";*
4 *"old geezer";*
5 *"old pig";*
6 *lecherous;*
7 *"Disgusting old man";*
8 *"depraved old pervert";*
9 *"Walrus dick/prick!"*
10 *"You goat!"*
11 *"Sugar Daddy";*
12 *lechery.*

Хуй моржовый!

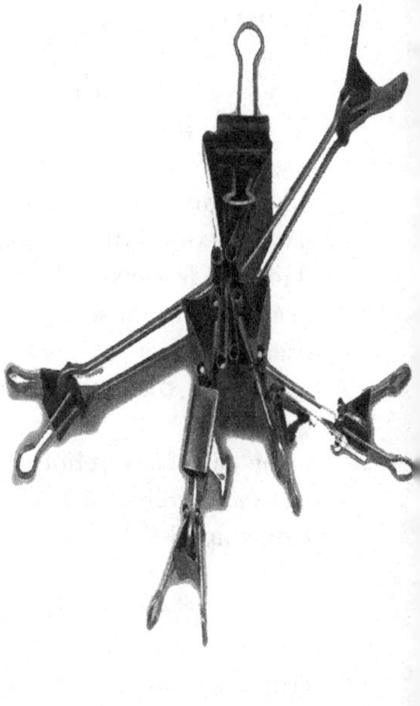

clipman image: GobQ/T. Warburton y Bajo

DOG FUCKER, GOAT FUCKER, HORSE FUCKER, CAT FUCKER, SHEEP SHAGGER (& BESTIAL VARIATIONS) σκιλογαμιμενε

AFRIKAANS hondenaaier *;
sognaaier **;
leeunaaier [4];
heiënanaaier [5]
ALBANIAN Të qiftë arusha. [6]
ARABIC/MOROCC. Takōl zep ala hamar. [7]
BOSNIAN Jebat koze! [8]
BULGARIAN чобан / choban [9]
CATALAN Ves a follar ovella! [10]
CROATIAN / SERB jebač kerova *;
јебач керова / jebač kerova *
DANISH hvalknepper [11]
DUTCH paarden neuker [2];
kippeneuker [12];
mierenneuker [13]
FINNISH vuohenraiskaaja [14];
Äitisi nai poroja. [15]
FRENCH T'est qu'une sale pute qui se met des chiennes et du chat dans le cul. [16]
GAELIC, SCOTS Bidh do mhàthair a' daireadh le eichan. [17]
GERMAN Kuhbumser [3];
Ziegenbumser [14]
GREEK, MOD. σκιλογαμιμενε / skilo-gamimene *
HINDI / URDU backarchōdu [14]
ICELANDIC rolluríðari [9];
kattasjúgari [18]
ITALIAN pecorina [9]
JAPANESE 獣姦するの人 jūkan suru no hito [19]
LITHUANIAN šuo´pisa *;
avie pisa [9]
NORWEGIAN saueknuller [9];
Pul en katt! [20]

POLISH Pies cie jebal! [21]
PORTUGUESE foda dos cachorros *;
foda da cabra [14]
ROMANIAN muist de oşareci [21]
RUSSIAN Еби корову. / Ebí koróvu. [22];
ядрёна мыши / yadrona mysh´ [23]
SINHALA gas kariya [24]
SPANISH coge perro *(m)* / coge perra *(f)* *;
coge cabra [14];
Chingate un caballo [25];
Coge burra [26]
SWEDISH Din mama suger norsk svan pitt. [27];
valfisk knullare [11];
hundknullare *
TAGALOG kantutero ng tsunggo [2]
WELSH Ffwcio dy gath i fyny´r pen ol. [28]

* *dog-fucker;*
** *"pig/sow fucker";*
2 *"monkey fucker";*
3 *"cow fucker";*
4 *"lion fucker";*
5 *"hyena fucker;*
6 *"May a bear fuck you!"*
7 *"Eat donkey dick/cock!"*
8 *"Go fuck goats!"*
9 *"sheep shagger";*
10 *"Go fuck sheep!"*
11 *"whale fucker";*
12 *"chicken fucker";*
13 *"ant-fucker";*
14 *"goat shagger/fucker";*
15 *"Yr mother fucks reindeer!"*
16 *"Y're a crappy whore who shoves dogs & cats up yr ass/arse!"*
17 *"Yr mother fucks horses";*
18 *"cat sucker";*
19 *"into bestiality";*
20 *"Fuck a cat!"*
21 *"Even the dog fucked you!"*
21 *"rat fucker."*
22 *"Fuck a cow./Go fuck a cow."*
23 *"Mouse fucker";*
24 *"Tree fucker."*
25 *"Go fuck a horse."*
26 *"Donkey fucker/Donkey Show Star."*
27 *"Yr mother sucks Norwegian swan dick/cock."*
28 *"Fuck yr cat up the ass/arse."*

DRAG QUEEN, TRANSVESTITE, SHE-MALE (& VARIATIONS) хажинқиз

AFRIKAANS fopdosser *; fopvrou *

ARABIC sharmute [2]

CANTONESE yàmyèuhng yàhn **

CROATIAN Jebi si svog travestita u guzicu. [3]; Jesi ti promijenio spol? *(m)* / Jesi ti promijenila spol? *(f)* [4]

DANISH pølse i svøb [5]

FINNISH tätisetä **; transvestiittishow [13]

FRENCH grande folle *; travelot *; trav *; trans **; folle [5]; femme à pedes [6]

GERMAN Zwitter **; Zwitterhaft [7]

GREEK, MOD. τραβεστί / travestí *

HINDI / URDU chhakka *; hidja **; zankha **

ICELANDIC dragdrottning *; klæðskiptin-gur *

INDONESIAN banci *; ratu *; bencong **

ITALIAN travestito *

JAPANESE ネコ neko [9]

KANNADA jyoggya **

LATIN saltatrix tonsa **

MALAYU mak´nyah *; bapuk *

MANDARIN 爱穿着异性义务的人 ai chuānzhuó yìxìng yìwù de rén *; 阴阳人 yīn yáng rén **

NORWEGIAN trans **

PORTUGUESE / BRAZ. traveco *; buceta caralhuda **

RUSSIAN трансвестúт / tranvestít *

SOMALI labēbe [8]

SPANISH Loca *

SWAHILI mcheza nachi mwanmme

SWEDISH tranvesit *

TAGALOG fasífica falayfáy / fasífica falayfáy fofongay *; binabáe *; hormonáda **

TELEGU kojja langa **

THAI gà'teu'i *; buàap **

TURKISH ipne **; bad asl kuni [10]; kuni [11]

UZBEK хажинқиз / hajiqiz [11]

WELSH dourywiog [8]

ZULU útracy [12]

* *"drag queen";*
** *"She-male/transexual";*
2 *"queen bitch";*
3 *"Fuck yr drag queen transvest. ass/arse."*
4 *"Did you have a sex change operation?"*
5 *"Wrapped sausage";*
6 *"Daft queen";*
7 *"fag hag";*
8 *"Androgyne";*
SOMALI, WELSH: "she-male, hermaphrodite";
9 *"cat";*
10 *"Evil Back-stabbing Queen";*
11 *"fem queen";*
12 *"She-male," Gay Township Zulu term;*
13 *"Drag act"; FINNISH: "drag show."*

image: GobQ/T Warburton y Bajo

DRUGS & THEIR BEDRAGGLED & DEBAUCHED DRUGGIES (& VARIATIONS) 葉っぱ中

AFRIKAANS Patsy Cola *;
Christina **;
dagga [2];
giggle gracie [2]
ALBANIAN kokaín kurve [3];
narkoman *(pl., narkomani)* [4]
ARABIC raked afa alsahad [5];
mudmin(-un) [4];
takya [6];
iknak / iknaakit [7]
BASQUE kokaina *;
kosto [8]
BENGALI pagla garod [9];
chitograstha [10];
gulikhor [11];
afimkor [4];
neshakhor [12]
BULGARIAN гадна друсалка / gadna drusalka [13]
BURMESE kohdìng [14]
CANTONESE daaihmàh [2];
hāai fán [15];
fán dong [16];
fán hùhng sī néuih lòhng [17];
fāt dāk [18]
CATALAN maria [2];
haixix [8]
CROATIAN narkoman [4]
CZECH poiva marihuany [12];
narkoman [4];
DANISH crackluder [3];
narkoluder [19];
crackbarn [21];
narkoman [4];
hasvrag [22];
Fyre en fed. [23];
græs / tjald [2];
galar [2];
DUTCH heroinehoer [19];
huisdealer [23]
FARSI khumori *; boteh-ye shâhdâneh [2]; motâd [4]; bang [8];
mafangi [10]
FINNISH narkomaani / narkkari [4];
pilviveikko [5];
nisti [11]
FRENCH chichon / marie-jeanne, la [2];
chef de marijuana [12];
courir le dragon / chasser le dragon [5];
drogué sale [24];
l'acid [39]
FRENCH (VERLAN) techi [2]
GAELIC, IRISH cócaon *;
marachuan [2];
andúileach drugaí [4]
GAELIC, SCOTS diasganach salach [24]
GERMAN Tüte [2];
Rauschgiftsüchtige [4];
Gib mir mal die Tüte rüber. [25]
GREEK, MOD. κάππα / káppa *;
μαριηουανα / marihouana [2];
Γοματακια / komatakia [26]
HEBREW dafuk [26];
mastul [27]
HINDI / URDU charashi [12];
gāngawala [28]
HUNGARIAN eksztázi [17]
ICELANDIC dópisti [4];
spítthaus [11];
hasshaus [12];
eiturlyfjasali [29]
ITALIAN tossico *(m)* / tossica *(f)* [4];
spinellato *(m)* / spinellata *(f)* [12];
Si fanno di crack. [30];
inalazione di colla [31]
JAPANESE ポン中 ponchū [11];
汚いヘロ中 kitanai herochū [24];
葉っぱ中 happachū [32];
ポン中 女郎 ponchū jorō [33]
KHMER th´nuhm gow´dēn [14]
KOREAN ch´wi han [26]

MALAYU ketagih candu / tagih candu [4]
MANDARIN 大麻 dàmá [2];
瘾君子 yǐn jūn zǐ [4];
安非他明有药瘾者 ān fēi tā míng yǒu yào yǐn zhě [11];
可卡因有药瘾者 kěk-yīn yǒu yào yǐn zhě [34];
MARATHI aphimī / aphimyā [4]
NAHUATL tecochtlazalli [26]
NORWEGIAN narkotiker [4]
POLISH narkoman *(m)* / narkomanka *(f)* [4];
pojebany [26];
Narkoman pierdolony ty! [35]
PORTUGUESE casqueiro *(m)* / casqueira *(f)* [10];
maconeiro *(m)* / maconeira *(f)* [12];
sujo viciado *(m)* / suja viciada *(f)* [24];
maconeiro de bosta *(m)* / maconeira de bosta *(f)* [36]
RUSSIAN травка / travka [2];
сидеть на игле / sidet´ na igle [4];
навеселе / navesele [26]
SERB / UKRAINIAN наркоман / narkoman [4]
SLOVENIAN porkafiks [37]
SPANISH zacate ingles [2];
puta de llelo [3];
narcomano [4];
moto [2];
SWAHILI kokeini *;
mtumiaji wa madawa [4]; l
ewa [26]
SWEDISH kokain hora [3];
knarkare [24];
brassrökare [12]
TAGALOG éseng **;
bató **;
chimís [2];
chongki-chongki [2];
durugista [4];
twennypabe [17];
bern [22];
túlak [29];
bátak [31]
THAI Jà sòop mǎi? [25];
ya bâh **;
TURKISH müptelâ [4]
UZBEK хумори / xumori [4];
банги / bangi [12];
мазахо ьрак хайол. / mazaxo´ rak hayol [38]
WELSH ymroddi [4]

* *"coke/cocaine";*
** *"crystal/crystal meth/speed";*
2 *"joint, pot, grass";*
3 *"coke/crack whore";*
4 *"junkie";*
5 *ARABIC: "Chasing the clouds" = opiate or kif high; FINNISH: "One who flies w/ the clouds" = druggie/ junkie; FRENCH: "chase/chasing the dragon";*
6 *"Den of repose";*
7 *"Got fucked up...," Tunis. dial.;*
8 *"hashish";*
9 *"crack house";*
10 *"crack head";*
11 *"tweaker";*
12 *"pot-head, druggie";*
13 *"stupid junkie";*
14 *"codeine";*
15 *"shoot up heroin";*
16 *"dope den";*
17 *"ecstacy";*
18 *"mandrax, 'downer'";*
19 *"junk whore";*
20 *"crack-baby";*
21 *"pot-wreck," stoner;*
22 *"Burn a fat spliff";*
23 *dope dealer, operating out of coffee shop;*
24 *"dirty junkie";*
25 *"Pass me the spliff."/"You want a hit/toke?";*
26 *"fucked up, stoned";*
27 *"stoner";*
28 *hashish dealer;*
29 *dope dealer";*
30 *"They're crack heads."*
31 *"huffing";*
32 *"leaf addict";*
33 *"meth whore";*
34 *"coke addict";*
35 *"Fucking junkie!"*
36 *"shit-head pot-smoker";*
37 *"Pig's shot of heroin";*
38 *"Pipe dream"/Farsi loan word.*
39 *"acid/LSD".*

大麻

DRUNKARD / ALCOHOLIC / LUSH (& VARIATIONS) 烂醉

AFRIKAANS dronklap * ;
Harry / Hairy [2]
ALBANIAN dehúr *
ARABIC sakrān *
ARMENIAN zuart´ *
BASQUE hortiputz * ;
zurrutero *
BELARUSIAN пьяний / p´yany *
BENGALI matal *
BOSNIAN / SERB pijan * ;
пијан / pijan *
BULGARIAN алкохолик / alkoholik *
CANTONESE jáugwái *
CATALAN pet [3];
els pets [4];
enganxar um sego [5]
CREOLE/HAITIAN sou *
CROATIAN alkoholičar *
CZECH opilec *
DANISH drukkenbølt * ;
tømmemænd [6]
DUTCH dronken *
ESTONIAN purjus *
FARSI mast * ;
araqxo´r
FINNISH juoppo * ;
pissaliisa [7];
baarian [8]
FRENCH allumé ** ;
dans les vignes du Seigneur [9]
FRENCH (VERLAN) foncedé [10]
GAELIC, IRISH ar deargmheisce [11];
ar na cannaí [11];
ar buile [11];
Tá do mháthair meisceoir. [12]
GAELIC, SCOTS misgear * ;
Tha do mhathair misgear. [12]
GERMAN / SW. ä Chlapf * ;
Häsch e Chappe aa? [13]
GREEK, MOD. μεθισμενος / methismenos *
HAUSA buggage *
HEBREW shikor *
HINDI / URDU nashīlā * ;
madāk *
ICELANDIC mígandi fullur [11];
pissfullur [11]
INDONESIAN / MALAYU mabuk *
ITALIAN ubriacone *(m)* / ubriacona *(f)* [14]
JAPANESE アル中 aruchū *
KOREAN chu-jŏng-gun
LATIN eribusa / eribusum *
LITHUANIAN girtas *
MALTESE sakran *
MANDARIN 烂醉 làn zuì [11]
MARATHI barala [15]
NAHUATL tlatahuanaliztli *
NORWEGIAN fyllik *
POLISH pijak *
PORTUGUESE o borracho *
QUECHUA machaq *
ROMANIAN beţiv *
RUSSIAN наебнуться / naebnut´sya [16]
SLOVENIAN pinajec *
SOMALI khamriya cab *
SOTHO, N. setagwa *
SPANISH borracho *
SWAHILI mlevi sugu *
SWEDISH fyllbult *
TAGALOG buratséro * ;
ponggáyan [16]
THAI mow * ;
kêe mow [17]
TURKISH alkollü *
UKRAINIAN алкогольний / alkohol'nyy *
UZBEK маст / mast * ;
пиёниста / piyonista [17]
VIETNAMESE nguòʾi say *
WELSH meddwyn *
YIDDISH shikkur [18];
vashnukad [16]
YORUBA ìmutíparra *
ZAPOTEC binni güe´ *

* *drunk/drunkard;*
** *"lit up";*
2 *"lesbian hangover";*

3 *"old drunken fart";*
4 *"The drunkards";*
5 *"stick a blindman";*
6 *"hangover";*
7 *"Piss-Alices";*
8 *"barfly";*
9 *"in the vines of the Lord";*
10 *"smashed, wasted, or stoned";*
11 *"pissed";*
12 *"Yr mother's a drunkard";*
13 *"Are you wearing yr drunk cap?"*
14 *"piss-head," drunkard;*
15 *"raving drunk;"*
16 *"falling down shit-face drunk";*
17 *"shit-face drunkard";*
18 *"drunkard" /Russ. loan word;*
18 *"goyem-drunk."*

DWARF / MIDGET (& VARIATIONS) νανος

AFRIKAANS dwerg *
ARABIC qazm *
ARMENIAN garjug *
BASQUE epoxt *
CANTONESE ngáijái *;
jyùyùh **
CATALAN lilliputench ** ;
nan *
CROATIAN / SERB patuljak *;
патуљак / patuljak *
CZECH trpaslík *
DANISH dvaerg *;
Sut dvaergepik din bøsseludende. [2]
DUTCH dwerg *
ESTONIAN lühike [3]
FARSI qad kutâh *;
kutuleh **
FINNISH kääpiö *
FRENCH nain *
GAELIC, IRISH abhac *
GERMAN Zverg *;
Knirps **
GREEK, MOD. νανος / nanos *
HEBREW gamad *
HINDI / URDU bāwan *
HUNGARIAN stöpszli [4]
ICELANDIC dvergur [5]
ITALIAN nano *(m.)* / nana *(f.)* *
JAPANESE 小人 kobito *
LATIN pumilio /pumilionis *
LITHUANIAN nykštu'kas *
MACEDONIAN изрол / izrod [6]
MALAYU orang katik *
MALTESE pinta [7]
MANDARIN 矮子 ǎizi *
MARATHI kirata *
NAHUATL tzapatl *
NORWEGIAN dverg *;
lilleput **
POLISH krótki [3]
PORTUGUESE anão *(m.)* / anã *(f.)* *

ROMANIAN pitic *
RUSSIAN карлик / kárlik *
SOTHO, N. ngopana *
SPANISH enamo *;
fenómeno [6]
SWEDISH dvärg *;
lilliput **;
infall [6]
TAGALOG burít *;
unáno **
THAI jàae *
TURKISH bodur *
UKRAINIAN хном / khnom *
UZBEK лилипут liliput **
VIETNAMESE vât nhó **
WELSH corrach *;
umbach **
YIDDISH pisher [8]
ZAPOTEC nachucu [3]
ZULU ishichwe *

* *dwarf/dwarfish;*
** *midget;*
2 *"Suck dwarf dick/cock you hunch-backed faggot";*
3 *"shorty";*
4 *"pipsqueak";*
5 *"gnome";*
6 *"freak";*
7 *"stubby"/"1/2-pint bottle";*
8 *per Harlan Ellison, "squirt, inexperienced person of no consequence."*

Лилипут

矮子

DYKE, LESBO/ LESBIAN (& VARIATIONS)

リリ族

AFRIKAANS lemon *;
letticus **;
beer [2]
ARABIC/TUNIS mibun *
BASQUE marikoia *;
lesbiana *
BOSNIAN lesbejka *
CANTONESE gēi pó *;
lēk néui *
CATALAN bollera *
CROATIAN lesbejka *
CZECH lesbička *
DANISH lesbik *;
lebbe *;
beton lebbe [3]
DUTCH viseter [4]
ESTONIAN vaiba sööja *
FARSI zané hamjenbâz *;
tabaqzan *;
lahâqeh *
FINNISH lesbo *
FRENCH gouine *;
caimoneuse [5];
brouteuse / brouteuse de touffe [6]
GAELIC, IRISH leispiach *
GAELIC, SCOTS leasbach *
GERMAN Lesbisch *;
Lesbierin *;
Futlecka [7];
Lesbe *
GREEK βλακο μυνου / vlako munou *
HAUSA 'yar madigo *
HINDI/URDU kusri aurat *
ICELANDIC lesbía *;
trukkalessa [5];
lesbískur *;
dækja **;
lessa *
ITALIAN lesbica *;
camionara [14];
raporto saffico [15];
lesicona [16]
JAPANESE レズ rezu *;
レズくさい rezu-kusai [8];
リリ族 riri-zoku [9]
KHMER ma'nōh guh'd·ey'srei *
MACEDONIAN педерка / pederka *;
лезбејка / lezbejka *
MALTESE ja lizbjana *
MANDARIN 女同性恋 nü tóngxìngliàn *
NAHUATL tecuilontiani [10]
NORWEGIAN lesbe *
POLISH lesba *
PORTUGUESE fufa *;
zapatão [11]
RUSSIAN лесби́йский / lesbíyskiy *
SERBIAN лезбејка / lesbejka *;
лезбача / lezbača *
SLOVENIAN lesbejka *
SPANISH lesbiana *;
cueca *;
tortillera [12];
torta [13];
cachapera [14]
SWAHILI msagaji *
SWEDISH lebb *;
lesbisk *;
flata *
TAGALOG felipe *;
lisbon *;
lirot *;
macha **;
pompiáng *;
jack **
THAI lét'bee'an *;
thàawn *
TURKISH sevici *
UKRAINIAN лесбійський / lesbiys'kyy *
VIETNAMESE lại đu'c;
con dê *;
(nguói) dô`ng-dâm nu *

* *lesbian, dyke;*
** *"butch dyke";*
2 *"bear" = hairy-backed butch dyke;*

レズくさい

3 *"concrete dyke";*
4 *"fish eater";*
5 *"truckdriver";*
6 *"nibble, grazer"; "muff nibbler/muff grazer";*
7 *"bitch-blower";*
8 *"stinking lesbian";*
9 *"lily tribe";*
10 *"switch-hitter";*
11 *"big shoes";*
12 *"tortilla vendor";*
13 *"cake," Arg.;*
14 *dyke, Venez.;*
15 *fem. "truck driver";*
16 *"Sapphic rapport";*
17 *"big lesbian."*

mural image: GobQ/N. Lehn

FASCIST! (& VARIATIONS) 走狗

AFRIKAANS fascist *;
Moras Poes **
ALBANIAN fashíst *;
Fashísti janë vegla të kapitalistëve! [2] ;
Milosh! [4]
ARABIC zolim [5];
ra´smālī [6]
BASQUE faxista *
BOSNIAN / CROATIAN / SLOVENIAN / SERB fašist;
фашист / fašist *
BULGARIAN фашист / fašist *;
шваб / švab [7];
мама ти да еба фашистка. / Mama ti da eba fashistka. [8]
CANTONESE faatsàisījyúyihjé *
CATALAN feixista *
CROATIAN /SERB Pička ti materina fašistička. [9];
Jebo naci papu. [10]
Пичка ти матерна фашстичка. / Pička ti materina fašistička. [9];
Јебо наци папу./ Jebo naci papu. [10]
CZECH faistick *;
nacista [7]
DANISH fascistisk *
DUTCH fascist *
FARSI fâshist *
FINNISH fasisti *
FRENCH Fasciste! *
GAELIC, IRISH faisistí *
GERMAN Volksdeutscher [11];
die Juden türken. / Türken klatschen. / Neger klatschen. [12]
Faschist *;
GREEK, MOD. φασίστας / fasístas *
HUNGARIAN fasiszta *
ICELANDIC fasisti *
ITALIAN fascista *
JAPANESE ファシスト fashisuto *
LATVIAN fašists *
LITHUANIAN fašistas *
MACEDONIAN фашист / fashist *
MANDARIN 法西斯主义者 fǎxīsīzhǔyìzhě *
走狗 zǒugǒu [19]
POLISH faszysta *
ROMANIAN fascist *
RUSSIAN фашист / fašist [13]
SERBIAN усташа / ustaša [14]
SPANISH ¡Pinchi fascista! [15]
SWAHILI a kifashisti *
SWEDISH Jävla fascistisk! [15]
TAGALOG CIA [16]
THAI lim huàa ròon ràaeng [18]
TURKISH faşist *
UKRAINIAN фашист / fašyst *
UZBEK фашистча / fašistča *;
миллий хавфсизлик хизмаи / milliy xavfsizlik xizmai [18]
VIETNAMESE phát-xít *
WELSH ffasistaidd *
YORUBA amòna *
ZULU umuntu ohambisana neqemu elithanda ukuba umbuso uphathwe ngumuntu-munye *

* *fascist/Fascist!;*
** *Swamp Cunt" = "M. P., Military Police";*
2 *"Fascists are just Capitalist Tools!;*
3 *tyrannical, oppressive;*
4 *"Miloch!" = Slobodan Milosovich! —intensive oath throughout Balkans;*
5 *tyrant;*
6 *"capitalist";*
7 *"Nazi";*
8 *"Fuck yr fascist mother!"*
9 *"Fascist motherfucker!"*
10 *"Fuck the Nazi Pope!"*
11 *Germ. Nazi fifth columnists;*
12 *"Stomping Jews" / "Stomping Turks" / "Stomping blacks" = racist skin-head advocation;*
13 *"Fascist German";*
14 *W.W. II Croatian fascist;*
15 *"Fucking fascist!"*
16 *"certified Imelda Acolyte" = fascist kiss-ass/arse;*
17 *Muslim extremists.*
18 *Uzbek secret police;*
19 *"Running dog".*

FAT ASS/ FAT ARSE, FATSO (& VARIATIONS)

ηονδρο κολε

AFRIKAANS gwabba [2]
ALBANIAN topolák (m) / (f) topoláke **
BENGALI motku *;
kutar baicha haramjada botla [3]
BOSNIAN debela kravo [4]
CANTONESE fèih lóu (m) / fèih pòh (f) [5];
fèih hāi [6]
CATALAN gros *
CROATIAN tlustoprd *
CZECH tuk *
DANISH fede nar [7];
fed swin [8];
Din fede nar. [9];
Din fede bondeknold. [10]
DUTCH dikzak *;
De reet heeft haar eigen ver vakbond steward. [11]
ESTONIAN paks *
FINNISH tankki **;
pasku **;
laardiperse [12];
selluperse [13]
FRENCH gros lard *;
pouffiasse [14]
GAELIC, IRISH tóin ramhar *
GAELIC, SCOTS tòin reamhar *
GERMAN Fettarsch *;
fethaltig **
GREEK, MOD. ηονδρο κολε / hondro kole *
HEBREW duba **
HINDI mōtā *;
motōmal *
ICELANDIC fitubolla *;
skvaprass [15]
INDONESIAN gemuk *
ITALIAN culone (m) / culona (f) *;
grassone (m) / grassona (f) *;
bighellonare *
JAPANESE デカ尻 dekajiri *;
デブセン debusen [16]
KANNADA dhappa thika *
KAZAKH толлик пидарас / tollik pidaras [2]
LATIN edax rerum [17]
LITHUANIAN storas [18];
boba [19]
MACEDONIAN дебељуца / debelyutza *
MANDARIN 胖子 pàngzi *
MARATHI acaḻōbā *
MONGOLIAN будуун / buduun *
NORWEGIAN bollingmoer [18]
POLISH gruby **
PORTUGUESE gargantua *;
bolão [2]
ROMANIAN umflat *
RUSSIAN толстозадый / tolstozádyy *
SLOVENIAN len *
SOTHO, N botšwa *
SPANISH culón *;
panzon *;
gordon **;
papayona [21]
SWAHILI enye unene *
SWEDISH tjockis *;
fetto *
TAGALOG bìik *;
jabba-hut **
UKRAINIAN грязь / hriaz [22]
URDU motōmal *;
Dharti ka bojh [23]
VIETNAMESE (má) phinh-phính *
WELSH cont tew [6];
Y haliwr mawr tew! [24]
YORUBA sísanra **
ZAPOTEC riroo **;
nachaabá **

* *fatso/fat-ass/arse;*
** *"tubby" / "chubby";*
2 *"fat-ass/arse faggot";*
3 *"fat bastard";*
4 *"fat cow";*
5 *"fat guy / fat gal" —gender specified w. (m) or w. (f);*

6 *"fat cunt";*
7 *"fat jerk"/ "fat ass/arsehole";*
8 *"fat swine";*
9 *"You fat jerk."/ "You fat ass/arsehole.";*
10 *"You fat hick/redneck."*
11 *"Yr fat ass/arse has its own union steward."*
12 *"lard ass/arse";*
13 *"cellulite ass/arse";*
14 *"fat bag";*
15 *"flabby ass/arse";*
16 *"fatty fetishist" – "Fatty Specialist";*
17 *"fat ass/arse glutton";*
18 *"lazy fat ass/arse";*
19 *"fat bitch";*
20 *"blimp";*
21 *"fat twat/fat pussy," Cub.;*
22 *"fat slob";*
23 *"unnecessary weight on the Earth" = fatso;*
24 *"You big fat wanker!"*

デブセン

illustr., © 2008, Graham Willoughby

FETISHIST, SHOE FUCKER, PURSE FUCKER (& VARIATIONS)

靴なめ魔

AFRIKAANS klismaphilia **;
retifism [2];
Wendy Bangles [3]
ALBANIAN lëpírës *
DANISH fetich *
FARSI maraz *;
falakeh [4]
FINNISH kähärä [5]
FRENCH fétichiste *;
un lèches-bottes **
GERMAN Schuhbumser [6];
Geldbeutelbumser [7]
ICELANDIC náriðill [9]
ITALIAN feticista *
JAPANESE デブセン debusen [10];
靴なめ魔 kutsuname-ma [11];
足なめ魔 ashiname-ma [12]
KOREAN net byuntae [13];
babariman [14]
LITHUANIAN ishkrypelis [15]
MANDARIN 恋脚癖人 lián tóng pǐ rén [16]
NORWEGIAN skopuler [6]
PORTUGUESE foda da zapata [7];
foda da bolsa [8]
RUSSIAN фетишист / fetišist
SPANISH fetichista *;
mamamdor de dedo [17];
coje-zapato [6];
coje-bolsa [7];
coje-tacones [18]
SWEDISH fetischist *
TURKISH fetişist *
UKRAINIAN фетiшист / fetišyst *

* *fetishist;*
** *enema fetish;*
2 *"boot-licker";*
3 *"shoe & boot fetish";*
4 *"handcuffs";*
5 *"bastinado" = foot torture, whether recreational or political;*
6 *"kinky";*
7 *"shoe-fucker";*
8 *"purse-fucker";*
9 *"necrophilia";*
10 *"fatty specialist";*
11 *"shoe-licking devil";*
12 *"foot-licking devil";*
13 *"internet pervert";*
14 *"kinky pervert";*
15 *"sexual deviant";*
16 *"foot fetishist",*
17 *"toe sucker";*
18 *"high-heels fucker."*

image: GobQ/T. Warburton y Bajo

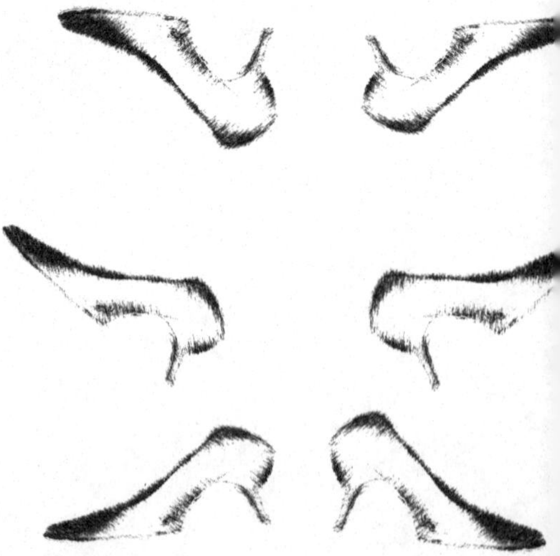

FINK,
GRASS,
INFORMER,
STOOL
PIGEON
(& VARIATIONS)

προδοτις

AFRIKAANS nuusdraer *
ARABIC far **
BASQUE informatzaile *
BELARUSIAN сука / suka **
CANTONESE gwái *;
gàansai [2]
CATALAN informador *;
delator *
CROATIAN izdajìca;
druker [3]
CZECH udava *;
zrádná krysa **
DANISH stikker *
FARSI khabarchin *
FINNISH ilmiantaja *
FRENCH bourrique *;
agent provoqueteur [6]
GAELIC, IRISH sceithire *
GAELIC, SCOTS brathadair *
GERMAN Berichsterstatter *
GREEK, MOD. προδοτις / prodotis *
HINDI / URDU kabri *;
bhedi *;
jasōs *
ICELANDIC heimilðarmadur
ITALIAN informatore (m) /
informatrice (m) *
JAPANESE 裏切り者 uragirimono [4]
MALAYU hantu polis [5]
MANDARIN 告发某人 gàofā mǒurén [5]
NORWEGIAN hjemmelsmann *
POLISH informator *
PORTUGUESE informatante *
ROMANIAN denuntător *
RUSSIAN мент / ment [6];
менти / menti [6]
SERBIAN издајица / izdajìca
SOTHO, N mmegi
SPANISH informador *;
solplón *
SWAHILI mbega *
SWEDISH tjällare *;
goltupp *
TAGALOG kumantà *;
ngúso´ *
TURKISH ihbarcı *
UKRAINIAN інформатор / informator *
UZBEK чақимч / chaqimch *
VIETNAMESE ngu ói thông-tin *
WELSH hysbysywr *
YIDDISH shtinker *
YORUBA olófófó *
ZULU umcebi *;
umzekeci *

* *"fink/grass/informant/informer";*
** *"rat/rat fink";*
2 *"spy";*
3 *"snitch";*
4 *backstabber/traitor;*
5 *police informant;*
6 *police/militia agent*

FUCK (& VARIATIONS) **еби**

AFRIKAANS naai * ;
goensch * ;
klomp pomp [2] ;
pomp *
ALBANIAN shkërdhej *
ARABIC nek *
ARMENIAN kunel * ;
bornigil * ;
miatsunel *
BASQUE larru * ;
larru jo *
BENGALI bash mara * ;
chōd *
BOSNIAN / CROATIAN jebi *
BULGARIAN еби / ebi *
BURMESE lo *
CANTONESE díu *;
bōk yéh *
CATALAN boixar *;
cardar *;
catxar *;
follar *;
barrinar [3]
CZECH oustat *;
ukat *;
rychlovka [4]
DANISH pule *;
knep *;
bunkepul [2]
DUTCH beurt *;
neuk *;
naaien *
ESTONIAN keppima *;
nikkuma *;
nussima *
FARSI zenâ *;
FINNISH nussia *;
naida *
FRENCH foutre *;
ficher *;
baiser *;
fourrer [5];
sacrer [22]
FRENCH (VERLAN) niquer *
GAELIC, IRISH bualadh craiceann [6];
streachailt leathair [7];
an sá deas [8];
feisigh *
GAELIC, SCOTS dàirich *;
bualadh craiceann [6];
faigh muin *
GERMAN ficken *;
besorgen *;
bollern *;
nageln [9];
orgeln [10];
böckle [29]
GUJARATI / HINDI / KANNADA / URDU chōd *
HINDI / URDU chodnha *;
chut *
marna *;
atkana *
HUNGARIAN baszni *
ICELANDIC dráttur *;
uppáferð *;
ríða *;
serða *
INDONESIAN kongkek *;
ngentot *;
martole jonjong emahi [11]
ITALIAN scopa *;
scopata *;
fottuto *;
fungula *;
chiavata *;
fottere *;
scopare *;
vangare *;
chiavare *;
montare [12];
sbattere [13];
sverginare [14];
trombare [15];
pincare [30];
sveltina [4]
JAPANESE やる yaru [16]

KHMER choi *
KOREAN shibal *
LATIN concubitum *;
futuere *;
futuo *;
raptus regaliter [18]
LITHUANIAN lachui *;
ishdulkint *
MALAYU iut *;
ngongkek *
MALTESE f'oxx *;
haqq *
MANDARIN 操 cào *;
干操 gàn cào *
MARATHI tujha *
MONGOLIAN ща / sha *
NAHUATL ahuilnemi *;
ahuilnemiliztli *
NORWEGIAN faen *;
jævla *;
pule *
POLISH jebać *;
przernać *;
pierdolić *;
przelecieć *
PORTUGUESE foder *;
afogar o ganso [19];
trepar [17] *
ROMANIAN futui *;
fute *
RUSSIAN ебать /ebát *
SERBIAN јеби/jebi *
SLOVENIAN jebaj *
SOTHO, N kopana *;
bofa *;
tlema *;
gwela *
SPANISH culear *;
casquete *;
chingar *;
echar un polvo / Echemos un polvo! [4];
mojar el churro [20];
coger [23];
pichar [24];
quimbar [25];
ponchar [26];
ingar [27];
pisar [28]
SWAHILI fanya mapenzi *
SWEDISH knulla *;
jävla *
TAGALOG chóndot *;
ginaláw *;
hindot *;
iyót *;
kamíhan *;
pitpítkáma *;
swák *;
tótwak *;
yarián *
TAMIL otha *
TELEGU denga *
THAI yet *
TURKISH Siktir! [31]
UKRAINIAN трахати / trakhkaty *;
штуркати / šturkaty *;
юбати / yubaty *
UZBEK сикиш / sikish *;
VIETNAMESE đị̲t me *;
đụ̲ má *;
giao-hợp *
WELSH ffwc *
YIDDISH schtupp *
YORUBA se àgbere *;
se panságà *
ZULU bhebha *;
ukuhlanganna *;
ukubhebha *;
hlobobgo [21]

* *"fuck";*
** *"pump";*
2 *"cluster-fuck/gang bang";*
3 *"drill";*
4 *"Pulverize" / "Have a quickie" P. Ric.; "Let's have a quickie/fuck!" Col.;*
5 *"stuff, bury";*
6 *"skin-hitting";*
7 *"stretching leather";*
8 *"the pleasant stabbing";*

9 *"nailing";*
10 *"playing the organ";*
11 *"standing fuck";*
12 *"mount," woman on top;*
13 *"bang";*
14 *"fuck a virgin";*
15 *"play the trumpet," Tuscan.;*
16 *"do"; try (can also mean to do someone in)*
17 *"fuck/screw," Braz.;*
18 *"royally fucked/screwed";*
19 *"drown the goose," Braz.;*
20 *"dip the pastry," Cast.;*
21 *"thigh fucking";*
22 *"fuck/fucking," Queb.;*
23 *"grab/grasp," Arg.;*
24 *"fuck/screw," Col.;*
25 *"fuck/screw," Cub.;*
26 *"fuck/screw," Pan.;*
27 *"fuck/screw," P. Ric.;*
28 *"fuck/screw," Salv.;*
29 *"fuck/screw," Germ./Sw.;*
30 *"fuck/screw," Lombard.;*
31 *"Fuck you!" / "Fuck off!"*

GobQ/T. Warburton y Bajo

やる

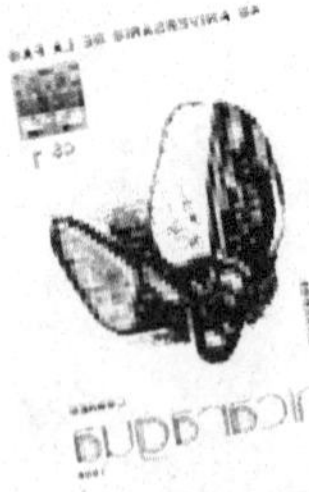

FUCK YOU / FUCK YOURSELF (& VARIATIONS) 操你

AFRIKAANS Fok jou! *
ALBANIAN Të qifsha. *;
Të qiftë miza kali. [2];
Të qiftë Milosh! [3]
ARABIC Cūs! *
ARABIC / TUNIS. Yātek asba. * ;
Imshi neyyek. **
ARMENIAN Kunem kez. *
BENGALI Bokachoda. *
BOSNIAN Jebi se. *;
Jebo te pokemona. [4]
BULGARIAN Еби се. / Ebi se. *;
Върви да се ебеш. / Vurvi da se ebiš. **
CANTONESE Díu néih *;
Ngóh díu néih go hāi! [5]
CATALAN Que et follin! *
CREOLE / MAURIT. Bour toi. *
CROATIAN Jebi se. * ;
Jebi se s vibratorom od lezbača. [6];
Jebi sve na svom brzom biranju na mobitelu. [7];
Jebo svoj usrani pank rock bend. [8];
Jebo svoj sunčan dan. [9];
Jebo te Milosovič. [10]
CZECH Jdi do prdele! [11]
DANISH Knep dig selv! ** ;
Du kan kneppe dig selv i røven med en lego-klods! [12]
DUTCH Je kunt de pot op. ** ;
Ga rukken. **
ESTONIAN Mine perse! *
FARSI Gaê damet! *;
Kiram tu maz-habet.[1]
FINNISH haista vittu [14];
Vittu mä tapan sut! [15]
FRENCH Vas te faire foutre! *
J'encule Foucault! / J'encule Baudrillard! [22]
GAELIC, IRISH Focáil leat. * ;
Téigh trasna ort féin. **
GERMAN Fick dich! / Fegg di! *
GREEK, MOD. σαλτα γαμισυ / salta gamisu **
HEBREW Lech tiezdayen. **
HINDI / URDU Tere ko chōdun. *
HUNGARIAN Baszódj meg! *
ICELANDIC ríddu ter ;
Ríddu þér. **;
Vaddírassgat. **
INDONESIAN Ngentot lu! *
ITALIAN Va´ a farti fotere! *;
Brutto stronzo! * ;
Scopa tutti nel tuo fonino. [7]
Fottiti! *
JAPANESE ザッケナヨ！ Zakkenayo! *
KAZAKH котакка кет! / Kotakka ket! *
KOREAN Yumago. *
LATIN Futue te ipsum. *
LITHUANIAN Valink nachui. **
MACEDONIAN Оди еби се. / Odi ebi se. *;
Крв да ти ебам / Krv da ti ebam. [16]
MANDARIN 操你。 Cǎo nǐ. *
NORWEGIAN Faen ta deg. *;
Pul deg selv. **
POLISH Pierdol sie! **;
Czochraj bobra! **
PORTUGUESE / BRAZ. Se fode! *;
Vão se fuder! [17];
Foda-se e morra-se. [18];
Que se foda essa merda. [19]
ROMANIAN Fututi! *;
Futu-te Dumnezeu! [20]
RUSSIAN Ебаться! / Ebat´sya! **
Ебай всех в твоей мобильник! / Ebay vsex v tvoey mobil'nik! [7]
SERBIAN јеби се! / Jebi se! * ;
Бог те јебо! / Bog te jebo! [20]
SLOVENIAN Jebaj se! *
SPANISH ¡Chinga te! / ¡Jode te! *;
¡Friege te! *
SWAHILI Nenda kutomba, nakata tatu. [21]

SWEDISH Fan också! *;
Jävlar! *
TAGALOG Hindót mo! *;
Ngatngát. *
TURKISH Siktir! *
THAI Yet màang. *
TURKISH Siktir! *
VIETNAMESE Đu me. **
WELSH Dos i ffwcio. **
YIDDISH Schtupp ir. *

* *"Fuck you!" / "Fuck off!"*
** *"(Go) Fuck yourself!"*
2 *"May the horsefly fuck you."*
3 *"May Slobodan Milosovich fuck you."*
4 *"Pokemón fucked you."*
5 *"Fuck you, man!"*
6 *"Fuck you with a dyke's dildo!"*
7 *"Fuck everyone on yr cell/mobile phone speed dial!"*
8 *"Fuck your shitty punk rock band!"*
9 *"Fuck your shinshiny day."*
10 *"Milosovič fucked you."*
11 *"Go to the ass/arse!" = fuck you;*
12 *"Fuck yourself up the ass/arse with a Lego brick!"*
13 *"Fuck yr religion!"*
14 *"Go sniff a cunt!" = "Fuck you!"*
15 *"Fuck yr religion!"*
16 *"Fuck your gene pool."*
17 *"Fuck all of you!"*
18 *"Fuck yourself, then die!"*
19 *"Fuck this shit!"*
20 *"God fuck you!" / "God should fuck you!"*
21 *"Fuck yourself, in triplicate!"*
22 *"Fuck Foucault!" / "Fuck Baudrillard!"*

FUCK YOUR GOD! / FUCK GOD!: **SEE: GOD, FUCK**

Ебат
ься!

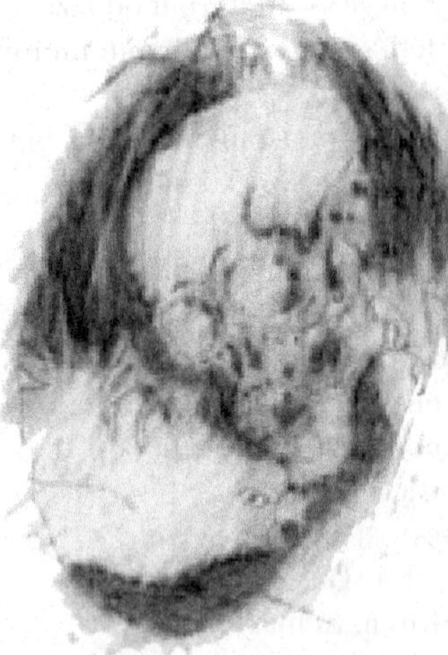

illustr., © 2008, Graham Willoughby

FUCK YOUR MOTHER/ FUCK YOUR SISTER, MOTHERFUCKER/ SISTERFUCKER (& VARIATIONS)

Ίαμισε τιν μανα σου!

AFRIKAANS Nai jou moeder *; moeder-naaier / mamanaaier **; Jou suster naai vir kaas-en-wyn. [2]

ALBANIAN Nëne qim! **; Mótër qirë [3]; Famíjeqir [4]

ARABIC / TUNIS. Nēk amok. *

ARMENIAN Kunem mered. *

BENGALI chōdmarani **

BOSNIAN Jebem ti mater! *; Jebem sestru! [5]

BULGARIAN Мама ти да еба фашистка./ Ma-ma ti da eba fašistka. [6]

CANTONESE Díu néih jímuih! [5]

CATALAN Hugo Sanchez! [7]

CROATIAN / SERB Jebo ti Tarzan baba! [8]; Pička ti materina fašistička. [5]; Jebem ti mater. *; Јебо ти Тарзан баба!/Jebo ti Tarzan baba! [8]; Пичка ти материна фашистичка./Pička ti materina fašistička. [5]; Јебем ти матер./Jebem ti mater. *

CZECH Mamrd! **

DANISH Knep din mor! *; en gal moderkneppe [9]

DUTCH Ga je moeder neuken! *

ESTONIAN Emakeppija. **

FARSI Madar gendu. **

FINNISH Pulunnussija! [10]

FRENCH Va voir ta mére. *

FRENCH (VERLAN) Nique ta mère. *

GAELIC, IRISH Feisigh do mháthair. *; Feisigh do dheirfiúr. [5]

GAELIC, SCOTS Dàirich do mhathair. *; Bidh do mhàthair a' daireadh le Caitiligich / Pròsdanaich / Calvinich / Sassanaich. [11]

GERMAN Mami ficka. **; Geh fick deine Schwester. [5]

GREEK, MOD. Ίαμισε τιν μανα σου! / Gamise tin mana sou! *

HINDI / URDU Mādhar chud! / Māchud! *; bhanchud [3]

HUNGARIAN Baszd meg az kurva disznó anyádat! [12]

ICELANDIC Ríddu mömmu þinni! *; Ríddu systur þinni! [5]

INDONESIAN Mandipantat! **

ITALIAN Figlio di puttana. [13]; Vai in mona di tua sorella! [14]

JAPANESE テメーの母をやれ！ Temē no haha o yare! *; テメーの甥と姪をやれ! Temē no oi to mei o yare! [15]

KOREAN um chang seki **

LATIN Matris futuor! **

LITHUANIAN Mo´tin krushys! **

MACEDONIAN Да ти ебам мајката!/Da ti ebam majkata! *

MANDARIN 操 你 妈. Cào nǐ mā. *; 你妈了操尝毛主席! Nǐ māle cào cháng mao zhǔ xí! [16]

NORWEGIAN Mul mora di! *; Mora-puler! **

POLISH matkojebca **; siostrojebca [3]

PORTUGUESE Su canna! *; Cabrão **; Sua irmã dá a bunda o dia inteiro. [17]

ROMANIAN Futi-ti matii! *; Futu-ti icoană matii. [18]

RUSSIAN Передай, ёб твою мать, водку!/ Peredáy, ëb tvoyú mat' vódku! [19]; Ебене матери!/Ebéne máteri! [20]

SLOVENIAN Jebi si pofukano mater. [20]

SPANISH ¡Chinga tu madre! *; Chinga-do sin madre. [21]; ¡Chinga tu hermana! [5]

SWAHILI Kuma mama yako nakala

tatu. [22]
SWEDISH Knulla din morsa! *;
Skit-stövel! **
THAI Hèe mâae mang. *;
Yet mâae! **
TURKISH Anasıken. **
UKRAINIAN Юб твою мать. / Yub tvoyu
mat´. *
UZBEK Онайне скаий. / Onayne skaiy. *
VIETNAMESE Đô Mâ mày. *
WELSH Cnuchu fy mam. *

Юб твою мать.

* *"(Go) Fuck yr mother!" / "I fuck yr mother!"*
** *"Motherfucker!"*
2 *"Yr sister fucks for cheese & wine";*
3 *"Sister fucker";*
4 *"Fuck yr family";*
5 *"(Go) Fuck yr sister!" / "I fuck yr sister!";*
6 *BULG: "Fuck yr fascist mother!" / CROAT./SERB.: "Fascist motherfucker!";*
7 *Hugo Sanchez" = Madrid soccer legend & notorious muthahfuckah;*
8 *"Tarzan fucked yr grandmother!"*
9 *"mad motherfucker";*
10 *"pigeonfucker"=motherfucker;*
11 *"Yr mother fucks Catholics / Protestants / Calvinists / Englishmen!"*
12 *"Fuck yr pig whore mother!"*
13 *"Motherfucker!" / "Son of a whore!"*
14 *"Go to yr sister's cunt!"*
15 *"Fuck yr nieces & nephews!"*
16 *"Yr mother fucked Chairman Mao!"*
17 *"Yr sister fucks all day long!"*
18 *"Fuck yr mother's icon!"*
19 *"Pass the 'Fuck-yr-mother' vodka!"*
20 *"Fuck yr fucked mother!"*
21 *"Motherless fuck!"*
22 *"Fuck yr mother in triplicate!"*

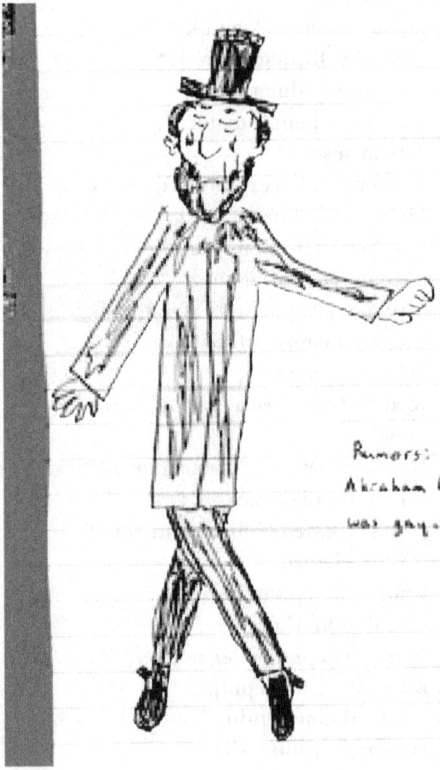
Rumors:
Abraham Li
was gay.
Liz Swados

テメーの母をやれ！

GAY,
FAGGOT/FAG,
QUEER,
LIMP
WRIST,
SISSY/
SISSY MARY
(& VARIATIONS)

підарас

AFRIKAANS moffie *;
moffinia *;
skeef *;
Nanette *;
koekblik [2]
ALBANIAN bytheqir *
ARABIC mahmoun *;
mibun *
ARMENIAN gyot *
BASQUE marikoi *;
atzelari *;
marixtu *
BELARUSIAN підарас / pidaras *
BENGALI makundo *;
neka *
BOSNIAN pederu *
BULGARIAN медена питка/medena pitka *;
педал /pedal *
CANTONESE geilóu
CATALAN marieta; maripili; fogó [3]
CROATIAN peder *;
pederčino *
CZECH buzerant *;
teplous *
DANISH bøsse *;
bøsserøv *;
bøssekal *;
svans *
DUTCH bruinwerker *;
flikker *;
mietje
aarsridder [4];
bilnaad acrobaat [5];
naadsensei [6];
bil spier cosmonaut [7];
darmtoerist [8]
ESTONIAN lilla *;
FARSI hamjesbâz *;
kuni *
FINNISH hinuri *;
hinaaja *;
fägis *;
ruskean rein ritari [4]
FRENCH pédé *;
tante [9];
tapette [3];
marcher à voiles et à vapeur [10]
FRENCH (VERLAN) ètappe [3]
GAELIC, IRISH aerach *
GAELIC, SCOTS gèidh *;
gille-tòin [11]
GERMAN Schwuler *;
Schwudi *;
Schwuchtlä *
GREEK, MOD. αδηλφή/ adhelfí [12];
ανεμοόμυος / anemómyos *;
κάππα / káppa *;
μοδερντεκνο / moderntekno [13]
HEBREW dohef batahat *;
batachat *;
egzozan *;
mitromem *
HINDI / URDU gando *;
chikna *
HUNGARIAN buzi *;
köcszög [3]
ICELANDIC hommi *;
hommamömmuríðari [14];
álfur *
INDONESIAN wandu *
ITALIAN frocio *;
cesso *;
puppo *;
recchione *;
bucaiolo *;
culattone [15];
effe / zia [3];
essera del'altra spondabanchina [27]
JAPANESE おかま okama [16];
バラ族 barazoku [17]
KAZAKH кизстеке / kizsteke *

KHMER kathūy
KOREAN dorang
LITHUANIAN pyderas *;
pedikas *;
gaidys *
MACEDONIAN педер / peder *;
весел / vesel *;
ведар / vedar *
MALAYU semburit *
MALTESE trinkatur *;
imcaqqam *;
toqbi *;
pufta *
MANDARIN 同性恋 tóngxìngliàn *;
玻璃 bōli *;
余桃 yútáo *;
同志 tóngzhì [18]
MARATHI battebaja *
MONGOLIAN гомо / gomo *
NAHUATL cuiloni *;
cihatic *;
tecuilon-tiani [19]
NORWEGIAN soper *;
feier *;
tarmturist [8];
bærsjhølpuler [20]
POLISH ciota *;
pedal *
PORTUGUESE baiola *;
baitolo *;
bichinha *;
bicholha *;
franga *;
panascoide *;
paneleiro *;
viado *;
viadão *
ROMANIAN bulangiu *;
poponar *
RUSSIAN клубника / klubníka *;
хуеплет / khüeplet *;
жопник / žópnik *
SERBIAN педе / pede *
SLOVENIAN feget / fegi *;
peder *;
ritolizeć [21]
SOTHO, N punya *
SPANISH puto *;
cacorro *;
maricón *;
maricon de playa [22];
pato [23];
mariposo / mariposa [24];
picaflor [25];
marica [28];
joto [29];
colisón [30];
mamalón [31] *;
afeminado [32];
parchita [33];
del otro bando [34]
SWAHILI mahanithi *;
basha *;
shoga *;
msenge *;
wasenge *
SWEDISH bög *;
bögjävel *;
homofil *
TAGALOG acheng *;
tsa bon thóy yangyáng *;
badápdidáp *;
chaplók *;
dadang *;
héchos *;
labák *;
manáy *;
níkya *;
pabukó *;
shóki *;
THAI àaep jit *;
dtòot *;
gaé *;
lek thàawn *;
saét lek *
TURKISH götoş *;
kuni [3]
UKRAINIAN москал / moskal´ *

UZBEK хажиқиз / hajiqiz *;
VIETNAMESE bon *
WELSH hoyw *
YIDDISH faygala *
YORUBA erù igi *;
ìdì igi *
ZULU imbube *;
nongolozi *;
zelda *

おかま

* *"gay/faggot/queer";*
GERM.: Schwudi/Schwuchtlä. Sw. dial.;
** *black queer;*
2 *"cake tin," effeminate gay/faggot/queer;*
3 *bot. gay;*
4 *"ass/arse-knight";*
5 *"butt-crack-acrobat";*
6 *"butt-crack-sensei";*
7 *"Butt-muscle Cosmonaut";*
8 *"colon-tourist";*
9 *"aunt";*
10 *"navigating by sail & steam"= bi-, AC/DC;*
11 *"arse-boy";*
12 *"sister";*
13 *"modern child," young queer;*
14 *"gay motherfucker;*
15 *"ass/arse-bandit";*
16 *"shallow pot";*
17 *"rose tribe";*
18 *"comrade"— term now confined to Politburo back-benchers & Chinese queers;*
19 *"bi/switch-hitter";*
20 *shit-hole fucker;*
21 *ass/ arse-licking faggot;*
22 *"beach faggot," Castil.;*
23 *"duck," Cub;*
24 *"butterfly," Guat. & Mex., respectively;*
25 *"flower-picker," Mex.;*
26 *"fairy," "queen."*
27 *"from the opposite riverbank/quay";*
28 *"Queen," Arg., Col., Pan"*
29 *"One-Eyed Jack";*
30 *"Collision," Ch.;*
31 *"Cock/dick-sucking faggot," Cub.;*
32 *"femme faggot";*
33 *"femme faggot," Venez.;*
34 *"On the other side"/ "In the other faction."*

GAY BAR, GLORY HOLE (& VARIATIONS)

το γαγ βαρ

AFRIKAANS chacha palais *;
carousel **;
slangpark **;
kloon sone [3]
CATALAN quartto fosc [2]
CROATIAN / SERB 'gay' noće klubove *;
гај ноће клубове / 'gay' noće klubove *
CZECH homosexuální kluby *
FRENCH ballet bleu, le [5]
GERMAN Schwulen-klub *;
Lesben-kneipen-Klub [6]
GREEK, MOD. το γαγ βαρ / "to-gay var" *
HUNGARIAN meleg szórakozóhelyeket *
ICELANDIC
INDONESIAN tempat 'gay' mankal *
ITALIAN il bar dei froci / il locale per froci *;
ripostiglio [4]
JAPANESE ゲイ・バー / gei bā *
KHMER bā suhm-rahp ma-nōh *
POLISH kluby dla gejów *
PORTUGUESE zona [4]
RUSSIAN кладовка / kladovka [4]
SLOVENIAN homosekualski bar *
SPANISH club de mariposa *
SWAHILI baa ya mahanithi *
TAGALOG cása *
THAI bah gay *
VIETNAMESE quán mà gió'i *

* *"gay/queer bar/club/disco/venue";*
** *"public loos/lavatories where gays fuck & suck & frolic & form conga lines & put on a show";*
2 *"fuck room";*
3 *"clone zone," gay club/bar;*
4 *"glory hole";*
5 *"daisy-chain/clump-fuck/group grope with very very very young boys";*
6 *"lesbian/dyke bar/club/disco/venue."*

GEEK, NERD (OR NURD), FOUR-EYES, SKINNY TIE (& VARIATIONS) ботаник

AFRIKAANS mofgat *
BENGALI padaku *;
keblakanto *
CANTONESE sei ngáan gwāi *
CATALAN coco *
CROATIAN smokljan *
CZECH blbec *;
poutov kejklí *
DANISH nørd *;
brilleabe **
DUTCH mafkees *;
engerd *
ESTONIAN jobu *;
FINNISH nörtti *
FRENCH taré *;
quatre-yeux [2]
GAELIC, IRISH ceathair-súile [2];
ríomhchláraitheoir [3]
GAELIC, SCOTS ceithir-sùilean [2];
neach-compiutaireachd [3]
GERMAN Niete *
HEBREW chnun *;
laflaf *
HINDI padhaku *;
computer ka keeda [4]
ICELANDIC nördi *; gík *
ITALIAN sfigato *(m)* / sfigata *(f)* *;
fanatico del computer *(m)* / fanatica del computer *(f)* [4];
quatrocchi [2]
JAPANESE オタク otaku *;
マニア mania [5];
A系 A-kei [6]
KAZAKH лох / loh [7]
KOREAN je-su up nuen nom [7]
LATVIAN lohs/losene
LITHUANIAN nevykelis
MACEDONIAN изрод / izrod [8]
NORWEGIAN dust
POLISH robotnik [9]
PORTUGUESE quatro olhos [2]
ROMANIAN martalog [7]
RUSSIAN ботаник / botanik [10];
мутар / mutar [11]
SPANISH pariguallo *;
bobolon *;
quatro-ojos [2]
SWEDISH försagd *;
menlös *
TAGALOG nerdo *
THAI koh' bpèern lae chèeuy [12]
URDU sankī [13];
char ānkhonwala [2]
UZBEK ишқибоз / ishqiboz *
YIDDISH nebish *;
shtick holtz [14]

* *"geeky nerd/nurd, nerdy/nurdy geek";*
** *"glasses monkey",;*
2 *"four-eyes";*
3 *computer programmer;*
4 *computer geek,;*
5 *obsessive maniac;*
6 *tech-toy geek who hangs out in Akihabara, Tokyo's tech toy district;*
7 *"loser";*
8 *"freak";*
9 *"workaholic yuppie/workaholic";*
10 *"botanist"=nerd/nurd";*
11 *"neurotic worry-wart Jewish brainiac";*
12 *"clueless & awkward nerd";*
13 *"oddball/eccentric";*
14 *"dull bore with no personality.*

A系

GO TO HELL (& VARIATIONS)

Вирви в Ада!

AFRIKAANS Gaan te Hel! *
BASQUE Zoaz infernua! *;
Pikutara joan. *
BENGALI Pude mar! *
BOSNIAN/CROATIAN Idi do djavola! *
BULGARIAN Вирви в Ада!/Vyrvi v Ada! *
CANTONESE Séi lāa! *
CROATIAN/SERB Idi do djavola! *;
Иди до дјавола!/Idi do djavola! *
DANISH Gå ad Helvede til! *
DUTCH Loop naar de Hel! *
ESTONIAN Mine põrgu! *
FARSI Boro be jahanam! *
FINNISH Painu helvettiin! [2]
FRENCH Va à l'enfer! *;
Allez à l'enfer! *
GAELIC, IRISH Go hIfreann leat! *;
Imigh sa diabhal! **;
Go dtachta an diabhal thú! [3];
Do bhháltaí don diabhal. [4]
GAELIC, SCOTS Rach chun an donais! **;
Rach chun an diosg cruaidh nan donais! [4]
GERMAN Fahr' zur Hölle! *;
Geh zum Teufel! *;
Scher dich zum Teufel! *
GREEK, MOD. Ας τό διαολό!/As tó diaoló! **
HEBREW Lech laazazel! *;
Tisaref be evadon! [6]
HINDI/URDU Mar sāle! *
HUNGARIAN Menj a fenébe! *;
Menj a picsába! ;
Rohadj meg! [7]
ICELANDIC Farðu til Helvítis! *
ITALIAN Andare all' inferno! *
JAPANESE 地獄へ行け! Jigoku e ike! *
KOREAN Toejora! *
LITHUANIAN Eik velniop! *
MALAYU Pergi mampus! *
MANDARIN 去地狱! Qù dìyù! *
NORWEGIAN Dra til Helvete! *
POLISH Idź do Piekla! *
PORTUGUESE Vai pro inferno! *;
Come merda e vai pro inferno! [8]
RUSSIAN Во пизду!/Vo pizdu! [9]
SLOVENIAN Spizdi v kurac! [10]
SPANISH Vete al infierno! *
SWEDISH Dra åt Helvete! *
UKRAINIAN Чорт тебе бери/Čort tebe bery! [11]

* *"Go to hell!"*
** *"Go to the devil!"*
2 *"Fuck off to hell!"*
3 *"May the Devil choke you!"*
4 *"Go to the Devil's hard disk!"*
5 *"Yr cunt to the Devil!"*
6 *"Burn in Hell!"*
7 *"Rot in Hell!"*
8 *"Eat shit & go to Hell!";*
9 *"Go to pussy!"*
10 *"Go to cock!/Go to dick!"*
11 *"The Devil take you!"*

地獄へ行け!

GOB, SPIT
(& VARIATIONS)

AFRIKAANS spoeg/spoog *
ARABIC başqa *
BASQUE listu *;
eldertu [2];
adurreztatu [3]
CANTONESE léu/lēu *;
háuséui [4]
CATALAN escopir *
CREOLE/HAITIAN krache *
CROATIAN/SERB ražanj *;
ражанј/ražanj *
CZECH prskat *;
mžít *;
slintat [3];
DANISH sprutte *;
savle [3];
spyt [4]
DUTCH spuwen *
ESTONIAN sülgama *
FINNISH Kakista ulos! [9]
FRENCH crépiter *
GAELIC, IRISH smugairle *;
seile [4]
GERMAN Speichel *(m)* / Spucke *(f)* [4]
GREEK, MOD. (το) σάλιο/ (to) oáleo
GUJARATI thōk [5]
HAUSA miyau [4]
HEBREW reer [4]
HINDI/URDU Tere bahin ki shalwār main thōk phainkun. [6]
ICELANDIC slefa [2]; hráki [4];
ITALIAN sputo/sputare *;
sbalordito **
JAPANESE 唾 / tsuba
KOREAN ch´ĭm paet´-da *
LATIN exspuĕre [9];
in facium inspuĕre [10]
LATVIAN spļaut *
LITHUANIAN seílės [5]
MACEDONIAN плука/pluka *
MALAYU berludah/ludah *
MANDARIN 唾液 / tuòyè *
NAHUATL iztlameyatl [3]
NORWEGIAN savl [2];
vrøvel [2];
rør [2]
POLISH ślina *; pluć *
PORTUGUESE escarrar *;
babarse [3];
cuspe [4];
"proibido cuspir" [7]
ROMANIAN scuipat [4]
RUSSIAN слюна́! / slyuná [4];
"плева́ть воспреща́еця" /
"plevát´ vospreščáetsya" [7]
SLOVENIAN Plunem nate! [8]
SOMALI candhuufo *
SOTHO, N mare [4]
SPANISH escupir *;
babosear/babear [3]
SWEDISH saliv [4];
Vräka ur sig! [9]
TAGALOG lumurâ *;
maglawáy [2]
THAI grà ak [11]
TURKISH Tükürük açıkla! /
Tükürük söyle! [9]
UKRAINIAN плюва́ти /
plyuváti *
UZBEK туфла/tufla *
VIETNAMESE cái xiên *
WELSH poer *;
glafoeri [2];
poeryn [4]
YIDDISH spei´en **
YOEME/YAQUI chitwatte *
YORUBA itọ ẹnú [4]
ZAPOTEC ruchá xhinni *
ZULU fela *;
phumisa *;
bhibhizela [2]

* *"spit"; ITAL. "gob";*
** *"gobsmacked";*
2 *"slobber";*
3 *"drool";*

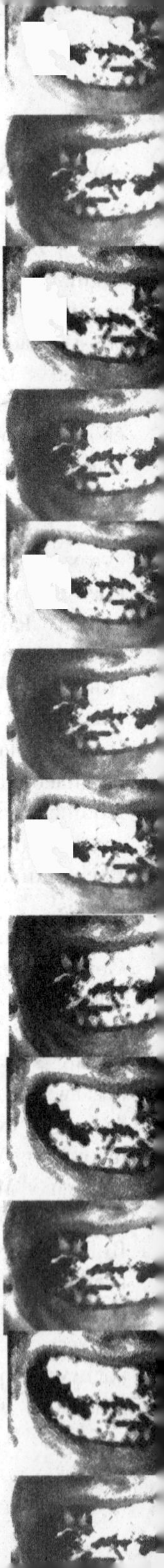

4 *"spittle";*
5 *"saliva/sputum";*
6 *"I spit in yr sister's blue jeans!"*
7 *"Spitting prohibited";*
8 *"I spit on you!" / "Spit on you!";*
9 *"Spit out"; TURK: "Spit it out!";*
10 *spit in somebody's face;*
11 *spitting up blood.*

"плева́ть воспреща́еця"

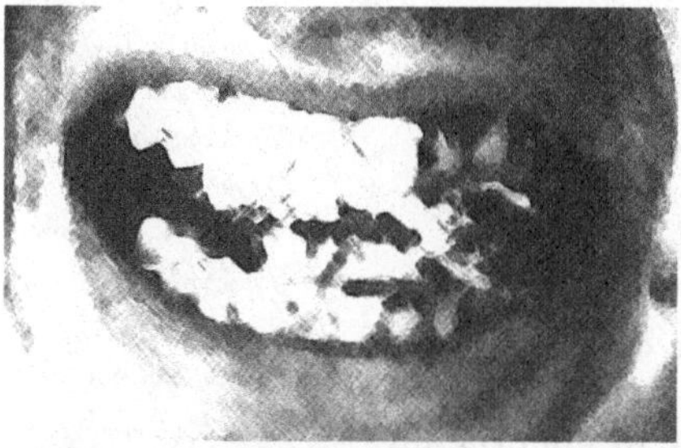

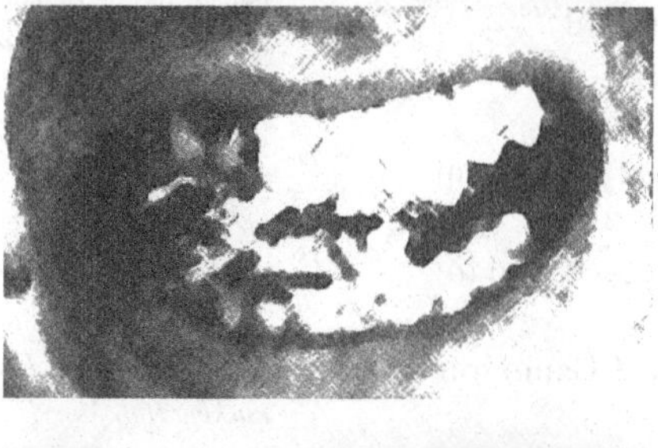

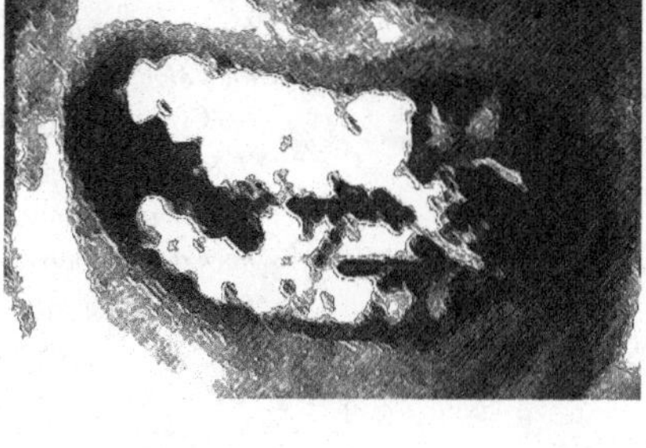

images: GobQ/M. Clarke

GOD!, FUCK/ GOD!, FUCK YOUR GOD! (& VARIATIONS)

Γαμο το θεο.

AFRIKAANS Naii jou Jesus. *
ALBANIAN Ta qifshä Zotërin tënd. **
ARABIC/TUNIS. Nān rabb bōk. [2]
BOSNIAN Jebem ti Boga! / Jebem ti Allah! **
CATALAN Mecàgum el Déu que et va fotre! [3]
CROATIAN/SERB Bog te jebo. [4]; Jebo naci papu. [5]
Бог те јебо / Bog te jebo. [4];
Јебо наци папу./ Jebo naci papu. [5]
DUTCH Ga je God kneuken! **
FINNISH Äitisi nai Kristus. [6]
FRENCH J'encule Dieu! **;
J'encule le pape nazi! [5];
J'encule ta scene de nativite! [7];
J'encule ton bebe Jesus dans sa creche! [8]
GAELIC, IRISH Focáil an Pápa. [9];
Gab-haidh 'sé sa thóin in ainm Dé, an Mac, is an Spiorad Naomh! [10]
GAELIC, SCOTS Gabhaidh e 'sa thòin ann an-t ainm nan Tighearna. [11]
GERMAN Jesus im Stuka! / Jessas im Stuka! [12]
GREEK, MOD. Γαμο το θεο./ Gamo to theo. **;
Γαμο τον αντιχριστο. / Gamo ton antichristo. [13];
Γαμα σταυρος σου./Gama stavros sou. [14]
ICELANDIC Heilagur mömmuriðill. [15]
ITALIAN Va funcuolo Dio e tutte i santi! [16];
Santo cazzo! [17];
Porca madonna! [19]
MACEDONIAN Да ти ебам бозество. / Da ti ebam bozestvo. **
MALTESE Haq alla. **;
Haq al minestra madonna. [19];
F'oxx madre Teresa! [20]
MANDARIN 操你祖宗十八代! Cào nǐ zǔ zōng shí bā dài! [21]
ROMANIAN Futu-te Dumnezeu. [4]
SLOVENIAN Jebem ti Boga na križu! [22];
Jebem ti vse svete! [23]
SPANISH ¡Pinche evangelizador! [24];
¡Chinga la purmísima hostia! [25]
SWEDISH Jävla evangelist! [24]
YIDDISH Schtupp elohim! / Stup elohim! **

* *"Fuck yr Jesus!";*
** *"Fuck God!"/ "(Go) Fuck yr God!"/ "Fuck the God!"; GREEK: "I fuck yr God.";*
2 *"Damn yr father's God";*
3 *"I shit on the God who fucked you!"*
4 *"God should fuck you!" / "God fuck you!";*
5 *"Fuck the Nazi Pope."*
6 *"Yr mother fucks Jesus Christ."*
7 *"Fuck yr Nativity scene!"*
8 *"Fuck yr baby Jesus in a creche!"*
9 *"Fuck the Pope" — popular 1980s Dublin graffito;*
10 *"He takes it up the ass/arse in the name of the Father, the Son, and the Holy Spirit/Ghost."*
11 *"He takes it up the ass/arse in the name of the Lord."*
12 *"Jesus in a Stuka." — 2nd. vers., Bav. dial.*
13 *"Fuck yr Antichrist!"*
14 *"(I) Fuck yr cross!"*
15 *"(Holy motherfucker!"*
16 *"Fuck God, Christ, & all the saints!"*
17 *"Holy dick!" = Holy Fuck!;*
18 *"Fucking Holy Mary!" / "Fucking Madonna!" / "Pig Madonna!"*
19 *"Fuck the minestroni Virgin Mary / Madonna!"*
20 *"Fuck Mother Teresa!"*
21 *"Fuck yr 18 Generation-ancestors!"*
22 *"(I) Fuck yr God on the cross!"*
23 *"(I) Fuck all yr saints!"*
24 *"Fuck the most holy Communion wafer!"*
25 *"Fucking evangelist!"*

GOD DAMN / DAMN / DAMN YOU / GOD DAMN YOU

(& VARIATIONS)

畜生!

ALBANIAN Lanét qofsh!
BASQUE Madarikatu(a)! **
BENGALI Jahanname jao!
BOSNIAN / CROATIAN Bog te zajebi!
CZECH Zaklení! [2]
DANISH Sikke noget møg! [3]
DUTCH Godverdomme!
ESTONIAN Kurat! [2]
FARSI Khak bar saret!
FINNISH Helvetti!
FRENCH Bordel de Dieu! ; Je m'en fous et je m'en contrefous! [4]
GAELIC, IRISH Dia damnú ort!
GAELIC, SCOTS Dia gonadh ort!
GERMAN Gottverdammt!
HINDI Lānat hai!
ICELANDIC Djofull! [2]
INDONESIAN Jamput! [2]
ITALIAN Dannazione! [2]
JAPANESE 畜生! Chikushō! [5]
LATIN Vae! [2]
MALAYU Allah mati terdir diri! [6]
MANDARIN 他妈的! Tā māde! [7]
NORWEGIAN Svarte! [2]
POLISH Kurcze!
PORTUGUESE Maldição! [2]
RUSSIAN Проклятие! / Proklyatie! [2]
SERBIAN Бог зајеби! / Bog zajebi!
SLOVENIAN Jebela cesta! [2]
SPANISH Que Dios te chinga! [2]
SWEDISH Fan ta dig!
UKRAINIAN Шлях трафуть! / Šlakh trafyt'! [9]
URDU Tujh pe Khuda ka qahar barse!
VIETNAMESE Vô lê! [2]
YIDDISH Gut zol oyf im onshikn fin di tsen makes. [10]

* *"Goddamn you!"*
** *"Goddamn!"*
2 *"Damn!"*
3 *"Damn this load of dirt!"*
4 *"I fuck & counterfuck myself!"*
5 *"Beast!;*
6 *"Allah curse you & kill you where you stand!"*
7 *"His mother!"*
8 *"God screw you!/God fuck you!"*
9 *"God damn them all!*
10 *"God should visit upon him the 10 plagues."*

illustr., © 2008, Graham Willoughby

HIPPIE ヒッピー
(& VARIATIONS)

AFRIKAANS hippie *
CANTONESE hēi pèi sih *
CATALAN grenyes [2];
txolles [2];
cabells llargs *
CZECH hipík **
DANISH hippie * ;
hippie tøs [3]
blomsterbarn [4];
hallal-hippie [5]
DUTCH hippie *
FINNISH hippi * ;
kettutyttö [6]
FRENCH hippeoisie [7]
GERMAN Hippie * ;
amtlicht propper [8]
HINDI / URDU naye fashan kā [9]
ICELANDIC hippi * ;
bóhem [10];
mussu-hippi [10]
ITALIAN hippy *
JAPANESE ヒッピー hippī *
PORTUGUESE hippy *
RUSSIAN хиппеоисие / hippeoisie [7]
SPANISH hippy maricón [11]
SWAHILI hipi *
SWEDISH hippy *
TAGALOG pihíps * ;
jéproks [7]

хиппеоисие

* *"hippie";*
** *"hipsters/hip";*
2 *"long hairs";*
3 *"hippie girl/hippie chick";*
4 *"flower child";*
5 *"Hippies naively embracing all cultures";*
6 *"tree-hugging hippie girl/tree-hugging hippie chick";*
7 *"Trustafarian(s)/Trust fund hippie(s)" = hippeoise" / "hippeoisie";*
8 *"cool, groovy, hip";*
9 *"trendy";*
10 *"tree hugger";*
11 *"hippie faggot."*

image: GobQ/M. F. McAuliffe

HORNY, HOT こふん
(& VARIATIONS)

AFRIKAANS jags *;
yetta **
ALBANIAN epsh *
ARABIC/TUNIS. shāhett *
BASQUE adardun *;
emagale *;
emajoera *;
gogor *;
haragikoi *
CANTONESE hàah sāp [2]
CATALAN sortit (m) / sortida (f) [2];
calent [3]
CROATIAN/SERB vru ; вру / vru [3]
CZECH madrený *
DANISH liderlig *;
vild i varmen [4]
DUTCH geile *;
botergeil *;
geilneef [4]
FARSI kosô (f) [2]
FRENCH puffiasse [2];
canon [3];
à tomber [5]
marcher à voiles et à vapeur [6];
un paillason [7];
FRENCH (VERLAN) Ce mec est chelou. [8]
GAELIC, IRISH te [3]
GAELIC, SCOTS druiseil *;
te [3]
GERMAN geil *;
saugeil *;
tierisch geil *;
affengeil *
GERMAN, SW. giggerig *
GREEK, MOD. γαβλα /gavla *
HEBREW harman *
HINDI/URDU garam māl *;
masala [3]
ICELANDIC graður *;
kynæstur *

INDONESIAN/MALAYU gatal *
ITALIAN assatanato (m) /assatanata (f) [4];
allupato(m) /allupata (f) [9]
JAPANESE こふん kofun [3]
KOREAN jukjuk-pangpang [3]
MANDARIN 性欲 xìng yù *
MARATHI jhimparī [2]
NORWEGIAN fittfaen [4]
PORTUGUESE lascivo *;
quente [3]
ROMANIAN mananca *;
excitat (m) / excitata (f) *
RUSSIAN ебливый / e eblívyy *;
пиздастрадáтель -я / pizdăstradátil' (m) [10];
поблядýшка -и / păblidúshkă [7];
SPANISH arrecho (m) /arrecha (f) *;
pelotas michinados [9]
SWEDISH kåt *
TAGALOG demónyo *;
mahílig *;
malíbog *

* *"horny/hot";*
** *"horny gay/faggot/queer";*
2 *horny slut (male or female);*
3 *hot (& bothered) (& horny);*
4 *wild in heat; ITALIAN: sexually possessed;*
5 *hot for, falling for;*
6 *"navigating by sail and steam", bi-, AC/DC;*
7 *"easy lay, fucks ALL around"; FRENCH: "doormat";*
8 *That guy's louche/rough trade., Verlan.*
9 *"hungry & horny & desperate as a wolf"; unlucky in finding the perfect other horny man/woman;*
10 *"cunt-sufferer," hot & horny & bothered ;*
11 *blue balls;*

HUNCHBACK/ HUMPBACK
(& VARIATIONS)

AFRIKAANS geboggel
ALBANIAN kurizdálë
CANTONESE tòhbut
CATALAN geperut
CROATIAN / SERB grbavač ; грбавач / grbavač
CZECH hrbáč
FARSI quz
FINNISH kyttyräselkä
FRENCH arrondié
GAELIC, IRISH cruiteachán
GAELIC, SCOTS croitean
GERMAN Buckel ; Bucklige
GREEK, MOD. καμποίρης / kampoíres
HINDI / URDU thaddā
ICELANDIC kroppinbalur
ITALIAN gobbo *(m)* /gobba *(f)*
MALAYU bongkok
MANDARIN 驼背 tuóbèi
MARATHI kubadahai
NORWEGIAN pukkelrygget
POLISH garbus
PORTUGUESE corcunda
ROMANIAN cocoşat
SOTHO, N lehutla
SPANISH jorobado
SWEDISH puckelrygg
THAI kàawm
TURKISH kambur ; kambur kimse
UKRAINIAN хорб / khorb
VIETNAMESE lung gù
WELSH cofngrwm ; gwargrwm
ZULU isifumbu

Liz Swados

Mel Gibson's first animated feature.

驼背

IDIOT (& VARIATIONS) олигофрен

AFRIKAANS domkop *
ARABIC ahbal *
ARMENIAN abush *;
debil *
BASQUE inozo *;
kaiku *;
tentel *;
zozo *
BELARUSIAN піздабол / pizdabol *
BENGALI gadha *
BOSNIAN budalo *;
idiote *
BULGARIAN олигофрен / oligofren *;
тапак / tapak *
CANTONESE baahkchì *
CATALAN borinot *;
capsigrany *;
gamarús *;
imbecil *;
pastanaga *;
sapastre *;
tros de quòniam *; ximplet *
CREOLE/HAITIAN idio *
CROATIAN / SLOVENIAN idiot *;
kreten *;
svinje [2]
CZECH blbec *;
debile *;
iqvac *
DANISH idiot *;
tåbe *;
forpulede idiot [3];
jubleidiot [4];
tågehoved [5]
DUTCH badmuts *;
idioot *;
kalf *; oetlul *;
rand-debiel [6]
FARSI ahmaq *;
kodan *;
nadân *
FINNISH älykääpiö *;
pässi *;
tanopää *
FRENCH gogol *;
idiot *;
le roi des cons [7]
GAELIC, IRISH amadán *
GAELIC, SCOTS amadan *
GERMAN Bert [6];
Fischkopf [8];
Oberarsch [9];
Blädl [19];
Depp [19];
Lööli [21];
Fetznschädl [20];
GREEK, MOD. ουλακας / ovlakas *
HEBREW tembel *
HINDI / URDU badirchand *;
bakland *;
buddhū *;
ullū kā patthā [6]
HUNGARIAN húgyagyú [10]
ICELANDIC fáviti *;
fifl *;
hálfviti [11];
heimskingi *
INDONESIAN blo'on *;
tollo *
ITALIAN idiota *;
budiùlo [17];
pistola [18]
JAPANESE まぬけ manuke *;
おぼけ oboke *;
どん臭い donkusai [12];
馬鹿 baka [22];
アホ aho [23];
アホンダラ ahondara [23]
KAZAKH акмак / akmak *;
KOREAN bbadori (m) / bbadsŭni (f) *
LATIN impos animi *
LATVIAN cirvis *
LITHUANIAN debilas *;
durnius *;
kretinas *
MACEDONIAN идиот / idiot *

MALAYU mangkuk hanyun *
MALTESE ja condom mċarrat [13]
MANDARIN 傻子 shǎzi *
MARATHI arbakha *;
khuḻakaṯa * ;
apārā *;
MONGOLIAN мулгуи / mulgui *
NAHUATL ahquimati *;
xolopihtli *
NEPALI harami *
NORWEGIAN idiot *;
jævla idiot [14];
kronidiot [15]
POLISH debil *(m)*/debilka *(f)* *;
kretyn *(m)* / kretynka *(f)*
PORTUGUESE abestado ;
abilolado ;
otario *;
cagalhão [24] ;
neba / nécio [25]
QUECHUA mana allin yuyayniyuq *
ROMANIAN capac *;
nătăflet *;
prost *(m)* / proasta *(f)* *
RUSSIAN мудак / mudak *;
мудило / mudilo *;
опездол / opezdol *
SERBIAN идиот / idiot *;
свинје / svinje [2]
SINHALA modaya *
SOTHO, N sesotho *
SPANISH idiota *;
cutre *;
cerebro de cuño [15];
capullo [26] ;
imbécil [27];
güeón [27]
SWAHILI mjinga *;
zuzu *
SWEDISH kuk *;
CP *;
jävla idiot [14]
TAGALOG gúng-gong *;
hunyángo *;
TAMIL muttal *
THAI kòn ngôh *
TURKISH geri zekâlı kimse *;
salak *
UKRAINIAN ідіот / idiot * ;
пустувáти / pustuváty [27]
UZBEK ахмок / akhmok *
VIETNAMESE ngu-ngóc *
WELSH twpsyn *
YIDDISH schmendrick / shmendrake *
YORUBA aláìkwé *;
mùgò *;
pè *
ZAPOTEC ique chonga *
ZULU isiphoxo *;
isithutha *

* *"idiot" / "idiotic";* ** *"shit-cunt";* 2 *"wild pig";*
3 *"fucked-up idiot";*
4 *"happy idiot";*
5 *"foggy-headed";*
6 *DUTCH: "Complete idiot"; GERM: "Total idiot";*
7 *"The king of cunts";*
8 *"fishhead"= hick from northern BDR;*
9 *super-ass/arse;*
10 *piss-head;*
11 *halfwit;*
12 *"Stupid smelling," Kansai/Osaka;*
13 *"ambulatory torn condom";*
14 *fucking idiot;*
15 *crown-idiot;*
16 *cunt-brain*
17 *Any stupid idiotic ass/arsehole from the <u>other</u> town, Tusc.;*
18 *"Pistol," Lombard.;*
19 *"idiot"/"idiotic," Bav.;*
20 *"idiot"/"idiotic," Vien.;*
21 *"idiot"/ "idiotic," Sw.;*
22 *"ba=horse; ka=deer"—According to Chinese legend, a fuckwit ancestor of Dick Cheney (i.e., a Qin dynasty king) went hunting; upon seeing a deer, he shouted, "Horse," & earned the nickname "Baka";*
23 *"idiot"/ "idiotic," Kansai/Osaka;*
24 *"stupid ass/arsehole," Braz.;*
25 *"too stupid," Braz.;*
26 *"bud" / "dick-head" / "stupid ass/arsehole," Castil;*
27 *"idiot" / "jerk" / "ass/arsehole," Chil.;*
28 *"fool."*

JUNKIE, DIRTY JUNKIE (& VARIATIONS) ヘロ中

AFRIKAANS verslaafde *
ALBANIAN narkomán *
ARABIC Raked afa alsahab... **
BASQUE drogazale *
BENGALI afimkhor *;
gulikhor *
BULGARIAN гадна друсалка / gadna drusalka *
CANTONESE douhyáuh *;
yáhn gwanjí
CATALAN drogadicte *
CROATIAN / SERB narkoman *;
наркоман / narkoman *
CZECH narkoman *
DANISH narkoman *
DUTCH heroinehoer [2]
FARSI khumori *;
motâd *
FINNISH narkkari / narkomääni *;
pilviveikko **;
nisti *
FRENCH drogué sale [3];
fixer, se / schnouffer, se [4];
schnouffe, la [6];
courir le dragon / chasser le dragon [7];
toxico *
GAELIC, IRISH andúileach drugaí *
GAELIC, SCOTS diasganach *;
diasganach salach [3];
tràill-dhrogaichean *
GERMAN Rauschgiftsüchtige *
ICELANDIC dópisti *;
eiturlyfjasjúklingur *;
fíkill *
ITALIAN tossico *(m)* / tossica *(f)* *
JAPANESE 汚いヘロ中 kitanai herochū [3];
ヘロ中 herochū [4]
MALAYU ketagih candu *
MANDARIN 瘾君子 yǐn jūn zǐ *
MARATHI aphi<u>n</u>ya *
NORWEGIAN narkotiker *
POLISH narkoman *(m)*/narkomanka *(f)* *
PORTUGUESE viciado *(m)* / viciada *(f)* *
SERBIAN наркоман / narkoman *
SLOVENIAN porkafiks [6]
SOTHO, N lamala *
SPANISH narcomano *
SWAHILI mtumiaji wa madawa ya kulevya *
SWEDISH knarkare *;
narkoman *
TAGALOG baníg *
UZBEK хумори / humori *
VIETNAMESE ngu ó·i nghiên *
WELSH ymroddi *

* *"junkie";*
** *"Chasing the clouds" = opiate or kif high;*
FINNISH: "One who flies w/ the clouds" = druggie/ junkie;
2 *heroin whore;*
3 *dirty junkie;*
4 *"shoot up/get a fix";*
5 *"pig's fix/pig's shot of heroin";*
6 *"heroin, smack, china white/shit";*
7 *"chasing the dragon"*

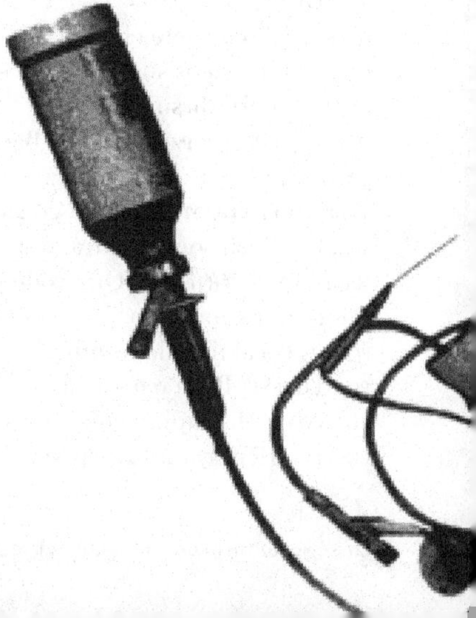

image: GobQ/ T. Warburton y Bajo

KISS MY ASS/ARSE, LICK MY ASS/ARSE (& VARIATIONS)

Полизи ми шупак

AFRIKAANS Siug aan my aambeie en wag...[2]
ARABIC Bus tezi. * ;
Telhasi tezi. **
BOSNIAN Poljubime u tamnicu! [3]
BULGARIAN Челуни ме оцад! / Čeluni me otzad!
CROATIAN Polizi mi šupak. **
CZECH Polib mi prdel. * ;
Vyli mne prdel. **
DANISH Kys mig i røven! *; Sut min behårede røv, din vatpik! [4]
DUTCH Lik mijn reet. **
FRENCH Lèche mon cul! **
GAELIC, IRISH Póg mo thóin. *
GAELIC, SCOTS Pòg mo thòin. *
GERMAN Leck mich am Arsch! **
HEBREW Nashek li et hatachat. * ;
Lech timtsots tahat! [5]
HUNGARIAN Nyald ki a seggem. **
ITALIAN Baciami il culo. *
JAPANESE 俺のケツをなめてくれ！ Ore no ketsu wo namete kure! *(m)* **;
あたしの尻をなめてちょうだい！ Atashi no shiri wo namete chōdai! *(f)* **
LATIN Potes meos suaviari clunes. [6]
LATVIAN Laizi dirsu. **
MACEDONIAN Бачими го газот. / Bačimi go gazot. *;
Лижими го газот. / Lizhimi go gazot. **
MALTESE Busli sormi ala francisa. [7]
MANDARIN 亲我的屁股。Qīn wǒde pìgu. *
NEPALI Mero chak kha. [8]
POLISH Pocaluj mnie w dupe. *
PORTUGUESE Beija o meu cú. *
ROMANIAN Ma pupi in cur. *
RUSSIAN Поцелуй меня в сраку! / Potselúy menyá v sráku! *
SERBIAN Полизи ми шупак. / Polizi mi šupak. **
SLOVENIAN Zaleti se v rit. *
SPANISH Besa mi culo. *;
Chupe mantequilla de mi culo! [9];
Metele mas lengua! [10]
SWEDISH Kyss mig i arslet. *
TELEGU Nā gudda nāku. **
TURKISH Götumu yala. **
UKRAINIAN Узни мене. / Uzny mene. *
WELSH Sychu fy penol fi. **
YIDDISH Kush in toches arein. *

* *Kiss my ass/arse.*
** *"Lick my ass/arse."*
2 *"Suck on my hemerrhoids and wait."*
3 *"Kiss my caboose!"*
4 *"Suck my hairy ass/arse; you stupid wanker!"*
5 *"Go suck ass/arse!"*
6 *"You may kiss my ass/arse."*
7 *"French kiss my ass/arse."*
8 *"Eat my ass/arse."*
9 *"Suck butter from my ass/arse!"*

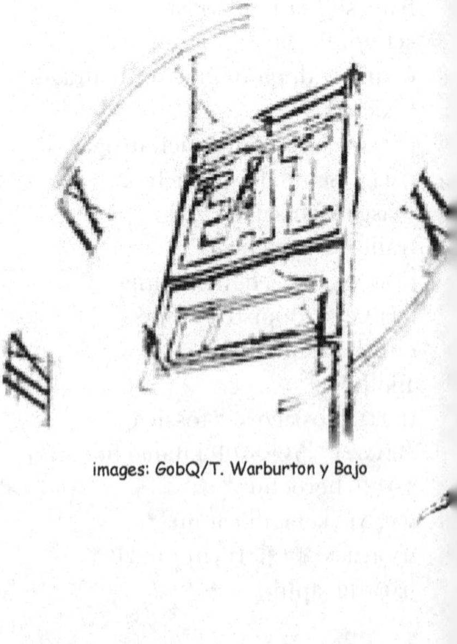

images: GobQ/T. Warburton y Bajo

LAZY-ASS/ LAZY-ARSE, LAZY (& VARIATIONS) 不老者

AFRIKAANS traag *;
luilak *
ALBANIAN dembélë [2]
ARABIC tanbal **
ARMENIAN s'uyl *;
t´uyl *
BASQUE lodi *;
alfer *;
zuri *;
geldo *;
fardel *
BELARUSIAN лянiвы/lyanivy *
BENGALI Adhagodha! [3]
BOSNIAN líjen *
BULGARIAN мурзелиф/murzelif *
CANTONESE láahngwattauh [2]
CATALAN mandrós *;
gandul *
CROATIAN leniv/ lijen *;
lenivost **
CZECH linyý *;
nečinný *;
pomalý *;
lenoch [2]
DANISH dovenlars [2]
DUTCH Wees niet zo lui. [4];
luie schoft/luie schoften [5];
lui *
ESTONIAN laisk *
FARSI tanbal *;
soyaparvar [6]
FINNISH laiska *;
haluton [7]
FRENCH flemmarde, e *;
paresseux, a (m)/ paresseuse, a (f) *;
GAELIC, IRISH giolla na leisce **;
fuar-chúiseach [8]
GERMAN Du fauler sack! [9];
abpoofen [10]
GREEK, MOD. Μη τεβελιαξις/Mi teveliazis. [4]

GUJARATI ä ḷas **
HEBREW 'atse̲l *
HINDI/URDU harāmkhōr [11];
kāmchor
HUNGARIAN mintha élnél
ICELANDIC ónytjungur [8];
letingi/leti-blóð **;
sinulaus [8]
INDONESIAN/MALAYU malas *
ITALIAN pigrone/pigrona [2];
apatico [8];
bighellonare [11];
ambiopia [13]
JAPANESE 不老者 furōsha [11]
KOREAN ke-ŭ-rŭ-da **
LATIN ignavusaum *;
/entusaum [8]
LATVIAN slinks *
LITHUANIAN storas [14];
shliuzhas [12];
rupuzhe [15]
MACEDONIAN мрзлив/mrzliv *
MALTESE ghazzien *
MANDARIN 懒惰的人 lănduòde rén *
MARATHI aca̲lōbā/aca̲lōjī [14];
a̲las ̃ī/ja̲dabharata *
NAHUATL tlatziuhcayotl *
NEPALI alcchi *
NORWEGIAN dovenpels/lathangs [2];
bollingmoer [16];
nedbrytende [17]
POLISH leniwy *;
apatycyzny [8]
PORTUGUESE preguiçoso (m)/preguiçosa (f) *;
indiferente [8]
ROMANIAN murzelif *;
nebăgător [7];
nesimţire [8]
RUSSIAN халявщик/khalyavščik [11];
филон/filon [18];
филонить/filonit´ [19]
SERBIAN ленив/leniv *

трoм / trom [7]
SLOVENIAN len *
SOTHO, N botšwa *
SPANISH apático [8];
flojo *(m)* / floja *(m)* [18];
Hüevon [20];
papayona [21]
SWAHILI vivu *
SWEDISH slö / slöfok / lätting [2];
håglös [7];
likgiltig [8];
nervklen [22]
TAGALOG hubyá *;
gásti [3];
waláng-siglá [8]
THAI gèe´at khràan *;
khwehng khàang [7];
jeùut jàang [8];
khràan [23]
TURKISH tembel *;
miskin *
UKRAINIAN лінивий / linyvyý *
UZBEK дангъаса / dang´asa *;
дангасалик / dangasalik *;
қоьл / qoʼl [12];
лаванд / lavand [6];
ишсиз / ishsiz [24]
VIETNAMESE l `am biêng / biêng nhác *
WELSH dioglyd / didoreth *;
defrater [8]
YIDDISH foil *;
golem [12]
YORUBA òle *
ZAPOTEC nachaabá *
ZULU isibhaca *;
i(li)-bhaxakezi [25]

* *"lazy" / "lazy-ass/arse";*
** *laziness;*
2 *"lazy-bones";*
3 *BENG.: "Good-for-nothing lazy bum/beast!"; ICEL.: "Good-for-nothing lazy ne'er-do-well!" TAGAL.: "Good-for-nothing parasitic lazy-ass/arse loafer & goof-off bum!";*
4 *"Don't be so lazy";*
5 *"lazy bastard" / "lazy bastards";*
6 *"lazy-ass/arse, shiftless";*
7 *"listless";*
8 *"apathetic";*
9 *"You lazy bastard!"*
10 *"lazy, dozing off, napping";*
11 *HIND. / URD.: "dole blodger/bludger"; ITAL.: "lazy scrounging bum"; JAP.: "bum"; RUSS.: "dead-beat";*
12 *"sluggard" / "slug"; UZBEK: "slothful"; YIDD.: "clumsy sluggard";*
13 *"lazy eye";*
14 *"lazy fat-ass/arse";*
15 *"toad";*
16 *"lazy sub-fucking-moronic fat-ass/arse slob";*
17 *"enervating";*
18 *RUSS.: "lazy-ass/arse lug"; SPAN.: "lazy-ass/arse slacker";*
19 *"looking occupied at work while doing fuck-all";*
20 *"lazy-ass/arse big-balls/bollocks-for-brains idiot";*
21 *"Big Fat Lazy-ass/arse Cunt," Cub.;*
22 *"neurasthenic";*
23 *"aloof, detached, lazy";*
24 *"out of work, unemployed";*
25 *"Super-lazy-ass/arse."*

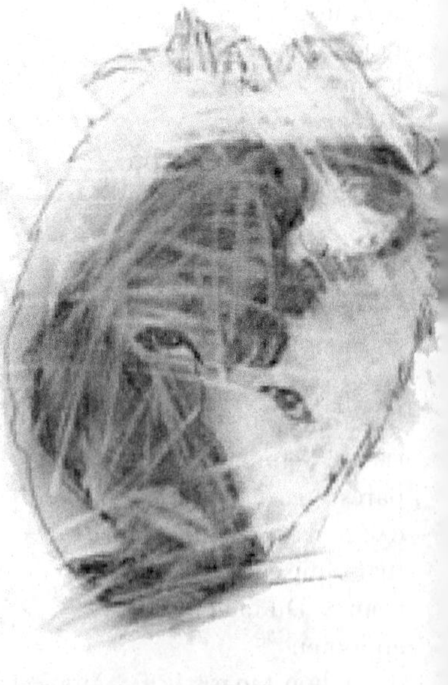

illustr., © 2008, Graham Willoughby

LIAR, MIND FUCKER, PATHOLOGIC LIAR, MORAL IDIOT (& VARIATIONS) лажов

AFRIKAANS leuenaar *;
Leonora **
ARABIC kazzob *
ARMENIAN sidakhos *
BASQUE gezurti *;
gezurjario *
BELARUSIAN хлус /khlus *
BENGALI jhuta *
CANTONESE daaihpaauyáu *
CATALAN mentider *
CREOLE/HAITIAN màntè *;
djòlè *
CROATIAN / SERB lažov *;
jeba misli [4];
лажов / lažov *;
јеба мисли / jeba misli [4]
CZECH cikán *
DANISH løgner *;
løgnhals [2]
DUTCH leugenaar *
ESTONIAN valetaja *
FARSI kâzeb *
FINNISH valehtelija *
FRENCH menteur *(m)* / menteuse *(f)* *
GAELIC, IRISH bréagadóir paiteolaíoch [5];
bréagadóir *
GAELIC, SCOTS breugadair galarach [6];
breugadair *
GERMAN Lügner *
HINDI paidaishi jhōta [7];
jhōta *
ICELANDIC lygari *
ITALIAN bugiardo *(m)* / bugiarda *(f)* *;
fregniacciaro [10]
JAPANESE 嘘つき usotsuki *;
病的な嘘つき byōteki na usotsuki [5]
KOREAN kŏ-jit mal jaeng-i *
LATIN mentiri *
LITHUANIAN melagis *
MALAYU kecing berapi [4];
dajal *
MANDARIN 说谎者 shuōhuǎngzhě *
NAHUATL tlapicqui *
NORWEGIAN løgner *
POLISH kłamca *
PORTUGUESE mentiroso *(m)* /mentirosa *(f)**;
mente-foda [4]
ROMANIAN mincinos *
RUSSIAN пиздун / pizdún [3]
SPANISH mentiroso *(m)* / mentirosa *(f)* *
SWAHILI mwongo *
SWEDISH lögnare *;
mytoman [4]
TAGALOG echoséro *(m)* / echoséra *(f)* *;
índyan [8]
TELEGU abaddālakoru *
THAI khót *;
kón làayo [9]
TURKISH palavracı *
UKRAINIAN брехун / brekhun *;
патологчний брехун / patolohichnyy brekhun
UZBEK лофчи / lofchi *
VIETNAMESE ngu'ò'i nói dô'i *
WELSH celwyddwr *
ZULU umqambi-manga *;
umuntu onamanga *

* *liar;*
** *gay liar;*
2 *"liar neck";*
3 *wimp, pussy;*
4 *mind-fucker;*
5 *pathological liar;*
6 *chronic liar;*
7 *liar by birth;*
8 *bullshit artist;*
9 *evil, dishonest ass/arsehole;*
10 *"cunting liar," bullshitter, gossip.*

LIMP DICK: **SEE DICK, LIMP**

MIND FUCKER, PATHOLOGIC LIAR, MORAL IDIOT: SEE LIAR

MISER/ MISERLY, STINGY, MEAN-SPIRITED
(& VARIATIONS)

керпеден

AFRIKAANS schnora *; gierigaard *
ALBANIAN kurnáce *;
BASQUE eskuitxi **
BENGALI kipte *
BULGARIAN керпеден / kerpeden *
CANTONESE guhohngwái *;
CATALAN avar *; gasiu *
CZECH lakomec *
DANISH nærrigrøv [2]; gnier *
DUTCH krentekakker [3]
ESTONIAN ihnuskoi *
FINNISH saituri *
FRENCH pisse-vinegar [4]
GAELIC, IRISH sprionlóir *
GAELIC, SCOTS crìnean *
GERMAN Geizhals *
GREEK, MOD. τσιγούνις / tsigounis *
HINDI, URDU mōtichiriyā [5]
ICELANDIC nánös *
ITALIAN avoro *(m)*/avora *(f)* *
JAPANESE けち kechi [6]
KOREAN in-saek-han saram *
MACEDONIAN стиснат / stisnat [6]
MALAYU medit [6]
MANDARIN 守财奴 shǒucáinú *
NAHUATL tzotzocatl *
NORWEGIAN gjerrigknark *
POLISH skąpy **
PORTUGUESE avaro [7]
ROMANIAN sgârcit [6]
SLOVENIAN porkadu [8]
SOTHO, N sejato *
SPANISH tacaño **; avaro [7]
SWAHILI bahili [6]
SWEDISH snål **; ondsint **
TAGALOG bató **
THAI kêe něe'o [9]
TURKISH tamahkâr [6]
UKRAINIAN скнара / sknara *
UZBEK калхамаж / kalkhamaj [10]
VIETNAMESE ngừơi hà-tiên *
WELSH cybydd *
YIDDISH schnora*; kamtsen *; khazer [11]
YORUBA ahun *
ZAPOTEC guibí *; nazí [6]
ZULU umuntu ombanyileyo *; unqodoyi *

* *miser ;*
** *tight-fisted;*
2 *tight-ass/arse;*
3 *raisin-shitter;*
4 *vinegar-pisser;*
5 *miserly moneybags;*
6 *stingy;*
7 *avaricious;*
8 *pig's soul;*
9 *sticky shit;*
10 *turd beetle;*
11 *greedy pig.*

守财奴

MOTOR MOUTH, CHATTERBOX, BLABBERER
& VARIATIONS)

бабакун

AFRIKAANS Elsie Geselsie **;
babelkous *
BASQUE berritsu *;
hitzontzi *
BELARUSIAN пиздзиук / pizdziuk *
BENGALI kathar khoi phote *
CANTONESE jūngyi king-gái ge *
CATALAN xerraire *
CROATIAN klepetalo *
CZECH tbetalka *
DANISH sludrechatol *
ESTONIAN jutukas *
FARSI verâj *
FINNISH lörppö *
FRENCH ballibard *(m)* / ballibarde *(f)* *
GAELIC, IRISH cabaire *
GAELIC, SCOTS cobhar mu bhus [2];
glibheid *
GERMAN Schwaadlappen [3]
HINDI / URDU bakchōd *
ICELANDIC kjaftakvörn *
með munnræpu *
skrafskjóða *
ITALIAN Non raccontar fregne! [11];
chiaccierone *(m)* / chiaccierona *(f)* [4]
JAPANESE ベチャベチャ becha becha *
LITHUANIAN patarshka [5]
MALAYU petis *
MARATHI cāṯaḻa *
NAHUATL tzatzini [6]
POLISH gadatliwy *
PORTUGUESE bacharel *;
boca grande [7]
ROMANIAN bârfitor *;
limbut *
SERBIAN брбљати / brblyati *
SOTHO, N mmalabadi *
SPANISH mamon [8]
SWEDISH pratkvarn *;
sladdertacka *
TAGALOG chikadóra [9];
daldákina *
TURKISH boşboğaz *
UKRAINIAN бабакун / babakun *;
балазіка / balazika *
UZBEK чакакли / chakakli *;
VIETNAMESE cái máy mól *
WELSH clebreau *;
clebryn *
YIDDISH ploidersak [10]
YORUBA elejo *
ZULU i(li)khasi *;
i(li)photwe *

* *motor-mouth, chatterbox;*
** *"Elsie, the little chatterer," gay term;*
2 *froth about the mouth;*
3 *"Chatterbox," Köln dial.;*
4 *blabberer;*
5 *female chatterbox;*
6 *loudmouth;*
7 *big mouth;*
8 *motor mouth, braggart;*
9 *girl who likes to tell tall tales;*
10 *"chatterbag";*
11 *"Dont' talk 'cunt'!" = Don't talk bullshit.*

NIHILIST
& VARIATIONS) ニヒルスト

AFRIKAANS nihilist *
CANTONESE hèuimòuhjyúyih yàhn*
DANISH / NORWEGIAN / SWEDISH nihilist *
DUTCH nihilist *
FRENCH nihiliste *
GERMAN nihilist *
ICELANDIC níhílisti *;
gereyðingarsinni *
ITALIAN nichilista *
JAPANESE ニヒルスト nihirisuto *
MANDARIN 悲观主义者 bēiguān zhyǔi-yìzhě **
PORTUGUESE nihilista *
RUSSIAN нигилист / nigilist *
SPANISH nihilista *
TURKISH nihilist *
UKRAINIAN нігіліст / nigilist *
WELSH nihilydd *
ZULU mphikaqethuke *

* *nihilist;*
** *pessimist.*

NOSEY,
SEE:
BOSSY,
NOSEY

illustr., © 2008, Graham Willoughby

PEEPING TOM, VOYEUR
& VARIATIONS) βανεστερεγε

AFRIKAANS voyeur *
CROATIAN / SERB voajer *;
воајер / voajer
CZECH voajér *;
kukátko **
DANISH vindueskigger *
DUTCH voyeur *
FARSI chesm charân *
FINNISH tirkistelijä *;
tirkistysesitys **
FRENCH voyeur *
GAELIC, IRISH Seán an Spléachaidh [2]
GAELIC, SCOTS Iain an Caogadh [2]
GERMAN Glotzer *
GREEK, MOD. βανεστερεγε / vanesterege *
ICELANDIC gluggagægir *
ITALIAN guardone *
JAPANESE のぞき nozoki *
のぞき魔 nozoki-ma [3]
MANDARIN 窥视的人 kuīshìde rén *
NORWEGIAN kikker *
PORTUGUESE espreitador *
RUSSIAN человек / chelovek *
SPANISH mirón *
SWEDISH snuskgubbe *
TAGALOG bósero *;
mambobósò *;
usbíng *;
tòro-tóro **
TURKISH röntgenci *
UKRAINIAN надто цікава допятлива людиана / nádto tsikáva (dopyátlyva) liudyána

* *Peeping Tom; voyeur;*
** *peepshow;*
2 *Peeping John;*
3 *peeping devil.*

PICKPOCKET, 手手手 THIEF
(& VARIATIONS)

AFRIKAANS sakkeroller *
ARABIC ganav *;
haramī *
ARMENIAN ki'sagahad
BASQUE lapurtxo *;
litxarrero *
BENGALI pocket-mār *;
chohr *
CANTONESE pahsáu *
CATALAN carterista *;
pispa *
CREOLE/HAITIAN vòlè *
CROATIAN džeparoš *;
karjerista *
CZECH kapesní zlodj *
DANISH lommetyv *
DUTCH zakkenroller *
ESTONIAN taskuvaras *
FARSI jibbor *
FINNISH taskuvaras *
FRENCH voleur à la tire *
GAELIC, IRISH peasghadaí *
GAELIC, SCOTS biothantach *;
meirleach *;
siolpadair *
GERMAN Taschendieb *
GREEK, MOD. ενας πορτοφολα / enas portofola *
HINDI, URDU jeb katrā *(m)* / jeb katrī *(f)* *
HUNGARIAN zsebtolvaj *
ICELANDIC vasaþjófur *
INDONESIAN pencopeti *
ITALIAN tagliaborse ** ;
borsaiolo *(m)* /borsaiola *(f)* *
JAPANESE スリ suri *;
チボ chibo *
KOREAN to-jŏk-nom *
LATIN fur * ;
homo trium litterarum [2]
LATVIAN veikalu zaglis *
LITHUANIAN vagis *
MACEDONIAN крадец / kradets *
MALAYU pencopit *
MALTESE halliel *(m)* / halleal *(f)* *
MANDARIN 手手手 shǒu *
NAUATL ichtequi *
NEPALI chor *
NORWEGIAN tyv *
POLISH kieszonkowiec *
PORTUGUESE batedor *(m)* / batedora *(f)* de carteira *
QUECHUA suwa *
ROMANIAN pungaş de buzunare *
RUSSIAN вор / vor *;
Арап / Arap [3]
SERBIAN џепарош / džeparoš *
SLOVENIAN tat *
SOTHO, N lehodu *
SPANISH carterista *
SWAHILI kibaka *
SWEDISH ficktjuv *
TAGALOG atibán *;
doróbo *
TAMIL cōrakan *
TELEGU dongana kodukka [4]
THAI ka mòoy luàang gra bpao *
TURKISH kankesici *
UKRAINIAN кишеньковий злодій / kyšenkovyy zlodiy *
UZBEK оғри / oghri *
VIETNAMESE tên móc túi *
WELSH pigwr pocodi *
YIDDISH ganev *
YORUBA olè *
ZAPOTEC gubaaná *
ZULU umkhuthuzi *;
isiguguli *

* *pickpocket; petty thief;*
** *cut-purse;*
2 *man of 3 letters = i.e., f-u-r.*
3 *"Arab" = blackamoor, petty thief*
4 *son of a thief.*

PIMP, PLAYER, WHOREMONGER 卖屄
(& VARIATIONS)

AFRIKAANS / DUTCH pooier *;
koppelaar *
ARABIC gawwad *
ARMENIAN pozavak *
BASQUE andraketari *;
emazain / putazain *;
BENGALI nagor *;
BULGARIAN сводник / svodnik *
CANTONESE gū yèh jái *
CATALAN alcavot *;
macarró *;
proxeneta *
CROATIAN / SERB podvodnik *;
подводник / podvodnik *
CZECH kuplí *;
pasák *
DANISH alfons *;
luderkarl *
FARSI jâkesh *;
kun kesh **
FINNISH parittaja *;
sutenööri *
FRENCH maquereau *;
souteneur *
GAELIC, IRISH fostaitheoir *
GAELIC, SCOTS maor-strìopach *
GERMAN Schlampenschlepper [2];
Zuhälter *
GREEK, MOD. δαβαγις / davagis *
HEBREW sarsur *
HINDI bhadhava *;
bhadwe ka awlat [3];
talal *
ICELANDIC melludólgur *
INDONESIAN germo *
ITALIAN magnaccia *;
puttaniere *
JAPANESE ヒモ himo *;
ポンビキ pombiki *
LATIN leno *
MACEDONIAN ебач / ebač *;
пичлеме / pičleme *
MALAYU barua *
MANDARIN 卖屄 mài bī [4]
MARATHI randapati *
NORWEGIAN / SWEDISH hallik *
POLISH alfonsie *
PORTUGUESE azeiteiro *;
chulo *
ROMANIAN curvar *;
pezevenghiu *
RUSSIAN альфонс / al'fóns *;
блядунь / blyádun' *;
наводчик / navódčik *;
сводник / svódnik *;
сводня / svódnjá [5]
SPANISH padrote *;
chulo *
SWEDISH sutinör *;
TAGALOG búgalu / búgaw / búgulo *;
kwékong *
THAI màaeng dáa *
TURKISH pezevenk *
UKRAINIAN звідник / zvidnyk *
URDU dalla *
UZBEK қoьшмачи / qo'shmachi * / [5]
VIETNAMESE ma-cô *
ZULU ofunela abanye izifebe *;
umbambelli *

* *pimp, player, whoremonger;*
** *gay pimp running gay whores;*
2 *slut-dragger; pimp-mobile;*
3 *son of a pimp;*
4 *sell pussy;*
5 *female pimp.*

illustr., © 2008 Graham Willoughby

PINKO COMMIE, COMMUNIST: SEE: ANARCHIST, PINKO COMMIE

PISS, PISSY, PISS HEAD (& VARIATIONS) ПИКЛИО

AFRIKAANS pis *
ALBANIAN shurrë *
ARABIC bol *
ARMENIAN qoz *
BASQUE txiza * ;
gernu *
BENGALI nongra / pocha * ;
Birokto kara! [2]
BULGARIAN пик / pik * ;
пиклио / piklio [3]
CANTONESE niuh * ;
niuh tàuh **
CATALAN pixa *
CROATIAN / SERB mokraća * ;
Piša na kanap! [2];
Pišam té. [4];
Pišam ti u krvotok. [5];
Pišo sam ti na majino mleko. [6];
мокраħа / mokraća *;
Пиша на канап! / Piša na kanap! [2];
Пишам те. / Pišam té. [4];
Пишам ти у крвоток. / Pišam ti u krvotok. [5];
Пишо сам ти на мајно млеко. / Pišo sam ti na majino mleko. [6]
CZECH chcát *
DANISH tis * ;
pis * ;
Pis af! [2];
Hvem har pisset på din sukkermad? [7]
DUTCH zijk *
zeldzame zijkzak [8]
ESTONIAN kusi * ;
kusipea **
FINNISH kusi *;
kusipää **
kusiaivo [9];
pissaliisa [10]
FRENCH pisse * ;
tête de pisse ** ;
chaude-pisse [11];
pisse-froid [12];
C'est comme si on pissait dans un violoncelle. [13]
GAELIC, IRISH mún * ;
Múnaim i mbainne do mháthair. [6]
GAELIC, SCOTS mùn * ;
ceann dhen mùn ** ;
Mùnaim sa' bhainne do mhàthair.
GERMAN Piß * ;
Pißkopf ** ;
Verpiß Dich! [2]
HUNGARIAN húgy / vizelet * ;
Elhúzza a belét! [2]
húgyagyú **
ICELANDIC hland / míga * ;
pissa * ;
Hypja sig! [2]
INDONESIAN air seni *
ITALIAN piscio *;
ubriacone **
JAPANESE 尿 nyō *
立ち小便 tachishoben [15]
LATIN urina *;
LATVIAN churāt *
MANDARIN 尿 niào *;
尿头 niào tóu **
MARATHI khata *
MONGOLIAN шаес / shaes *
NAHUATL axixtli / tlapiaztli *
NEPALI mōt *
NORWEGIAN piss *
PORTUGUESE mijo * ;
Mije em você! [4];
Mim mijo no leite da sua mãe. [6]
ROMANIAN piş * ;
Pişa-m-aş in gura ta. [16]
RUSSIAN (по) ссать / (po)ssat' * ;
(по) щать / (po) ščát' * ;

пишать / píšat' *;
Щать я на него хотел. / Ščat' ya na negó khotél. [17]
SLOVENIAN scavnića *;
Poščijem se nate! [4]
SOTHO, N moroto *
SPANISH meado *;
meado de la araña [11];
Tengo que miar que mis dientes flotan. [14];
SWAHILI mkojo *
SWEDISH Dra åt helvete! [2]
TAGALOG jínggel / jojó *
THAI bao *;
Bai hâi pón! [2]
UKRAINIAN пісся / pissya *;
VIETNAMESE nuóc tiểu *
WELSH Piso bant! [2]
YORUBA ìtò *

* *piss; SPANISH: piss/pissy coward;*
** *piss-head;*
2 *"Piss off!"*
3 *pants-pisser;*
4 *(I) piss on you.*
5 *"I piss in yr bloodstream."*
6 *"I piss in yr mother's milk."*
7 *"Who pissed on your sugar sandwich?"*
8 *"rare piss-bag";*
9 *piss-brain;*
10 *"piss-Alices";*
11 *gonorrhea; FRENCH: "hot piss"; SPANISH: "spider's piss" = VD;*
12 *"cold piss", i.e., cold fish; snotty;*
13 *"It was as if someone'd pissed in a cello."/Possible term of endearment in French pop music.*
14 *"I've gotta piss so bad my teeth are floating."*
15 *Taking a piss whilst standing up.*
16 *"I piss in yr mouth."*
17 *"I myself would piss on him."*

POT-HEAD, DRUGGIE:
SEE: DRUGS & THEIR BEDRAGGLED & DEBAUCHED DRUGGIES

PUNK, PUNKER (& VARIATIONS) панкер

AFRIKAANS punk *
BASQUE ardai *
CANTONESE yáhnfó ge yéh *;
tou jái [2]
CATALAN barbamec [3]
CROATIAN / SERB pank *; панк / pank *;
panker **; панкер / panker **;
Jebo svoj usrani pank rock bend! [4];
Јебо свој усрани панк бенд!/ Jebo svoj usrani pank bend! [4];
Dao Bog da ti pankeri svirali na sprovodu! [5];
Дао Бог да ти панкери свирали на споводру! /Dao Bog da ti pankeri svirali na sprovodu! [5]
CZECH pankov *
DANISH / FRENCH punk *;
punker **
DUTCH / NORWEGIAN / PORTUGUESE / SWEDISH punk *
FARSI qerti *
FINNISH punk *;
punkarri **
GAELIC, IRISH punc *
GAELIC, SCOTS puing *;
Ròc a-mach gu cruaidh! [6]
Bidh e a' dannsadh an *pogo* còmhla ri Fionn agus Oisean. [7]
GERMAN Punk *
GREEK, MOD. πανκ / pank *
ICELANDIC pönk / ræfill *;
pönkari **;
ræflarokkari **
ITALIAN punk *;
pogare [8]
JAPANESE パンク panku [9]
LITHUANIAN netikelis *
MANDARIN 朋克 péngkè *
SPANISH roquero **
SWEDISH punkare **
TAGALOG jéprox *;

kómiks [10]
TURKISH kav *
UKRAINIAN панк / pank * ;
трухляк / trukhliak * ;
шмаркач / shmarkach *
UZBEK агитацийа пункти / agitatsiya punkti [11]
WELSH pync *

* punk
** punker/punk rocker;
2 "pet rabbit" = punk, gay bottom;
3 boy w/o facial hair;
4 "Fuck your shitty punk rock band!"
5 "May God grant that punkers play at yr funeral!"
6 "Rock out hard!"
7 "He dances the pogo with Finn & Ossian."
8 to mosh / to pogo;
9 punk; also Japanese reference to petty sabotage;
10 tattooed all over like a walking comic book;
11 agit-punk; also, political agitation.

images: GobQ/T.Warburton y Bajo

PUSSY BRAIN,
SEE: CUNT/PUSSY-BRAIN / CUNT FACE / CUNT HEAD (& VAR.)

PUSSY, EAT/PUSSY, EAT BLOODY (& VARIATIONS)

お門食う

AFRIKAANS Suig my poes. [2]
BULGARIAN Лапаи ми путката. / Lapai mi putkata. [2]
CANTONESE sihk tāat *
CATALAN xuclar-la *
CROATIAN / SERB jedi pičku * ;
једи пичку / jedi pičku * ;
jedi krvavu pičku ** ;
једи крваву пичку / jedi krvavu pičku **
DANISH æd fisse * ;
råbe i mosen [3] ;
æd blodig fisse **
DUTCH beffen *
ESTONIAN laku vittu *
FINNISH ime vittu * ;
loskavittu [4]
FRENCH Mange ma chatte. [2]
Léche mon clito. [6] ;
brouter le cresson [7] ;
descendre à la cave [8] ;
le soixtante-neuf [5]
GAELIC, IRISH ith báltaí *
GAELIC, SCOTS ith pitean *
GERMAN iss Fotzen *
iss blutige Fotzen **
GREEK, MOD. απο πισο γλιψη το μυνι / apo piso glipse to muni *
GUJARATI chut na pakoda [9]
HUNGARIAN pinabubus [10] ;
Kurva anyád vérvörös picsáját! [11]
ICELANDIC éta píku * ;
Sleiktu píkuna á mömmu þinni. [12]
sleikja blóðuga píku **
INDONESIAN ciak wingkeng *
ITALIAN leccare la figa * ;
fare il sessantanove [5]
JAPANESE まこをなめる manko o nameru * ;
あいなめ ainame [13] ;
お門食う omonkuu [14]

LATVIAN pezhlaizisr [10]
LITHUANIAN kopinek medu *
MACEDONIAN лизипичка / lizipička [10]
MALAYU jilat lubang puki *
MANDARIN 舔阴 tiǎn yīn *;
吃豆腐 chī dòufu [15]
NEPALI puti chāt *
NORWEGIAN slikk fitte *;
fittesleiker [10]
POLISH robić minete *
PORTUGUESE coma buceta *;
lambedor das xotas menstruadas [16]
ROMANIAN mança pizda *
SPANISH bajar al pozo *(Col.)* [17];
coma panocha *;
el beso del payaso [19]
SWEDISH slicka fitta *
TAGALOG posisyon sa pagtatalik [5]
UKRAINIAN сосати / sosaty *
URDU Teri mane pudhi kā. [20]
WELSH llyfu cont *

* *eat pussy;*
** *eat bloody pussy;*
2 *"Suck my pussy." / "Eat my pussy."*
3 *"shout in the marsh";*
4 *"slurpie-cunt";*
5 *FRENCH / TAGALOG: "69"; ITALIAN: "Do a 69…";*
6 *"Lick my clit."*
7 *"graze the watercress";*
8 *"go down to the cellar";*
9 *"pussy entrée";*
10 *pussy-licker;*
11 *"Yr whore mother's blood-red cunt!"*
12 *"Go suckle yr mother's cunt!"*
13 *mutual licking;*
14 *stuff yr face at the honorable gate;*
15 *"eat tofu";*
16 *licker of menstruating cunts;*
17 *"descend to the well," Col. dial.;*
18 *"eat sweet bread," Mex.;*
19 *"the clown's kiss";*
20 *"You eat yr mother's pussy."*

PUSSY, HOT, & NYMPHO:
SEE: HORNY, HOT

PUSSY, RUB:
SEE: CLIT, CLITORIS

RAPE / RAPIST / GANG-RAPE / GANG BANG (& VARIATIONS) згвалтанне

AFRIKAANS vertragning *;
verktragter *;
roof [2]
ALBANIAN përdhunój *;
përdhunúes/i **;
Atij i ka rënë sapuní në burgje! [3]
ARABIC ightaşaba *
BASQUE bortxaketa *
BELARUSIAN згвалтанне / zgvaltanne *
BENGALI Āmake d´orshon rohrech´e. [4]
BOSNIAN silovange *
BURMESE Chuh-náw muh dáyng chíng kang yá de. *(m/gay)* ;
Chuh-má muh dáyng chíng kang yá de. *(f)* [4]
CANTONESE jehw *;
kèuhnngàan *;
hāai yáu [5]
CATALAN violar *;
forçar *
CROATIAN / SERB silovati *;
silovatelj **;
силовати / silovati *;
силоватeлj / silovatelj **
CZECH znásilnní *;
loupe *
DANISH voldtægt *;
bunkepul [6];
massevoldtægt [7]
DUTCH de verkrachting *;
ezel verkrachtende [8]
ESTONIAN vägistama *
FARSI tajâvoz *;
motejâvez **
FINNISH raiskaaja **;
motejâvez **

ruma huoranraiskaaja [10]
vuohenraiskaaja [9];
FRENCH violeur **;
sauter sur [16]
GAELIC, IRISH banéigean *;
éigneoir **
GERMAN Enfürung **
GREEK, MOD. ενας βιασμος / enas viasmos *
HEBREW anas **;
be´eelat keteenah [11]
HINDI / NEPALI balātkār *
HUNGARIAN megerő *
ICELANDIC nauðgun *;
brottnám *
ITALIAN stupratore **;
stupro di grupo [6]
JAPANESE ゴカン gokan *;
ゴカン魔 gokan-ma [12]
KOREAN kang-gan ha-da *
LITHUANIAN ro´pé *
MACEDONIAN силјвање / siljvanje *
MALAYU rogol *;
merogol *
MANDARIN 强奸 qiángjiān *
MARATHI dharsana *
NORWEGIAN voldtekt *
POLISH gałcić *
PORTUGUESE a violação *;
estrupo *;
estuprador **
QUECHUA alquchay *
ROMANIAN siluire *; rapiţă *
RUSSIAN Онá попáла под трамвáй. / Oná popálă păd tramváyy [13]
SINHALA
SLOVENIAN
SOMALI kufsi *
SOTHO, N kata / kato *
SPANISH violador **
SWAHILI kunibaka *;
ubakaji *;
mbakaji **
SWEDISH förstöra *;
våldtäktsman **;
kompaniknull [6]
TAGALOG dayukdók *;
atibán [14]
THAI kòm kĕun *;
gahn kòm kĕun *;
sóm [6]
TURKISH tecâvüzü **
UKRAINIAN ґвалтівання / gvaltiyvannya *
URDU zana bil-jabr *
UZBEK зоьрлаш / zo´rlash *;
номусга тегиш / nomusga tegish *
VIETNAMESE hãm hiếp *
WELSH trais / trais ar ferch *
YIDDISH trennen *;
farvg´valdiken *
YORUBA fi ipá mú *
ZULU ukuthumba *

* *"rape";*
** *"rapist";*
2 *"rape/date rape";*
3 *"He bent over to pick up his bar of soap in prison";*
4 *"I've just been raped";*
5 *"molestor of women";*
6 *"gang-bang/gang-rape";*
7 *"gang-bang with more gang-bangers gang-banging";*
8 *"donkey rapist";*
9 *"goat rapist";*
10 *"ugly whore rapist";*
11 *"statutory rape";*
12 *"rape devil";*
13 *"She fell under the gang-bang tram";*
14 *"roofie," date rape drug;*
15 *"x-x-x"/triple-x;*
16 *"leaping upon."*

强
奸

RETARD, MONGOLOID (& VARIATIONS) 傻瓜

AFRIKAANS vertraagde / gestremde *;
vertraagde kind / gestremde kind [2]
ALBANIAN njeri me fiskime *
ARABIC / TUNIS. mnayyak [3]
ARMENIAN tufta [4]
BENGALI gadha **;
bhabla **;
akat murkho **
BULGARIAN малоумник / maloumnik *;
кретен / kreten [19]
CANTONESE mauh léi *
CATALAN sapastre **
CROATIAN / SERB retardirana seljano *(m)* [5];
ретардирана селјано / retardirana seljano *(m)* [5]
CZECH nedomrd *
DANISH sinke *;
retarderet *;
tågehov-ed [6];
jubleidiot [7]
DUTCH spast *;
achterlijke *;
Je hebt het niveau van een koekje. [8];
Tering mongool! [9];
achterlijke tulp / achterlijke bloem [10]
FARSI `aqab oftâde *
FINNISH älykääpiö *
FRENCH retardé *(m)* / retardée *(f)* *
GAELIC, IRISH leathdhuine [12]
GERMAN Wappler [12];
Fischkopf [13]
GREEK, MOD. καθυστερημένος / kathisteriménos *
HINDI / URDU ullū kā patthā *
ICELANDIC Mongólíti [14]
INDONESIAN okak udang [15]
ITALIAN ritardato mentale / ritardata mentale *;
mongoloido [14]
JAPANESE どん臭い donkusai [16]
KAZAKH акмак / akmak **
KOREAN ae-ja *
LATVIAN debils *
LITHUANIAN nedatupetas *
MALTESE pacocc *
MANDARIN 傻瓜 shăguā [17]
MARATHI apārā [18]
MONGOLIAN мулгуи / mulgui **
POLISH kretyn *(m)* / kretynka *(f)* [19]
PORTUGUESE Mongolóide [14];
cabeção [20]
RUSSIAN Ефиоп / Èfióp [21]
SINHALA modaya [22]
SLOVENIAN kreten [19]
SPANISH ¡Pinchi retrasado! [23];
brea [24]
SWAHILI punguani [25]
SWEDISH mongo **;
miffo **
TAGALOG sinto sinto *;
abnoy *
THAI kòn ngôh **
TURKISH salak **
UZBEK эсар / esar [25]
VIETNAMESE ngu-ngốc **
WELSH hwyrhad *
YIDDISH schlemiel *;
schtumie [26]
YORUBA pè **
ZAPOTEC nada´gu´ **

* *"retard/retarded";*
** *"idiot/retard";*
2 *"retarded child";*
3 *"Fucked up retartd/Fucked retard";*
4 *"stupid/retard";*
5 *"retarded country hick";*
6 *"foggy head";*
7 *"happy idiot";*
8 *"You've got the brain-power of a cookie";*
9 *"Tubercular retard/Mongoloid!"*
10 *"retarded tulip/retarded flower";*
11 *"mental midget/fuckwit";*
12 *"half-person";*
13 *"incompetent retard," Germ./Vien. dial.;*
14 *"Mongoloid";*
15 *"shrimp brain";*

16 *"stupid-smelling," Osaka/Kansai;*
17 *"stupid melon";*
18 *"born feet-first";*
19 *"cretin";*
20 *"huge head," Braz.;*
21 *"Ethiopian";*
22 *"fool";*
23 *"Fuckin' retard!" Mex.;*
24 *"tar," Chil.;*
25 *"feeble-minded;" ;*
25 *"simpleton."*

SCAB, STRIKE-BREAKER, GOON, STORM TROOPS (& VARIATIONS)

子分

BASQUE grebausle **
CANTONESE dahtgīkdéui [4];
chànseun [2]
CATALAN esquirol *;
beneit [2];
babau [2]
CROATIAN / SERB štrajkbreher **;
штрајк-брехер / štrajkbrekher **
CZECH stávokaz *;
hulvát [2]
DANISH strejkebryder *;
struebrækker *
FARSI e´tesāb **
FINNISH rikkuri *;
iskujoukot [3]
FRENCH briseur de grève **
GERMAN Streikbrecher *;
Sturmtruppen [4]
GREEK μπράβοζ / mprávoz [2]
HEBREW mefeer *
ICELANDIC verkfallsbrjótur *;
glópur [2];
fylgismaður [2]
ITALIAN crumiro *(m)* / cruminira *(f)* *;
picchiatore [2];
squadra de picchiatore [5]
JAPANESE 子分 kobun [2]
MALAYU asykar penggempur [3]
NORWEGIAN streikebryter **;
stormtrop-per [4]
POLISH strajk za atakować [3]
PORTUGUESE disjuntor da batida *;
capanga [2]
ROMANIAN trupe cari dau asalt [4]
RUSSIAN штрейкбре́хер / štreykbrékher *;
приспе́шник / prisnéšnik [2]
SPANISH rompehuelgas *;
sustituir a un huelgista **
SWAHILI mvunja mgomo *
SWEDISH strejkbrytare *;
hejduk [2];
dumbom [2]
TAGALOG kabig [2];
tauhan [2]
TURKISH grev kırıcı işçe *;
amak kimse [2]
VIETNAMESE nguŏi phá cuộc dình-công *

* *"strike-breaker";*
** *"scab/scab worker";*
2 *"goon/hench-man";*
3 *"shock troops/ strike troops/thugs";*
4 *"stormtroops";*
5 *"goon squad."*

SENILE (& VARIATIONS) эсар

AFRIKAANS kinds *;
afgeleef *
ARABIC kharif *
ARMENIAN s´eratsum *
BASQUE txotxatuta *
BENGALI buro thubdo *;
jada bharat *
CANTONESE fùngkwòhngge **
CATALAN / DANISH / PORTUGUESE senil *
CROATIAN / SERB senilan *;
сењилањ / senilan *;
Je si se osenilio? [2];
Је си се осењиљо? / Je si se osenilio? [2]
CZECH staeck *
DUTCH seniel *
FARSI fartut *
FINNISH vanuudenöperö *
FRENCH sénile *
GAELIC, IRISH néaltraithe *
GERMAN Teletubbies zurück Winker. [10]
HEBREW seneelee *
HINDI / URDU Dimāg me bhōsna bhara hai. [3]
ICELANDIC elliær *
ITALIAN demenza [4];
rincoglionire [5]
JAPANESE 老衰な rōsui na *
MALAYU orang tua bangka [6]
MANDARIN 老态龙锺的 laotài lóng-zhōng de *
MARATHI vayōvrddha *
RUSSIAN маразматúчестий / marazmatíš-estiy *
SPANISH Senil ;
¿Eres senil? [7]
SWAHILI dhaifu *;
siotambua [8]
SWEDISH ålderdomssvag *
TAGALOG mahulí *
THAI cha ràa *
TURKISH bunak *
UKRAINIAN старечий / starečyý *
UZBEK эсар / esar [9]
VIETNAMESE già yê̇u *
WELSH oedrannus *;
methedig *
YEOME / YAQUI ka suak *
ZULU ukugaga *

* *"senile";*
** *"demented";*
2 *"Have you gone totally senile?";*
3 *"Yr brain's choked with sawdust";*
4 *"senile dementia";*
5 *"becoming senile";*
6 *"useless senile geezer";*
7 *"Are you senile?";*
8 *"oblivious";*
9 *"feeble-minded;*
10 *"He waves back at the teletubbies."*

illustr., © 2008, Graham Willoughby

SHAMELESS, (HAVE YOU) NO SHAME (& VARIATIONS) ずうずうしい

AFRIKAANS skaamteloos *
ALBANIAN i partup (m) / e paturp (f) *
ARABIC bi lā haya *
ARMENIAN anamot *
BASQUE lotsagaiztoko *
BENGALI dui kan kata *; nak-kan kata *
CANTONESE miji cháu *; háumithnpeth *
CATALAN poca-vergonya *; bandarra **
CROATIAN / SERB Sram te bilo! [2]; Срам те било! / Sram te bilo! [2]
CZECH nestydat *
DANISH / NORWEGIAN skamløs *
DUTCH Foei! [3]
ESTONIAN häbematu *
FARSI Khejâlet bekesh! [4]
FINNISH Häpeää! [4]
FRENCH éhonté (m) / éhontée (f) *; effronté (m) / éffrontée (f)
GAELIC, IRISH gan náire *
GAELIC, SCOTS dì-nàireach *
GERMAN unverschämt *
GREEK, MOD. θεν εηις τροπι / then ehis tropi [6]
HEBREW khasar *
HINDI / URDU Tumhein koi sharm nahi!? [2]
ICELANDIC blygðunarlaus *
ITALIAN svergognato *
JAPANESE ずうずうしい zūzūshii *
KOREAN yŏm-ch'i ŏp-nŭn *
LATIN salvo pudore *
LATVIAN nekaunīgs *
MALAYU tak silu-silu *
MANDARIN 无耻的 wúchǐ de *
MARATHI ujagira *
NAHUATL apinauhqui *
POLISH bezwstydny *
PORTUGUESE Sem vergonha! *; Gente sem vergonha! [7]
ROMANIAN neruşinat *; obraznic *
RUSSIAN бесстыдный / besstýdnyy *
SOTHO, N Mafee! [4]
SPANISH sin vergüenza *; descarado *
SWAHILI bila haya *
SWEDISH skamlös *
TAGALOG askád **; mapalabok [8]
THAI nàa dàan *; hèern grèerm **
TURKISH yüsüz *
UKRAINIAN безпардонний / bezpardonnyý *
UZBEK бэхайолик / behayolik *
VIETNAMESE khóng biết xấu-hổ *
WELSH digywilydd *; beiddgar *
YIDDISH chutzpah [10]

* *"shameless/Shameless!";*
** *"bitchy/cheeky/no shame";*
2 *"Have you no shame!?!?";*
3 *"Shame!"*
4 *"Shame on you!"*
5 *"effrontery";*
6 *"without shame";*
7 *"Shameless people!"*
8 *"over-the-top";*
9 *"shamelessness";*
10 *Per Harlan Ellison: "gall, brazen nerve, audacity, shamelessness, presumption-plus-arrogance, such as no other word, & no other language, can do justice."*

SHE-MALE, TRANSEXUAL:
SEE: DRAG QUEEN

SHIT, SHITTY (& VARIATIONS) тртушка

AFRIKAANS / DUTCH stront *; kak *
ALBANIAN muti *
ARABIC chrā *; ARMENIAN kak *
BASQUE kaka egin *; kaka *
BELARUSIAN хауно / hauno *
BENGALI bhagade *; bāl er chāt **
BOSNIAN / CROATIAN / SERB sranje *; govno *; сранје / sranje *; говно / govno *
BULGARIAN гувно / guvno *; мамка му́ / mamka mú *; лайно / layno *
BURMESE chi *
CANTONESE sí *
CATALAN caganer [4]
CREOLE/HAITIAN mede *
CZECH hovno *; sraní *; sraky *
DANISH lort *; skid [5]; bæ [6]
ESTONIAN sitt *
FARSI golole *; goh *
FINNISH paska *; paskamainen **; skeida [2]
FRENCH merde! *; merdeux [3]; étron [5]
GAELIC, IRISH / GAELIC, SCOTS cac *
GERMAN Scheisse! *; Scheissdrägg [7]
GREEK, MOD. σκατά / skatá *; σκατο / skato **
HEBREW charah *
HINDI / URDU pakhana *; Bakvās! *
HUNGARIAN szar **;
ICELANDIC kúkur *; skítur / skíta *; drita *; skítlegur **; kúkalabbi **; saur [2]
INDONESIAN berak *
ITALIAN merda *; stronzo [8]
JAPANESE クソ kuso *
KAZAKH бхогк / bhogk *
KOREAN ni-mi-ral *
LATIN fimus [10]; merda [10]; caco [10]; stercus [10]
LATVIAN suuds *
LITHUANIAN shudas *; meshlas *
MACEDONIAN сранје / sranje *; лајна / lajna *; тртушка / trtuška [5]
MALAYU berak *
MALTESE hara *
MANDARIN 屎 shǐ *
MONGOLIAN баас / baas *
NAHUATL sapa [3]
NORWEGIAN dritt *
POLISH gówno *
PORTUGUESE bosta *; merda *; fodeu [2]
QUECHUA q'upa [2]
ROMANIAN căcat *; căcacios **
RUSSIAN говно / govnó *; сраный / srányy **
SLOVENIAN govno *; drek *
SOTHO, N mampho [2]

SPANISH mierda *;
murrda *;
cagada *;
mojón [5]
SWAHILI mavu [2];
mavi [2]
SWEDISH skit *;
värdelöst **;
det suger **
TAGALOG ta´e **;
tékla´ [2];
ébak / état [2];
jabóng [2]
TAMIL khukhu *
THAI kêe*;
Ba! *
TURKISH bok *
UKRAINIAN гівно /givno [2];
засраний /
zasranyy [11];
дермо /dermo [12]
UZBEK поқ / poq [2]
VIETNAMESE cu´t *;
phán *
WELSH cach *
YIDDISH dreck [2]
YORUBA ìgbé [2]
ZULU amasimba *;
uthuvi *

* *"shit" / "Shit!";*
** *"shitty";*
2 *"crap; shit"; BRAZ.: "crap";*
3 *"crappy";*
4 *"shitty brat";*
5 *"turd";*
6 *"poop";*
7 *"shitty shit," Sw./Bern dial.;*
8 *"turd; also, shit-for-brains bastard; 'stronza' (f), turd, shit-for-brains bitch/cunt";*
9 *"shit/shitting";*
10 *"'Shit,' or 'To shit'," attributed to Ceasar's wife;*
11 *"shit-caked/shitty";*
12 *"fresh stinky shit."*

SHIT-HEAD / SHIT, FULL OF (& VARIATIONS)

Σκατο κεφαλε!

AFRIKAANS Jy is vol kak *
ALBANIAN Je një hale i vërtetë! [2]
ARABIC khrāwet [3]
ARMENIAN kaki gi'dor [4]
BELARUSIAN Ты хауно. / Ty hauno. [5]
BENGALI Thor matha gōe bora! [6]
BOSNIAN Seres na sve strane! [7]
BULGARIAN Миришеш на гъвна! / Mirišeš na guvna! [8]
CANTONESE Sí tàuh! **;
nóuh jōng sí [23]
CATALAN Pilo de merda! *(m)* /Piha de merda! *(f)* [9]
CROATIAN Govnaru! **
CZECH Kokot! **
DANISH Lortehoved! **
DUTCH Bloedpoepende skødehund. [10]
ESTONIAN Sitapea! **
FARSI Gho kordi! [2]
FINNISH Päässäsi tekee kusi patoja ja paska puroja. [11]
FRENCH Branleur! **
GAELIC, IRISH lán de cac **
GAELIC, SCOTS làn dhen cac *
GERMAN Scheisskopf! **
GREEK, MOD. Σκατο κεφαλε! / Skato kefale! **
HEBREW khhatikhhat khhara [4]
HINDI / URDU Bheje me gō bhara hai! [6]
HUNGARIAN gennyláda [12]
ICELANDIC kúkalabbi [12];
lygalaupur *
INDONESIAN Tai kucing! [13]
ITALIAN Cacacazzo! **;
Torta di Merda [14]
JAPANESE 便所虫 benjo mushi [15]
KAZAKH бхокшил / bhokshil **
KOREAN ship se-ki [4]
LATIN caput stercoris **

LATVIAN Kakja spiras! [13]
LITHUANIAN Sudo gábalas. [4]
MACEDONIAN Лјња глава / Lynja glava! **
MALAYU karung kosong *
MALTESE Harja kollok. [16]
MANDARIN 屎头 / shǐtóu! **
NAHUATL sapa [17]
NEPALI kukur kogu [18]
NORWEGIAN Drittsekk! [12]
POLISH Masz w głowie gówno! [6]
PORTUGUESE Cabeça-de-merda! **
ROMANIAN căcănar **
RUSSIAN Говнюкь! / Govnyuḱ! **
SERBIAN Говнару! / Govnaru! **
SPANISH ¡Cabeza de mierda! **
SWAHILI Matako yakona nuka kama mavi! [8]
SWEDISH Skithuvud! **
TAGALOG puro ta´e *
THAI farang kèenók [19];
kêe móh *
TURKISH Bok kafa! **
UKRAINIAN купа гівна /kupa hivna [20]
VIETNAMESE Đụ má! [21]
WELSH Pen cachi! **
YIDDISH Kucker! ** ;
schtick dreck [4]
ZULU inganckwane [22]

* *"full of shit"; AFRIKAANS: "You're full of shit."*
** *"shit head" / "Shit-head!"*
2 *"You're a real shit!"*
3 *"shit-heel";*
4 *"Piece of shit."*
5 *"You're worth shit-all."*
6 *"Yr head's filled with/full of shit!"*
7 *"You shit everything!"*
8 *"You reek of shit!"*
9 *"Shitty yuppie!"*
10 *"Blood shitting lap dog."*
11 *"In yr mind's eye, dams are built of piss & rivers flow w/ shit."*
12 *"Shit bag bastard!"*
13 *"Cat shit!"*
14 *"shit cake";*
15 *"shithouse bug";*
16 *"You're an A-1 all-shit."*
17 *"crappy, filthy";*
18 *"dip shit";*
19 *"bird shit foreigner";*
20 *pile of shit/shit pile;*
21 *"Shit bastard fuck!"*
22 *"cock-&-bull b.s."= totally full of primo bullshit;*
23 *"shit-for-brains."*

屎
头

SHIT, EAT / SHIT-EATER / COPROPHILIAC (& VARIATIONS)

Йай лайна

AFRIKAANS Eet kak. *
ARABIC Kul khara. *
ARMENIAN Shun kak utes. [2]
BASQUE gorozjale [3]
BENGALI Gō kah. *
BOSNIAN Jedi govna. *
BULGARIAN Йай лайна! / Jaj lajna! *
CANTONESE Sihk sí! *
CATALAN cagant llets [4]
CROATIAN Jedi govna. *
DANISH Æd lort. *
DUTCH kakzuiger [5]
ESTONIAN Söö sitta. *
FARSI Goh bokhor. *
FINNISH Syö paskaa! *;
Paskaa paahtoleivällä! [6]
FRENCH/QUEB. Mange donc un gros char plein d'merde! [7]
GAELIC, IRISH Ithe cac. *
GAELIC, SCOTS Ith cac. *
GERMAN Iss Scheisse. *
GREEK, MOD. Φαε σκατά! / Fae skatá!
HEBREW Kuli chara. **
HINDI / URDU Tu gō khai. *
ICELANDIC Ettu skit. *
INDONESIAN Makan tai. *
ITALIAN Mangia merda. [8]
JAPANESE クソでも食え / Kuso demo kue. *;
クソを食べる人 / kuso wo taberu hito [3]
KAZAKH Bhokti zep. *
KOREAN Dong muk-uh. *
LATIN Mande merdam. *
LATVIAN Izēd dirsu. *
MACEDONIAN Цади говна со магданос. / Dzadi govna so magdanos. [9]
MANDARIN 吃我的屎! Chī wǒ de shǒ! **
NORWEGIAN spedbarnsbæsjsniffer [10];
Gå og spis en kubæsj. [11]
PORTUGUESE Vai chupar merda, o seu filho da puta. [12]
ROMANIAN Minca-mi-ai căcatu. **
RUSSIAN Что Я в борщ нсрал, свто ли? / Čto ya v boršč nsrál, svto li? [13]
SERBIAN Једи говна. / Jedi govna. *
SPANISH Me cago en las pechugas de la puta Virgen Maria para que el Niño Jesús chupe mierda. [14];
caga cosina [15]
SWEDISH Dra åt helvete. *
TAGALOG Kain ta´e. *
UZBEK Боқимни епсан. / Boqimni yepsan. **
VIETNAMESE An cu´t ne con. [16]
WELSH Bwyta fy gachu. **
YIDDISH Kuck ind faall. [17]
ZULU Tsa mor kaka. *

* *"Eat shit";*
** *"Eat my shit/May you eat my shit";*
2 *"Eat dog shit."*
3 *"feasts on shit/coprophile";*
4 *"shitting milk";*
5 *"shit-sucker";*
6 *"Shit on a shingle!"*
7 *"So eat a truckload of shit!"*
8 *"Shit-eater."*
9 *"Eat shit with parsley";*
10 *"baby-shit-sniffer";*
11 *"Go eat cow-shit."*
12 *"Go suck on shit, you son of a bitch";*
13 *"Did you think I shat in the borscht, or what?"*
14 *"I shit on the whore Virgin Mary's tits so that baby Jesus can suck shit."*
15 *"burglar shitting in your kitchen";*
16 *"Go eat shit right now";*
17 *"Shit and fall on it."*

Φαε σκατά!

SLUT/
SLUTTY
HORNY
(& VARIATIONS)

AFRIKAANS slet *;
lugmatrass **
ALBANIAN zuskë *
ARABIC/TUNIS. attaya *;
māllma [2]
ARMENIAN poz *;
hazarag [3]
BASQUE nahastatu [3]
BELARUSIAN блйадз / bliadz *;
курва / kurva [4]
BENGALI jowhra *
BULGARIAN торба / torba *
CANTONESE hàahm sāp [5]
CATALAN calent [6];
anar calent [26]
CHABACANO querida [7]
CROATIAN Mama ti je drolja na Internetu. /
Baba ti je drolja na Internetu. /
Sestra ti je drolja na Internetu. /
Kćer ti je drolja na Internetu. [8]
CZECH děvka *
DANISH tøjte *
DUTCH greppeldel [9];
gratenkut [10];
geilneef [26]
ESTONIAN Libu selline. [11]
FARSI saliteh *;
koskesh [12]
FINNISH pikkupillu [13];
Pissaliisa [14]
FRENCH garce *;
sale pute [15]
FRENCH (VERLAN) Tassepé! [4]
GAELIC, IRISH sraoilleog *
GAELIC, SCOTS Tha thu 'nad luid. [11];
làir [27]
GERMAN/SW. Du bisch ä schlampä. [11]
GREEK, MOD. τσουλα / tsonla *
GUJARATI rhannd [4]
HEBREW sharmuta *
HINDI randi sāli *;
masala [6]
HUNGARIAN Jól ismerik. [16]
ICELANDIC drusla *;
lauslátur [3];
graður [6]
INDONESIAN perek *
ITALIAN scopatrice [3];
bocchinara [18];
assatanato [26]
JAPANESE ヤリマン yariman [15];
イエロー・キャブ iero-kyabu [19]
KANNADA chilali [20]
KAZAKH bliad´ [4]
KOREAN net ssang nyon [21]
LATIN lupa [4]
LATVIAN mauka *
LITHUANIAN shliundra *
MACEDONIAN Куратс / kurats *;
Курвариште / kurvarishte [26]
MALAYU jual pung'kuk *
MALTESE qahba *;
nittien [26]
MANDARIN 骚货 sāohuò [4]
MARATHI sepalu [6];
jogamma [15]
MONGOLIAN вашка / vashka [4]
NAHUATL ahuiani [4]
NEPALI alachina [3]
NORWEGIAN tispe *;
felleshøl [22];
fittfaen [26]
POLISH dziwka *
PORTUGUESE piranha *
ROMANIAN târfá [4];
târfá murdara [15]
RUSSIAN верушка / veruška *
SERBIAN дроља / drolya *
SINHALA hukanni *
SLOVENIAN kurba [4];
kurba na etone [23]
SOTHO, N leš aedi *
SPANISH cusca *;
arrecha [26];
puta [4]

SWEDISH slyna * ;
madrass [24]
TAGALOG bilasá *
TAMIL thevidya [4]
THAI ga'réé [4]
TURKISH pasakh kadin *
UKRAINIAN бръднуля / brudnulya *
URDU randi sāli *;
masala [6]
UZBEK гар / g´ar [4]
VIETNAMESE dàn bà nhếch nhấc bẫn-thĩu dĩ thoã
WELSH slebog *
YIDDISH nafkeh [4];
shikseh [25]
YORUBA àgbèrè [4]
ZULU i(li)vabakazi *

image: GobQ/L. Jamneck

ヤリマン

* *slut;*
** *"air-mattress," slutty gay S.African flight stewards;*
2 *slut, female pimp;*
3 *slutty, gets around/fucks around;*
4 *slut, whore, slutty bitch;*
5 *horny slut, male or female;*
6 *hot, horny, slutty;*
7 *mistress, slut;*
8 *"Yr mother/*
Yr grandmother/
Yr sister/
Yr daughter is an internet slut!"
9 *ditch slut;*
10 *"fish-bone pussy";*
11 *You slut;*
12 *worn-cunt slut;*
13 *Apprentice Teen Slut/Apprentice Teen Cunt;*
14 *"Piss-Alices," drunken teen sluts who piss themselves;*
15 *"dirty skanky slut";*
16 *"He/she fucks around";*
17 *"Yr mother's a slut";*
18 *slutty woman who gives great blow jobs;*
19 *"Yellow cab" slut;*
20 *"Super-slut." / "Super-whore.";*
21 *On-line slut/whore;*
22 *"free whore," slut;*
23 *bus token slut/whore.*
24 *"mattress";*
25 *gentile/goyem girl, & of course a slut;*
26 *hot horny male slut;*
27 *"a good shag," sexy, slutty.*

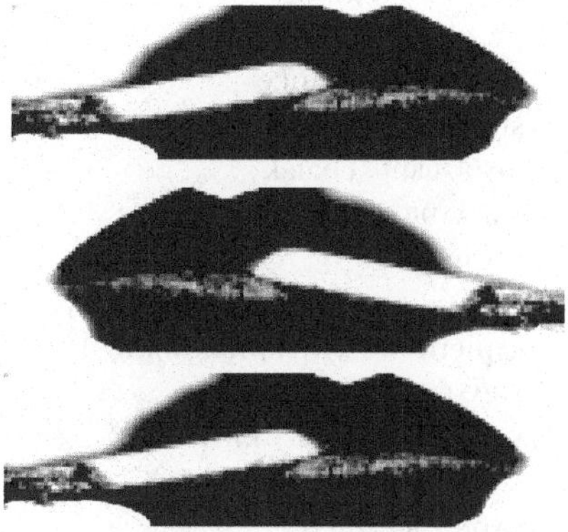
GobQ/T. Warburton y Bajo

SMART ASS / SMART ARSE, SARCASTIC (& VARIATIONS) **ИЛМОҚЛИ**

AFRIKAANS spottend *
ALBANIAN karderr **
ARABIC kinoya [2]; qil-kinoya [3]
ARMENIAN heqnagan *
BASQUE ozpin *
BENGALI chalu māl *; chalbāj *
CANTONESE fúngchi *; dai [4]
CATALAN coco [5]
CROATIAN pametnjakovič *
CZECH zatrpklý [6]
DANISH vise sig [8]
DUTCH sarcastisch *
ESTONIAN ebaviisakas [7]
FARSI kenyâyedâr *; masxraraomuz [9]
FINNISH pisteliäs *
FRENCH sarcastique *
GAELIC, IRISH searbhasach *
GERMAN Gscheidhaferl
GREEK, MOD. εχπινο κολέ /expino kolé [10]
GUJARATI naph´phat [16]
HAUSA mai gatse *; na zambo [2]
HEBREW laglegan<u>ee</u> [11]; shel la´ag mar [12]
HINDI / URDU chālāk [8]
ICELANDIC oskammfeilinn [13]; horugur [14]
ITALIAN cacazzo *(m)* / cacazze *(f)* *; sapientone *(m)* / sapientona *(f)* [10]
JAPANESE まいう maiu *
KAZAKH киртпаш / kirtpash [8]
KOREAN p' ung-ja-jŏk *
LATIN acerbus [15]
LATVIAN rupjš [16]
LITHUANIAN šiurkštus' [16]
MACEDONIAN прост / prost [16]; груб / grub [16]
MALAYU gambong [8]
MALTESE vulgari [16]
MANDARIN 尖刻的 jiānkè de *
MARATHI <u>t</u>anakā / <u>t</u>anakāra [17]
NAHUATL huiteyolihtlacoani *
NEPALI anādar [19]
NORWEGIAN viktigpare *
POLISH cham [20]
PORTUGUESE fulera *; grosso [16]
QUECHUA asichikuq [21]
ROMANIAN aspru [16]
RUSSIAN хитрожопый / khitrožópyy [22]
SERBIAN паметакови / pametakovi *
SOTHO, N yo makgakga [16]; tshotlo [19]
SPANISH payaso [23]
SWAHILI chale [24]
SWEDISH Besserwisser *
TAGALOG antipátiko *; lángmagu [10]
TELEGU viajokti [18]; via<u>n</u>gyamu [19]
THAI hèerm grèerm [25]
TURKISH istiha *
UKRAINIAN насиро всравсиа / nasyro vsravsya *
UZBEK рамзли / ramzli [15]; илмоқли / ilmoqli [26]
VIETNAMESE vô lễ [16]
WELSH gwawdiol *; anfoesgar [16]
YAQUI/YOEMI kaveta yo´oró [16]
YIDDISH oysvorf [27]
YORUBA òpe [16]
ZAPOTEC rudu [16]
ZULU -bhuqayo *; -eyisayo [16]

* *smart-ass/arse, sarcastic;*
** *cocky, rude male;*

2 *sarcastic/satirical piss-take;*
3 *satirically/sarcastically refer to;*
4 *mock sarcastically;*
5 *smart-ass/arse nerd;*
6 *sardonic;*
7 *rude & snotty;*
8 *show-off, smarty-pants/smart-ass/arse;*
9 *semi-mocking;*
10 *smart-ass/arse know-it-all;*
11 *derisive sarcastic mocking;*
12 *sardonic mockery;*
13 *flippant smart-ass/arse;*
14 *snotty;*
15 *acerbic;*
16 *rude;*
17 *scorpion sting, sarcastic;*
18 *double-entendre, innuendo;*
19 *sarcasm, contempt, rudeness, disdain;*
20 *rude jerk;*
21 *joker, clown, smart-ass/arse;*
22 *clever/smart-ass/arse;*
23 *clown, buffoon, smart-ass/arse;*
24 *comedian, smart-ass/arse;*
25 *cheeky, brazen, rude;*
26 *tongue in cheek;*
27 *ungrateful bum, scoundrel.*

SON OF A BITCH
(& VARIATIONS)

AFRIKAANS Kont se kind. **
ALBANIAN bir kurve *
ARABIC / TUNIS. Wild il qahbā! *
ARMENIAN Poz'i tula! *
BASQUE Putasemea. [9]
BELARUSIAN баджтрук / badžtruk [2]
BENGALI shuroer baccha *
BULGARIAN копеле / kopele [2]
BURMESE quey ma tha *
CANTONESE chūksàng *
CATALAN fill de puta *;
fill de verra [3]
CHABACANO ijo puta / ijo de puta *
CROATIAN kirvin sine [4]
CZECH čubčí syn *
DANISH rottebarn [5]
DUTCH smeerlap *;
kind van dertig homo's [6]
ESTONIAN lita poeg *
FARSI zantaloq *
FINNISH huoranpenikka [9]
FRENCH fils de pute *;
fils de chienne *
GAELIC, IRISH mac an bitseach *
GAELIC, SCOTS mac a' bhaobh *
GERMAN Hurnsohn *
GREEK, MOD. μουλε / moule [2]
HAUSA d'an iksa [2]
HEBREW ben zsona/elef *
HINDI / URDU kuti ka bacha *
HUNGARIAN rohadék [2]
ICELANDIC Tíkarsonr *;
Bastarður [8]
ITALIAN figlio di puttana *(m)* / figlia di puttana *(f)* [7]
JAPANESE アマの息子 ama no musuko *
KANNADA sōle magne [9]
KOREAN geseki *

LATIN canis filius *
LATVIAN cunjas beerns *
LITHUANIAN kales vaikas *
MACEDONIAN копиле / kopile [2]
MALAYU anjing kurap [10]
MANDARIN 混账 hùnzhàng *
MARATHI codica [9]
NAHUATL tepalconetl [11]
NEPALI randi ko chhoro *
NORWEGIAN Horeunge [12]
POLISH sukinsyn [8]
PORTUGUESE filho da puta [9]
ROMANIAN Fiu de căţea. / Fiu de târfa. *
RUSSIAN Суксин сын / Súksin syn. *
SERBIAN копиле / kopile [2]
SINHALA huththigay putha [4];
kariya [2]
SLOVENIAN kurbin sine *
SOMALI we'le [2]
SOTHO, N leswena *;
lepastere [2]
SPANISH hijoputa *(m)* / hijaputa *(f)* [7];
hijo de puta *(m)* / hija de puta *(f)* [7]
SWAHILI mwana haramu [2]
SWEDISH horunge [9]
TAGALOG Nampútsa! *
TAMIL virundali ku porandavaney [14]
TELEGU dongana kodukka [13]
THAI luog´ ga´rèe *
TURKISH orospu nin oğlum *
UKRAINIAN сучий син / suchyý syn *
URDU kuti ka bacha *
UZBEK итвачча / itvachcha *
VIETNAMESE dô chó dėh *
WELSH uffar gwirion *
YIDDISH schmuck [16]
YORUBA <u>omo</u> wèrè [17]
ZAPOTEC xiñi gui´xhi´ [18]
ZULU i(li)bhasitele [2]

* *Son of a bitch;*
** *Son of a cunt;*
2 *bastard;*
3 *son of a pig;*
4 *son of a whore;*
5 *rat child;*
6 *child of thirty faggots;*
7 *son/daughter of a bitch/whore;*
8 *son of a bitch, bastard;*
9 *son of a bitch/son of a whore;*
10 *sick dog/bastard/son of a bitch;*
11 *son of a whore, bastard;*
12 *child of a whore;*
13 *son of a thief;*
14 *son of a guest;*
15 *silly bastard;*
16 *son of a bitch, dick/prick, bastard, fool;*
17 *son of a madman/woman;*
18 *bastard child .*

混
账

SON OF A WHORE **курвин сиње**
(& VARIATIONS)

AFRIKAANS hoerkind *
ARABIC / MOROC. wild el gahbah *
ARMENIAN poz´i tega [5]
BASQUE putakume **
BENGALI khankir nati [6]
CANTONESE chūksàng **
CATALAN fill de vera [7]
CROATIAN / SERB kirvin sine *; курвин сиње / kurvin sine *
DANISH luderbarn *
DUTCH hoerenjong *
ESTONIAN hoorapoeg **
FARSI / UZBEK g'arvachcha *; гъарвачча / g'arvachcha
FINNISH huoranpenikka **
FRENCH fils de putain **; enfant de pute [3]
GAELIC, IRISH mac an striapach *
GAELIC, SCOTS mac a' bhean-strìopa *
GERMAN Hurensohn *
GREEK, MOD. γε τις πυτνας / ge tis putnas *
HEBREW ben zona / ben zsona *
HINDI / URDU randi ka bacha *
ICELANDIC hóruungi *
ITALIAN figlio di puttana *(m)* / figlia di puttana *(f)* [2]
JAPANESE 女郎の息子 jorō no musuko *
KANNADA sōle magne **
MARATHI codica **
NAHUATL tepalconetl [4]
NORWEGIAN horeunge [3]
PORTUGUESE filho de puta **
ROMANIAN fiu de curva *
SERBIAN курвин сиње / kurvin sine *
SINHALA vesìegay putha *
SLOVENIAN pičkin sin [8]
SPANISH hijoputa *(m)* / hijaputa *(f)* [2]; hijo de puta *(m)* / hija de puta *(f)* [2]
SWEDISH horunge **
TAGALOG anak ng puta *
UKRAINIAN шлюхий син / shl'ukhyy syn *
YORUBA o̱máàlè [9]

* *son of a whore;*
** *son of a bitch/whore; CANTONESE: son of a bitch;*
2 *son/daughter of a bitch/whore;*
3 *child of a whore;*
4 *son of a whore, bastard;*
5 *son of a slut;*
6 *whore's grandson;*
7 *son of a pig;*
8 *son of a cunt;*
9 *bastard, son of a whore.*

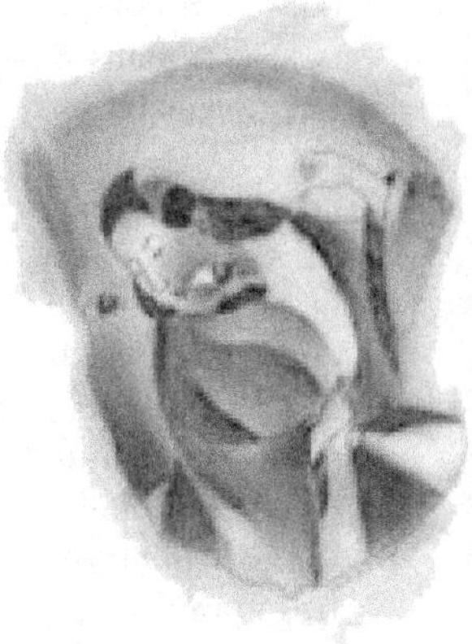

女郎の息子

illustr., © 2008, Graham Willoughby

SWINDLER/ SWINDLE (& VARIATIONS) бо́ямачи

AFRIKAANS verneuker *

ALBANIAN dallaveraxhínj *

ARABIC qalb **

ARMENIAN qoguni- [2]

BASQUE gezurti **

CANTONESE pinjí *

CATALAN estafador **

CROATIAN/SERB varalica *; варалица / varalica *

CZECH podvodník *; cikán **; zid [2]

DANISH / NORWEGIAN bedrager *

DUTCH oplichter *

ESTONIAN tüssaja *

FARSI lo´ttiboz *

FINNISH huijaus *

FRENCH escroc *(m)* *

GERMAN, VIEN. Pülcher *

GREEK, MOD. (ο)απατεωνας/ (o) apateonas *

HAUSA mazambaci *

HEBREW merameh [2]

HINDI / URDU ućakkā *

HUNGARIAN Roma *

ICELANDIC Þrjótur *

INDONESIAN penipu *

ITALIAN truffatore *(m)* / truffatrice *(f)* *; fregatura [3]

JAPANESE ぺてん師 / petenshi *

LATIN fraudare *

LATVIAN krāpšana *

MARATHI avararigabādî *

NAHUATL oniteixcuep [2]

POLISH oszustwo *

PORTUGUESE vigarista *

ROMANIAN pungaş *

RUSSIAN жу́лик / žulik *

SOTHO, N mohlalefetši *

SPANISH timador *(m)* / timadora *(f)* *; Ladrón que roba a ladrón tiene cien años de perdón. [4]

SWEDISH bedragare *(m)* / bedragurska *(f)* *

TAGALOG góyo *

TURKISH dolandirici *

UKRAINIAN шахраы / šakhray *

UZBEK бо́ямачи / bo´yamachi *

WELSH twyllwr *

YIDDISH gonif *

YORUBA arénije *

ZULU uwaka *

* *swindler, con artist, cheat; FINNISH: Swindle;*

** *swindler, gypsy;*

2 *cheating Jew;*

3 *swindle, fuck under;*

4 *"A thief who robs another thief gets 100 yrs free of grief." — prov.*

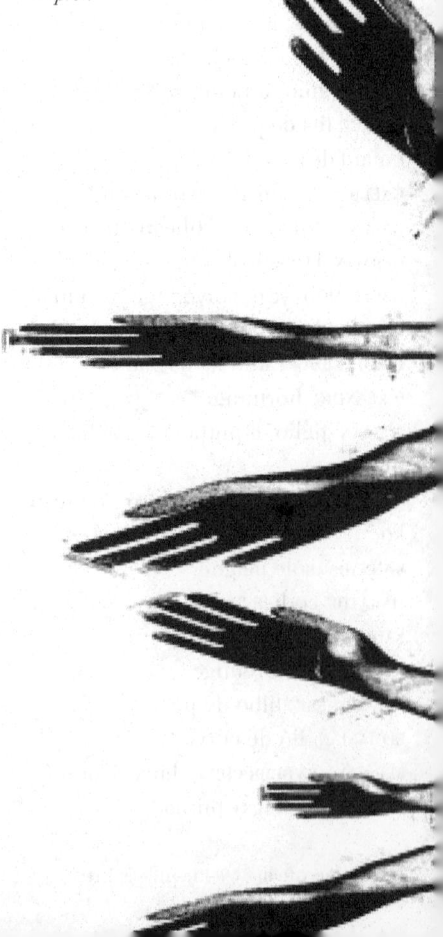

STUPID, DUMB-ASS / DUMB-ARSE (& VARIATIONS)

ηαζος

AFRIKAANS onnosel *
ALBANIAN torollák / torolláke *
ARABIC / LIBY. ahmaq *
ARMENIAN abush *;
yaram **
BASQUE kabroi **;
zozo *
BELARUSIAN дурний / durny *;
ныамй / ny-amy **
BENGALI foga *;
kebla-kanto **;
gobar ganesh [2]
BOSNIAN glup *
BULGARIAN тйпа пътка / typa putka [3];
проФан / profan **
CANTONESE sòh gāang *;
sòh hāi [3]
CATALAN beneit *;
tòtila **
CHABACANO / SPANISH bobo *;
tonto [4]
CREOLE / HAITIAN éstipid *;
gaga **
CROATIAN / SERB glup *;
глуп / glup *
CZECH krovák [5];
mad'ar [6];
turek [7];
hotentot [8]
DANISH dum *;
dumme kælling [5]
DUTCH sufkut [3]
ESTONIAN lollpea [4]
FARSI gij *
FINNISH tyhmä *;
pöljä **;
räpätäti [10]
FRENCH le roi de cons [11];
un historie conne [12];
bêtes *;
con [3]
GAELIC, IRISH gamal *;
dúr *
GERMAN Dumpfbacke **;
Teletubbies zurück Winker. [13]
GREEK, MOD. ηαζος / hazos *
GUJARATI salē gudheri *
HAUSA wawa *
HEBREW teepshee *;
frecha [9]
HINDI sali kuta *(m)* / sali kutti *(f)* [14]
HUNGARIAN seggfej *
ICELANDIC heimskingi *;
hemska belja [12]
INDONESIAN goblok *
ITALIAN coglione [16]
JAPANESE どん臭い donkusai *
KAZAKH dolbaeb [4]
KHMER pler *;
meah la bol yo *(m)* / me la bol yo *(f)* **
KOREAN babo *
LATIN stupidus *
LATVIAN muļķigs *
LITHUANIAN kvailys *
MACEDONIAN глуп(ав) / glup(av) *
MALAYU dungu *
MANDARIN 愚笨的人 yúbènde rén *
MARATHI adabanga *
MONGOLIAN teneg *
NAHUATL yolquimil *;
nontli **
NEPALI murkha *
NORWEGIAN tosket *;
bølgerta *(m)* *
POLISH gł'upi *
PORTUGUESE cabaço *;
pau no cú [17];
QUECHUA mana allin yuyayniyuq *
ROMANIAN prost *;
pizda proasta [3]
RUSSIAN Ефиоп / Èfióp *;
мудило / mudilo **
SINHALA modaya [4]

SLOVENIAN neumen *
SOTHO, N setoto *
SPANISH pendejo [18];
coño pendejo (m) / coño pendeja (f) [3]
SWAHILI pumbavu *
SWEDISH obegåvad *;
enfalding *
TAGALOG tiyópe *;
gági *;
tunggák [5]
TAMIL kaynay [4]
TELEGU koti guddha *
THAI ngôh *
TURKISH beyinisiz *
UKRAINIAN недолугий / nedoluhyý *
URDU chutiya *
UZBEK bishsiz *
VIETNAMESE ngu-ngô·c *
WELSH yn fytyn [4]
YIDDISH schmuck [19]
YORUBA fà *;
òkúyè [4]
ZAPOTEC naguidxa *
ZULU isibhukuza *;
isiphoxo [4]

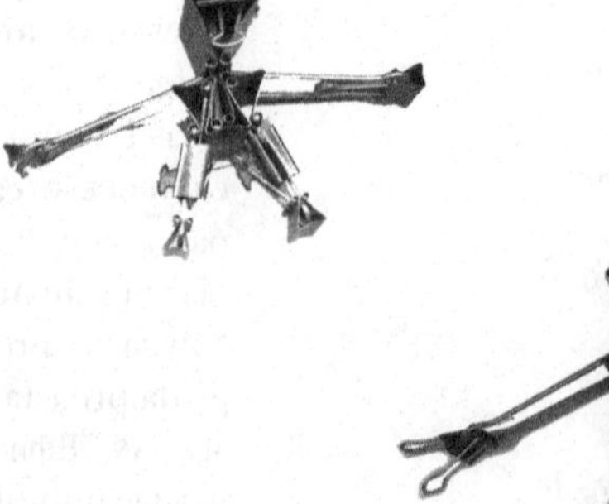

image: GobQ/T. Warburton y Bajo

* *"stupid, stupid ass/arse";*

** *"dumb-ass/arse"; CREOLE, HAITIAN: Imbecilic;*

2 *"Holy Fool";*

3 *"stupid cunt"; SPAN. /MEX.DIAL.: "stupid sub-moronic shit-for-brains cunt";*

4 *dumb, stupid, foolish;*

5 *"stupid bushman" = old school bigotry;*

6 *"cranky fuckwit Magyar Hungarian" = old school bigotry;*

7 *"stupid incoherent Turkman/Musselman/Arab" = old school bigotry;*

8 *"stupid incoherent African" = old school bigotry;*

9 *"dumb bitch, bimbo";*

10 *"air-head," ditzy girl";*

11 *"King Cunt," Absolute King of Stupidity & Idiocy;*

12 *"A Stupid Cunting Story";*

13 *"He waves back at the Teletubbies.";*

14 *"Stupid bastard!" (m) / "Stupid Bitch!" (f) ;*

15 *"Stupid cow!" / "Stupid bitch";*

16 *"Ball/bollock stupid," slobbering cousin to "stronzo";*

17 *"Stupid stick-up-the-ass/arse";*

18 *SPAN. /MEX.: "pendejo" = "stupid sub-moronic shit-for-brains ass/arsehole," or worse, depending on whether any pets or livestock are rectally bleeding; STD. SPANISH: "pendejo" = dumb-ass/arse, dork;*

19 *"dope/jerk/fool/s.o.b./prick/ass-/arsehole & so much more."*

[SUB-/DOM] SUBMISSIVE / BOTTOM: GAY / BI- / STRAIGHT (& VARIATIONS)

ネコ

AFRIKAANS Lucy *; Dinah [2]

BASQUE atzelari(a) [3]

CANTONESE wáan SM [4]

CATALAN fogó *

DANISH tøs [5]

DUTCH kontnicht [10]

ESTONIAN pepuvend [3]

FARSI / TURKISH kuni *

FINNISH homoperse [6]; tyynynpurija [7]

FRENCH tapette [8]

GERMAN Der Hinterlader [9]

GREEK, MOD. δήσκος / dískos [12]

HEBREW kariyot [7]

HINDI / URDU gānd marau *;

HUNGARIAN köcsög [14]

ICELANDIC undirgefinn [15]

ITALIAN busone *; recchione *; effe *

JAPANESE ネコ neko *; 受け身 ukemi *

KOREAN net mejo [16]

LITHUANIAN gaidys *; subindeshris [17]

MALAYU pondan *

MARATHI gā<u>nd</u>yē [18]

NAHUATL cuiloni *

PORTUGUESE frango assado [18]

RUSSIAN встать раком / vstat' rakom [19]

SERBIAN pederčino u crnoj koži [20]; педерчино у црној кожи / pederčino u crnoj koži [20]

SOTHO, N punya [3]

SPANISH muerdealmohadas [7]

SWAHILI unatombwa **

SWEDISH kuddbitare [7]

TAGALOG báyot *

TELEGU sanka nākuta [15]

UZBEK bachcha [11]; aka singli [13]

ZULU imbube [3]

* *gay bottom/submissive;*

** *straight bot./submis.;*

2 *"dildo empress";*

3 *versatile gay, top/bot., ass/arse-fuck buddy;*

4 *S&M sex;*

5 *submis. fem. bot.;*

6 *"ass/arse puppet";*

7 *"pillow biter";*

8 *"carpet-beater," bot. gay;*

9 *"Breech-loader," bot. gay;*

10 *"Ass/arse Knight," gay top/bot.;*

11 *"Dancing Boy," gay bot., catamite;*

12 *"like a 45 disc," plays both sides, top/bot. gay;*

13 *"Little brother";*

14 *"jar," bot. gay;*

15 *straight/gay bot.;*

16 *internet masochist;*

17 *sausage ass/arse;*

18 *"baked chicken," gay bot.;*

19 *"crayfish," bot.;*

20 *"Faggot leather-boy";*

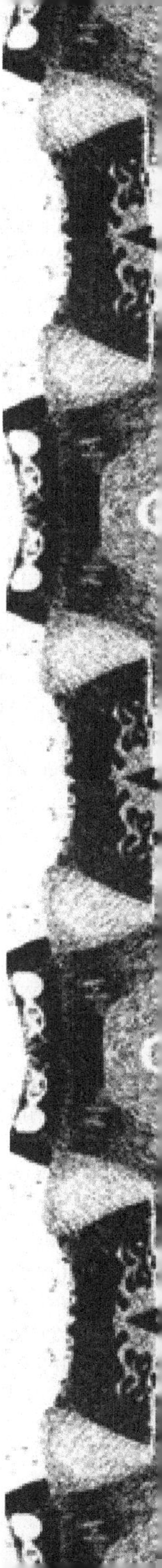

SUB-/DOM]
TOP/
DOMINANT:
GAY/
BI-/
STRAIGHT ЖОПНИК
(& VARIATIONS)

AFRIKAANS rektum ranger *;
dipstick trekker *;
delphinium *;
boudkapper [16]
ARABIC mu^{c}adhdhib(-ūn) [4]
BASQUE atzelari(a) [3]
CATALAN follador *
DANISH Herre [5]
DUTCH naadninja *;
naadsensei *;
naadyakuza *;
bilnaad acrobaat *;
vette ruigpoot [17]
ESTONIAN pepuvend [3]
FARSI / UZBEK bachchaboz [6]
FRENCH maîtresse [7]
GREEK, MOD. ψυκοτραγόπουρος /
psykhotraghópouros [8]
HINDI / URDU bumchod *
ICELANDIC drottnari [2]
ITALIAN culattone *;
Ho voglia di montare. [9]
JAPANESE 立ち役 tachiyaku [10]
NAHUATL tecuilontiani *
RUSSIAN жопник / žópnik *
SERBIAN педе / pede *
SOTHO, N punya [3]
SPANISH Buscar petróleo [11]
SWEDISH röv-knytkävs-knullare [13]
TAGALOG umbáw *
UKRAINIAN авра'ам / avra´am [12]
HINDI / URDU bumchōd *
UZBEK aka´si [14]
ZULU Ucitha isikathi sakho, nagama-
feleza! [15];
imbube [3]

* *top/dom., gay, ass/arsefucker;*
** *top/dom., straight;*
2 *top/ dom., gay/straight;*
3 *versatile gay, top/bot., ass/ arse-fuck buddy;*
4 *torturer;*
5 *"Master," gay/ straight;"*
6 *"Collector of dancing boys";*
7 *"Mistress" = dominatrix;*
8 *"Priest's soul," top/gay;*
9 *"I want to fuck on top!"*
10 *male kabuki actor, top;*
11 *"Drill for oil";*
12 *"ass/arse taker";*
13 *ass/arse fist-fucking;*
14 *"older brother," top, gay;*
15 *"Don't waste on him, he's straight!"*
16 *"Ass/arse chopper";*
17 *"dirty faggot leatherboy."*

S-&-M, ROUGH TRADE: GAY/ BI-/ STRAIGHT (& VARIATIONS)

Домина

AFRIKAANS 'bella queen [2];
Wendy bangles [3];
Sarie-&-Marie *;
bastinado [4]
ARABIC mu^{c}adhdhib / mu^{c}adhdhibūn [5]
BASQUE sadiko [6]
CATALAN sadisme [6]
CROATIAN pederčino u crnoj koži [7];
domina [8]
FARSI falakeh [4]
FRENCH maîtresse [8];
louche **
FRENCH (VERLAN) Ce mec est chelou. [9]
GERMAN / SW. Töfflibuebä [7]
ICELANDIC leðurhommi [7];
hnútasvipa [10]
ITALIAN marchettaro **
JAPANESE SM *
KOREAN net mejo [11]
SERB Домина / Domina [8]
SPANISH dominadora [8]
SWEDISH röv-knytkävs-knullare [12]
TAGALOG kuryénte [13]

* *S-&-M, sado-masochism;*
** *rough trade, w. signifying leathers, chaps, whips & handles;*
2 *gay dom. rough trade with "violence" issues, 3rd in police line-up;*
3 *hand-cuffs;*
4 *foot torture fetish/ beating soles of feet;*
5 *"torturer," somestimes S-&-M, sometimes strictly politics;*
6 *"sadistic"/"sadism";*
7 *leather boy/bike boy faggot;*
8 *dominatrix, usual wages, $60-600+/ hr., spanking very very very bad fascist motherfuckers in darker corridors of power;*
9 *"that dude's rough trade...."*
10 *cat-o'-9-tails;*
11 *on-line-masochist;*
12 *fist-fucking;*
13 *electroshock dick/cunt torture, S-&-M play.*

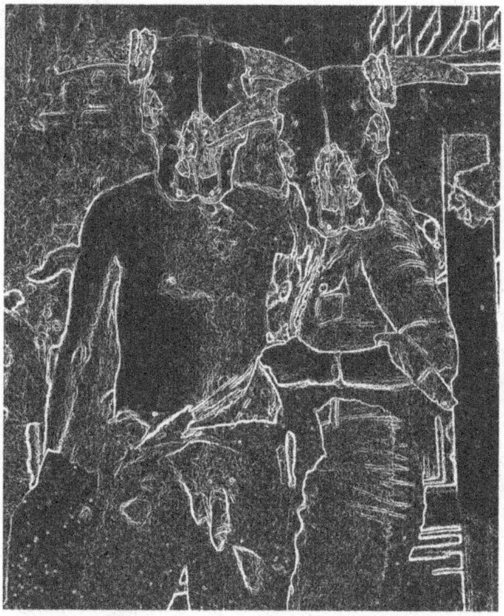

images: GobQ/T. Warburton y Bajo/Sabrina Canfield

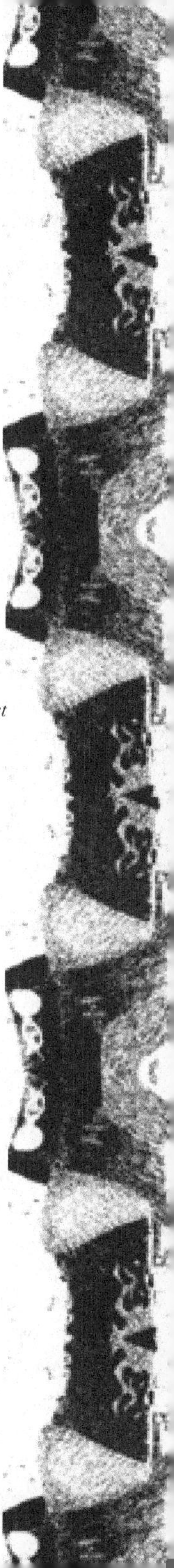

TIT/ TITTY, TITS/ TITTIES, BOOBS (& VARIATIONS) 馒头

AFRIKAANS tiete *;
Boude swaii en tiete skud! [3]
ALBANIAN cica **
ARABIC, LIBY./MOROC. bzazil *;
biz **
ARMENIAN yster *;
metz dzi-zik [2]
BASQUE ditiak **
BELARUSIAN / MACEDONIAN цички/cički *
BENGALI nimāi [4]
BOSNIAN / CROATIAN / SLOVENIAN / SERBIAN
sise *; сисе / sise *
BULGARIAN ци ци / tsi tsi
CANTONESE yúfohng **;
yùh dáan *
CATALAN mamelles *;
melons **
CZECH kozy *
DANISH babser *;
patter *;
store jader [5]
FINNISH tissit *;
nännipihan portsari [6]
FRENCH nénés *;
blobos **
GAELIC, IRISH cíocha *
GAELIC, SCOTS cìochan *
GERMAN Chürbis *;
Kiste, die *;
Hängentitten, die [7]
GREEK, MOD. μαστος / mastos *
HINDI pēshtan *
HUNGARIAN mell [8]
ICELANDIC brjost *;
INDONESIAN toket besar [9]
ITALIAN tette *;
cioccie [10]
JAPANESE オッパイ oppai *
KANNADA dhodda molay [2]
KHMER dahh *
LATIN mammas *
LATVIAN krutis *
MACEDONIAN цички вода / cički voda [12]
MALAYU ne´nen **;
tetek menglebeh [2]
MALTESE zejza *
MANDARIN 咪咪 mīmī [13];
馒头 mántóu [14]
NAUATL elchiquihuih **
NEPALI dudu *
NORWEGIAN pupper *;
brystpuler [15]
POLISH cycki *;
balony **
PORTUGUESE melharucos *
QUECHUA ñuñu *
ROMANIAN balcoane **
RUSSIAN сиски / siski *;
грудь / grud' *;
Мне нравится твоя прекрасная грудь! / Mnye nravitsya tvoya prekrasnaya grud'! [17]
SPANISH las tetas *;
chichis [2];
Haceme una cubanita. [15]
SWAHILI matiti **
SWEDISH pattar *
TAGALOG bámpers *;
kóplang *
TELEGU bāyilu *;
rommulu *
THAI òape [8]
TURKISH göğüs
UKRAINIAN cici /sisi *
URDU chhāti *;
dōdh *
UZBEK кòóкраклар /kòókraklar *
VIETNAMESE vú *
WELSH Bronnau fel bryniau Eryri. [17]
YORUBA abigèlaiya [2]
ZAPOTEC ca xidxi *
ZULU amabele *

* *tits/titties;* ** *boobs;*

2 *big tits/boobs;*
3 *"Swing yr ass/arse & shake yr tits!"*
4 *girl w./tiny tits;*
5 *"big jades";*
6 *nipple yard porter;*
7 *droopy tits;*
8 *tit/titty;*
9 *big titty;*
10 *"drops," tits;*
11 *"Spanish thing," titty-fuck/"Dutch fuck."*
12 *titty water;*
13 *"meow-meows";*
14 *"steamed buns";*
15 *titty-fuck; SPANISH: "Titty fuck me!"*
16 *"I like yr gorgeous boobs/tits!"*
17 *"Tits like the mtns. of Snowdon."*

TIT / TITTY FUCK (& VARIATIONS)

GERMAN Busengrapscher *
ITALIAN Spagnola **
SPANISH Hacer una cubana **
TAGALOG butingíng [2]

* *tit-grope;*
** *tit-fuck; SPANISH: "Titty fuck me!"*
2 *tit foreplay.*

TIT / TITTY, SUCK (& VARIATIONS) 哈咪咪

BENGALI Tor mar shāţi buni. [2] ; bānchosh [3]
CATALAN llepar els mongrons [4]
DANISH patte bryst *
GAELIC, SCOTS imlich sine [5]
JAPANESE オッパイをなめる oppai wo nameru [6]
MALAYU Hisap ne-nen saya. [5]
MANDARIN 哈咪咪 hā mīmī *
QUECHUA / BOLIV. ñuñuchiy *
ROMANIAN Suge-mi ai bacloane. [5]
RUSSIAN Мне нравитсяцеловать твою вкусный грудь. / Mnye nravitsya tselovat' tvoyu vkusniy grud'. [7]
SPANISH Chupa las tetas de tu puta madre. [8]

* *"suck tit/titty";*
2 *"Yr mother has 7 tits";*
3 *"nipple sucker";*
4 *"licking nipples";*
5 *"Suck my tits";*
6 *"lick tits";*
7 *"I like kissing yr delicious tits."*
8 *"Go suck on yr whore mother's tits."*

image: GobQ/N. Lehn

TWO-FACED, HYPOCRITE (& VARIATIONS) здразнітскі

AFRIKAANS vals [2]
ALBANIAN tradhtár [4]
ARABIC dhū wajhayn * ; muzawwir [3]
ARMENIAN tirz´um [4]
BASQUE gezurrezko [5] ; ausikilari [6]
BELARUSIAN здразнітскі / zdraznitski [4]
BENGALI jāliyat [6]
BOSNIAN izdajnički [4]
CANTONESE ngaihgwanjí **
CATALAN deslleial [4]
CROATIAN dvoličan *
CZECH pokrytek *; pomlouvat [7]
DANISH falsk *
DUTCH matennaaier [8]
ESTONIAN silmakirjalikkus *
FARSI do'ru *
FINNISH haukkuminen [6]
FRENCH faux *(m)* / fausse *(f)* *
FRENCH (VERLAN) seuf *
GAELIC, IRISH Tadhg an dá thaobh *
GAELIC, SCOTS leam-leat *
GERMAN doppelzüngig * ; Falsch *
GREEK, MOD. ενας επιθιχιας / enas epithixias [3]
HAUSA mai fuska biyu *
HEBREW doo partsoofee *
HINDI kamina [9]
HUNGARIAN alattomos kutya [10] ; alattomos kurva [10]
ICELANDIC undirförull *
INDONESIAN keliru [5]
ITALIAN falso [5]; doppio [12]
JAPANESE はっぽ美人 happo-bijin *
KOREAN sŏng-ŭi ŏp-nŭn *
LATIN bilinguisis / bilinguise *; malis animus [13]
LATVIAN liekulis *
LITHUANIAN gyvate *
MACEDONIAN издајник / izdajnik [15]
MALAYU bermuka muka
MALTESE falz [5]
MANDARIN 伪君子 wěijūnzǐ *
MARATHI bakadhyani [17]
NAHUATL moyectocani *
NORWEGIAN uopriktig *
POLISH obł'udnik *
PORTUGUESE dois-enfrentaram *
ROMANIAN trădător [4]
RUSSIAN гадука / gaduka [14]
SERBIAN дволичан / dvoličan *
SOMALI bēn [5]
SOTHO, N boradia [4]; ekago [4]
SPANISH de dos caras * ; falsa [5]
SWAHILI a'hila [18]
SWEDISH falsk [5]
TAGALOG balimbíng [19]
TELEGU rudrāk´sapilli **
THAI bpàak yàang jai yàang *
TURKISH ikiyüzlü *
UKRAINIAN зрадник / zradnyk [15]
URDU kamina [9]
UZBEK хавф-хатарли / khavf-khatarli [4]
WELSH dauwynebog *
YIDDISH tsvee´us *
YORUBA sehin sohun [20]
ZAPOTEC deche ná´ [18]
ZULU -mbalambili *

* *two-faced, hypocrite;*
** *hypocrite;*
2 *forked-tongue/two-faced;*
3 *phony/poseur;*
4 *treacherous;*
5 *false/insincere;*
6 *two-face back-biter;*
7 *back-bite;*
8 *backstabbing buddy-fucker-underer;*
9 *vicious/undependable;*
10 *backstabbing dog;*
11 *back-stabbing bitch;*
12 *double-dealing/double-faced;*
13 *malicious agendas;*

14 *snake-in-the-grass, serpent;*
15 *traitor;*
16 *false smiles;*
17 *sanctimonious fraud, pious ass/arsehole;*
18 *underhanded, back-handed;*
19 *five-faced hypocrite;*
20 *double-dealer.*

illustr., © 2008, Graham Willoughby

吐く

VENEREAL & SEXUALLY TRANSMITTED DISSEASES (VD & STD), AIDS / HIV, HERPES, CLAP, GONORRHEA, SYPHILIS, HEPATITIS, (& VARIATIONS)

СИДА

AFRIKAANS Auntie Aida *;
Auntie Aida-hoer [2];
sifilis **;
druiper [3];
geslagsiekte [9]
ALBANIAN / BOSNIAN / CATALAN / FRENCH / PORTUGUESE SIDA *
ALBANIAN sifulíz **;
gonorre [3]
zoster [6]; sëmundje venriane [9]
ARABIC a'ra-d naqsi 'l-mana-'ati 'l-muktasaba *;
zuh'ri **;
marađ tanâsúlî [9]
ARMENIAN frangakhd **;
BASQUE HIES / SIDA *;
frantzeseri **;
hazijario [3];
gibeleko [8]
BENGALI ayds *
BOSNIAN spolna bolest [9]
BULGARIAN СПИН / SPIN *
CANTONESE oijì behng *;
mùihduhk **
CROATIAN / SERBIAN SIDA *;
СИДА / SIDA *;
sifilis **;
сифилис / sifilis **;
gonoreja [3];
гонореја / gonoreja [3];
spolna bolesta [9];
сполна болеста / spolna bolesta [9]

CZECH / DUTCH / ESTONIAN / FINNISH / GERMAN / HUNGARIAN / ITALIAN AIDS *
CZECH lišej [6]
DANISH leverbetændelse [8];
kønssygdom [9]
DUTCH sifilis **;
heroine-AIDS-hoer [2];
gonorroe [3];
soa [6];
de leveronsteking [8]
ESTONIAN süüfilis **
FARSI eydz *
FINNISH typurri ** ;
immuunikato [4];
herpesperse [6];
sukopuolitautiperse [7]
FRENCH la chaude-pisse [5];
l'herpès [6];
l'hépatite [8];
maladie vénérienne [9]
GAELIC, IRISH SEIF / siondróm easpa imdhíonachta faighte *;
VEID / víreas easpa imdhíonachta daonna * ;
sifilis *;
GERMAN Tripper [3];
Geschlechtskrankheit [9]
GREEK, MOD. (το) ΑΙΔΣ / (to) AIDS ** ;
σύψιλη / sípsili **
HAUSA tsīdấ *;
tunjere **;
ciwon sanyé [3]
HEBREW agévet ** ;
hepatéetees [8]
HINDI / URDU bīmārī air havā *
HUNGARIAN nemi betegség [9]
ICELANDIC sárasótt **;
lekandi [3];
ábláster [6];
lifrarbólga [8];
kynsjúkdómer [9]
INDONESIAN radang hati [8];
penyakit kelamin [9]
ITALIAN la sifilide **;
sieropositivo [4];
lo scolo [5];
JAPANESE エイズ / eizu *;
梅毒 / baidoku **;
性病 / seibyo [9]
KHMER ayd / sída *;
roak swai **;
roak ra-lèe-uk t'larm [8];
gàam-ma-roak [9]
KOREAN mae-dok **
MALAYU siflis **;
penyakit perempuan / sakit kencing nanah [3]
MALTESE marda venerea [9]
NORWEGIAN kjønnssykdom [9]
PORTUGUESE sifilis **;
gonorréia [3];
uma doec a venérea [11]
ROMANIAN gonoree [3];
malerie [6]
RUSSIAN сифилитик / sifilitik **;
триппер / tripper [3]
венерик / venerik *(m)* / веперичка / venerička *(f)* [10]
SOMALI aydis *;
joonis [8]
SOTHO, N thosola ** ;
tsshipi [3]
SPANISH sifilis **;
meado de la araña [5];
enfermendades venereas [9]
SWAHILI ukimwi *
SWEDISH syfilitisk **;
gonorré [3];
HIV-smittad [4]
TAGALOG sakít sa batae **;
tulò / tulas [3];
sakít sa atáy [8];
THAI rôhk èd *
TURKISH frengi **
UZBEK СПИД / SPID *;
таносил касаллиги / tanosil kasalligi [9];
сариқ касалсиз / sariq kasalsiz [8]
VIETNAMESE bêhn SIĐA *;

WELSH clefyd gwenerol **; llid yr afu [8]
ZULU isifo sebuba **; isipatsholo [3]

*	*AIDS (aquired immuno-defficiency syndrome) / HIV (human immuno-deficiency virus);*
**	*syphilis; RUSSIAN, SWEDISH: "syphilitic";*
2	*AFRIKAANS: "AIDS-whore"; DUTCH: "heroin-AIDS-whore";*
3	*"clap" = gonorrhea;*
4	*HIV-positive, carrying the AIDS virus; SWEDISH: HIV-infected;*
5	*" hot piss" = clap/gonorrhea; SPANISH: "spider's piss" = VD;*
6	*herpes; FINNISH: "Herpes ass/arse";*
7	*'clap-ass/arse" = gonorrhea-ass/arse;*
8	*hepatitis;*
9	*VD;*
10	*"infected with some venereal disease or other";*
11	*"a* [venereal] *dose."*

κανο
εμετο

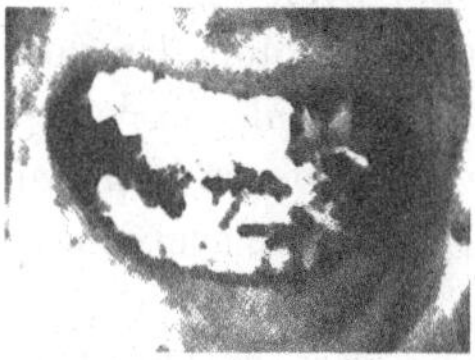

GobQ/M. Clark

VOMIT, SPEW, PUKE, THROW UP
(& VARIATIONS)

κανο
εμετο

AFRIKAANS opgooi *; braak *
ALBANIAN vjéll *
ARABIC qay´ *
ARMENIAN pisk'hel *
BASQUE goitika *
BENGALI ga guliye otha *
BOSNIAN povračati *
CANTONESE ngáutoumaht *
CATALAN també *
CREOLE/HAITIAN vomi *
CROATIAN povraćanje *
CZECH blití **; zvracení **
DANISH Tale i den store telefon. [2]; bræk *
DUTCH Ga kots drinken braksel. [2]
ESTONIAN oskendama *
FARSI bâlâ âvardan *
FINNISH oskentaa *
FRENCH gerber *; J´ai envie de te vomir dessus. [4]
VERLAN béger *
GAELIC, IRISH aisig ; Go n-aiseaga tú. [5]
GAELIC, SCOTS dìobhair *
GERMAN / SW. Ä pizza leggä. [6]; Muäsch chiisä? [7]
GREEK, MOD. κανο εμετο / kano emeto *
HAUSA amai *
HEBREW kee *
HINDI / URDUI ulṯi ānā *
HUNGARIAN (ki) hányi *
ICELANDIC æla * ; kasta upp [8]
INDONESIAN / MALAYU muntah *
ITALIAN vomito *
JAPANESE 吐く / haku *
LATVIAN unjavēmeklis *
LITHUANIAN vem´ti *

MALTESE (i)rrimetta *
MANDARIN 呕吐物 ǒutùwù *;
呕吐 ǒutù **
MARATHI ugdira<u>n</u>a *
NAHUATL tlahtoltecpantli **
NEPALI bāntā āyeko *
NORWEGIAN oppkast *;
kaste opp **
POLISH wymiotowac´
PORTUGUESE adjoelhando-se no santuário da porcelana [9]
QUECHUA Millanayawshanmi. [10]
ROMANIAN Vŏrasc in pizda lu mata. [10]
RUSSIAN травить. / travit´ [12];
Поехать в ригу. / Poekhat´ v rigu. [13]
SERBIAN повратити / povratiti **
SLOVENIAN Bruhal/bruhala sem. [14]
SOTHO, N mahlatša / hlatša *
SPANISH Estaban cantando huácala. [15];
Me puse verde. [16];
vuitrear; [17]
Se me/Se te vino el gato. [18]
SWAHILI matapiko *
SWEDISH bilåk/bilsjuk [19]
TAGALOG magsuká *;
magbugá *;
suka *
THAI ôo´ak *;
mow rót [19]
TURKISH kusma *;
kusmak **
UKRAINIAN блювати / bliuvaty *
UZBEK Қьусяпма/ Q´usyapma. [14]
VIETNAMESE phun ra *;
nôn *
WELSH chwydu *
YIDDISH varf *
YORUBA eebì **
ZAPOTEC rusidxi ɓa *
ZULU hlanza *

* *vomit;*
** *puke;*
2 *"Talk into the big phone";*
3 *"Go drink vomit";*
4 *"I'd like to vomit on you";*
5 *"I hope you vomit";*
6 *"Spew a pizza";*
7 *"Are you gonna throw up?"*
8 *"throw up";*
9 *"praying at the porcelain sanctuary";*
10 *"I feel like throwing up;*
11 *"I vomit on yr mother's cunt";*
12 *"lose yr lunch";*
13 *"going to Riga."*
14 *"I've been vomiting/throwing up";*
15 *"They were singing the barf song." /Mex. dial.;*
16 *"I turned green in the gills." /Mex.;*
17 *"barf like a vulture" /Peruv. dial.;*
18 *"I/You spewed like a cat." /Peruv.;*
19 *"car-sick."*

WATER SPORTS / GOLDEN SHOWERS / PISS-DRINKING (& VARIATIONS)

ВОДНИ спортове

AFRIKAANS gulde reënbui **
BULGARIAN водни спортове / vodni sportpveh **
CATALAN pluja daurada *
DANISH Toiletsex [3]
CROATIAN / SERB Napij mi se pišaline. [6];
Напиј ми се пишалине. / Napij mi se pišaline. [6]
ICELANDIC drekkur hland [4]
JAPANESE 尿を飲むヤツ nyō wo nomu yatsu [5]
SPANISH deportes acuáticos [7]
THAI chèe rót gan *

* *water sports/piss-drinking;*
** *"golden shower," giving/receiving thereof;*
2 *"piss-play";*
3 *"toilet-sex—any kinks";*
4 *"piss-drinking";*
5 *"piss-drinking dude";*
6 *"Drink my piss;"*
7 *"aquatic sports."*

WANK/ WANKER, JERK-OFF (& VARIATIONS) ηρογλικανο

AFRIKAANS manda *;
trek draad *;
sirkelnaii [2];
afskud [3];
ARABIC/TUNIS. booneeta *;
khart´Aa *;
BELARUSIAN драчзйцца/dračzycca *;
драчзйць/dračzyc´ **
BULGARIAN чекиа/chekia *;
чекидя/chekidja **;
ташак/tashak [4]
CANTONESE dáa fēi gēi [5]
CATALAN cascar-se-la [6];
palla mental [7];
pelar el plàtan [8];
els cincs fantastics contra el calvo [9]
CROATIAN/SERB drkadzijo [10];
дркадзијо/drkadzijo [10]
CZECH zmrd **;
honit ptáka [11]
DANISH Dogme-sex *;
pikspiller **;
Rive den af [6]
DUTCH rukker **
FARSI jaghul **
FINNISH runkata *;
runkkari **;
nukkepösky [12]
FRENCH branlette *;
branlage *;
coquin
de garce **;
branleur **;
se polir le chinois [13];
veuve [14]
GAELIC, IRISH láimh milis [15]
GAELIC, SCOTS brod *
GERMAN herunterholen *;
wischen [16]
GREEK, MOD. Μαλάκα!/Maláka! **;
ηρογλικανο/heroglikano [15]
GUJARATI muthia **
HINDI/URDU jaraqna *;
mu´t´th mārna *;
Apna hāth jagannath [15]
HINDI hast maithun [17]
ICELANDIC sjálfsfróun **;
fróa sér **;
rúnka sér **;
rúnkari **;
Runkadu ter! [18]
ITALIAN farsi una sega *;
farsi una pipa *;
Vati a fare una pipa! [19];
morto di seghi [20];
il segiolo [21];
toccarsi [22]
JAPANESE 千ずり senzuri [23]
KOREAN ta-ta-ri *
LATIN frico/fricare/fricui/frictum/fricatum *;
ire *;
ivi *;
itum *;
percieo *;
tero/terere/trivi/tritum *;
tracto/tractare *
LATVIAN Onaanists *
LITHUANIAN smachink *
MACEDONIAN дркајија/drkajija **
MALAYU melo´kok *;
MANDARIN 自慰 zì wèi *;
打手枪 dǎ shǎu qiāng [24];
打飛幾 dǎ fēijī [5]
NAHUATL matoca *
NORWEGIAN ronk *;
nappe løken [25];
Dra degi kugen. [26]
POLISH cisnąć se bulbe *;
walić końia [27];
walić niemiec [28]
PORTUGUESE bater uma punheta *;
punheteiro **

ROMANIAN a face laba *;
labagiu **
RUSSIAN дрочить / dročít´ **;
наяривать / nayárivat’ [29];
ебать в сухую / ebát v suxúju [30]
SOTHO, N shaya marete *
SPANISH hacerse la paja *;
gillipollas **;
pajiera **;
pelando el plátano [8];
Vete a jalar el pescuezo al pollo! [31]
SWAHILI punyeto **
SWEDISH runka *;
miffo **;
mongo **;
TAGALOG salsal *;
bionic *;
jakolero **
THAI chak jòo làa *;
chak wàao [32]
TURKISH patlıçanı okşamak *
UZBEK капак уриш / kapak urish *
VIETNAMESE su thu dam *
WELSH hiliwr *;
Y haliwr! **

* *"wank/jerk-off";*
** *"wanker!";*
2 *"circle wank/circle jerk";*
3 *"shake it off";*
4 *"one-bollock-wanker";*
5 *"do a jet plane" / "Hit the jet plane";*
6 *"bruise it" / "tear it off";*
7 *"mental wank";*
8 *"peel the banana";*
9 *"The Fantastic 5 vs. the Bald One";*
10 *"super wanker";*
11 *"chase the bird";*
12 *"puppet pants";*
13 *"polish the Chinaman;*
14 *"widow"—widowed dick/cock;*
15 *"sweet hand" / "My own sweet hand.";*
16 *"polishing";*
17 *"self-fucking;"*
18 *"Go wank!"*
19 *"Smoke a pipe."*
20 *"dead from sawing;"*
21 *"saw vendor"*
22 *"touch yourself/touching yrself;"*
23 *"thousand rubs";*
24 *"shoot a gun";*
25 *"pull the onion";*
26 *"pull on yr dick/cock/prick";*
27 *"batter the horse";*
28 *"batter a German;"*
29 *"strum";*
30 *"dry fuck";*
31 *"Go wring the chicken's neck/choke the chicken!"*
32 *"kite flying."*

ебать в
сухую

WANK, CLIT / CLIT RUB, SEE: CLIT, CLITORIS

WHORE, PROSTITUTE (& VARIATIONS) курва

AFRIKAANS hoer *
ALBANIAN kurve *
ARABIC / MALTESE qahba *
ARMENIAN agarka *;
poz **
BASQUE urdanga *
BELARUSIAN блиадз / bliadz **
BENGALI bārbodhu *
BOSNIAN / CROATIAN / HUNGARIAN kurva *
BULGARIAN мастия / mastiya **
BURMESE pathema *
CANTONESE gūng chi [3]
CATALAN bagassa *;
barjaula *
CHABACANO hostes **;
yede hostes [4]
CREOLE/MAURIT. sakal *
CZECH flandra [2];
děvka [2]
DANISH skøge *;
din omvandrende madras [5]
DUTCH stoephoer [6];
kankerhoer! / teringhoer! [7]
ESTONIAN hoor *
FARSI g´ar [2]
FINNISH portto *;
huora *
FRENCH conasse *;
putaine **;
morue / maquereau [8]
FRENCH (VERLAN) tassepé **
GAELIC, IRISH striapach *
GAELIC, SCOTS strìopach *
GERMAN Nutte, die *;
Strichmädchen [6];
Gertrud [2]
GREEK, MOD. μια πορνι / mia porni
GUJARATI maggi *
HAUSA karuwa *
HEBREW zonah *;
HINDI / KANNADA / NEPALI / URDU rāndi *
ICELANDIC Kanamella! [9];
hóra *
INDONESIAN sundel *;
lonte [10]
ITALIAN puttana *;
troia *;
battona [6]
JAPANESE 女郎 jorō *;
援助交際 enjo kōsai [11]
KAZAKH блиадч / bliad' [2]
KHMER s'rai som-peung *
KOREAN net ssang nyon [12];
shipcenchi *
LATIN meretrix *;
lupa **
LATVIAN mauka *
LITHUANIAN kekshe *
MACEDONIAN / SERBIAN курва /kurva *
MALAYU jalang *;
kupu-kupu malam [13]
MANDARIN 妓女 jì nü *
MARATHI sadharanastri [6];
murali [14]
MONGOLIAN яаньан / yanhan [2];
ваник / vanik [2]
NAHUATL cihuacuecuech *
NORWEGIAN hore *
POLISH kurwa *;
pizda [15]
PORTUGUESE puta *;
fazer a vida
POLISH kurwa *;
pizda [15]
PORTUGUESE puta *
ROMANIAN rapandula *;
curvă **
RUSSIAN курва / kúrva *;
потаскуха / potaskúxa [6];
блядь / blyád´ **
SINHALA patta vesie *
SLOVENIAN kurba *;
kuzla *
SOTHO, N sefebe *
SPANISH puta *;

pingona *;
la caída [17]
SWAHILI malaya *
SWEDISH gatflicka [6];
hora *
TAGALOG álpine *;
dónut *;
magdalena *
TAMIL varsai *
THAI ée dtwàa *;
ée dàawak *
TURKISH orospu *;
kahpe *;
fahişe *
UKRAINIAN шлюха / šl'ukha *
UZBEK тоток / totoq *;
jalab [2];
g´ar *
VIETNAMESE gái diểm *;
con dĩ *
WELSH hwren *
YIDDISH nafkeh [2]
YORUBA ajá *
YAQUI / YEOME antuari [2]
ZULU sifebe *

* *whore, prostitute;*
** *whore/bitch;*
2 *whore/slut;*
3 *"public toilet";*
4 *filthy whore/bitch;*
5 *"field mattress";*
6 *pavement-pounding street walker, on a mission from Dale Carnagie; PORT/BRZ.: "On the street"/ "Street life," as a whore as opposed to homeless;*
7 *cancer-whore/T.B.-whore;*
8 *"codfish"/ "mackerel," skanky whore;*
9 *"Yankee whore!"*
10 *Arabic whore;*
11 *teenyboppers turning tricks for extra cash;*
12 *internet whore/slut;*
13 *"fly-by-night whore";*
14 *temple whore;*
15 *whore, cunt;*
16 *"The Fallen One."*

WHORE, MALE / GIGOLO, HUSTLER (& VARIATIONS) ЖИГОЛО

AFRIKAANS Rita **;
Wandie [2]
ALBANIAN horr [3]
BOSNIAN / CROATIAN muška kurva *
BULGARIAN жиголо / jigolo *
CANTONESE kai daih *
CATALAN gigoló *
DANISH trækkerdreng *
DUTCH spermaslet [4]
FARSI zhigul *
FINNISH huoripukki [6]
FRENCH putain *
GERMAN / ITALIAN gigolo *
GREEK, MOD. πυσταρα / pustara *;
δαμδελαρή /damdelarí [7];
τεκνό / teknó [8];
κλούβα / kloúva [9]
HINDI / URDU randhwa [6]
HUNGARIAN buzikurva [3]
ICELANDIC karlhóra *;
fagamella **
JAPANESE ヤリチン yarichin *
MACEDONIAN курариште / kurvarishte *
MANDARIN 颜色狼 yánsè láng *
MARATHI ganda *
NEPALI randó *
PORTUGUESE puto *
ROMANIAN curvar *
SERBIAN мушка курва / muška kurva *
SPANISH chapero **;
puto **
SWAHILI laghai *
SWEDISH horbög **
TAGALOG kálban [6]

TURKISH tokmakçi *
UZBEK бачча / bachcha [5]
YORUBA asewo okùnrin *

* *gigolo, male whore, hustler;*
** *exclusively gay male prost.;*
2 *transvestite street walker;*
3 *male whore/scumbag fag pervert;*
4 *"sperm whore," male prost.;*
5 *"Dancing Boys";*
6 *rent boy, gay hustler;*
7 *"Dame de la rue;"*
8 *"Chicken," young gay male whore;*
9 *"paddy wagon," gay street hustler;*

WHORE, CRACK/ JUNK WHORE/ METH WHORE (& VARIATIONS) ポン中女郎

ALBANIAN kokaín kurve *
DANISH crackluder *; narkoludder **
DUTCH heroinehoer **
ICELANDIC krakkmella *(m)* / krakkhóra *(f)* *
JAPANESE ポン中 女郎 ponchū jorō [2]
SPANISH puto de llelo *(m)* / puta de llelo *(f)* **
SWEDISH kokain hora *

* *Coke/crack whore;*
** *junk/heroin whore;*
2 *meth whore.*

WHOREHOUSE, CAT HOUSE, BORDELLO (& VARIATIONS) бардакъ

ARABIC / TUNIS. bordeen **
BASQUE putexte **
BULGARIAN бардак / bardak *
FARSI fohishaxona *
GERMAN Puff, das *
NAHUATL netzinnamacoyan *
PORTUGUESE / BRAZ. puteiro *; zona [2]
ROMANIAN bordel **
RUSSIAN бардакъ / bardak´ *; заведение / zavedénie *
SPANISH Una casa de idolatría [3]; Una ramería *; Una casa libertina [4]
SWAHILI danguro *
THAI sàawng *
YIDDISH shandhoiz *

* *whorehouse;*
** *bordello;*
2 *whorehouse district;*
3 *"House of Idolatry";*
4 *"House of Libertines."*

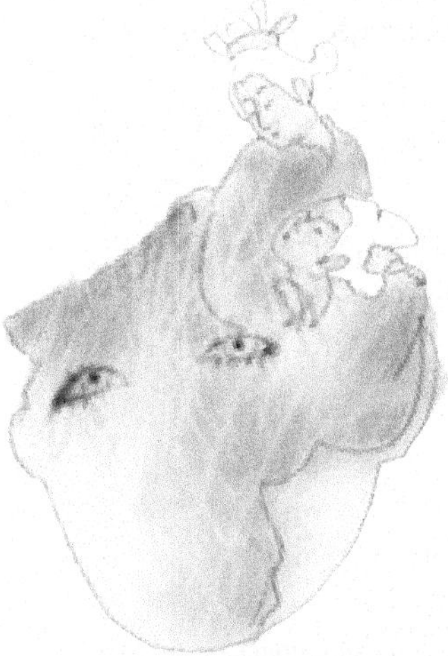

illustr., © 2008, Graham Willoughby

image: GobQ/Jaden Lowrey

XXX (TRIPLE-X): KINK, PORN, SEX TOYS (& VARIATIONS)

エロ・ビデ

AFRIKAANS ontkleedanser [4]; wendy bangles [17]
BASQUE ikuskaseta hirukoiztu-x **
CANTONESE hàahm pín **; gwāt chèung [18]
CATALAN cartelera turia **; consolador [12]; nina inflable *(f)* [13]; nino infable *(m)* [13]; boes xineses [15]; joguines sexuals [16]
CROATIAN / SERB vibratorom [12]; вибратором / vibratorom [12]
CZECH rukapouta [18]
DANISH nøgendanser [4]
FINNISH strippari [4] **; transvestiittishow [24]
FRENCH film porno *; strip-teaseuse *(f)* [4]; dessous sexy [11]; menottes [17]; gode [12]
GAELIC, IRISH porna [9]
GERMAN Stripteasetänzeren [4]
GREEK, MOD. ατριπτιςές / atripisés [4]
ICELANDIC fatafella [4]; nektardans [2]; klám hunder [6]; símasex [7]; gervi-getnaðarlimur [12]
ITALIAN per adulti *; pornazzo **; splog-larellista [4]; pedo-porno [10]; fallo [12]
JAPANESE エロ・ビデ ero-bide **; エロ・マンガ ero-manga [20]; エロ本 ero-hon [21]; エロ電 ero-den [22]; エロ・チカ ero-chika [23]
KOREAN net babariman [5]
MARATHI vāvācī maśī [14]
MANDARIN 脱衣舞表演者 tuōyīwǔ biǎoyǎnzhě [4]
NORWEGIAN stripteasedanserine [4]
RUSSIAN участница стриптиза / učástntsa striptíza [5]
SPANISH triple equís *; sexo en vivo [3]; coge burra [19]
SWEDISH penisattrapp [11]
TAGALOG tòro-tóro [3]
TURKISH striptiz *
VIETNAMESE thoát-y-vũ [5]; dâm-thư [9]

* *xxx-rated-film or magazine, Adults Only;*
** *xxx-rated video; or xxx-rated video store section;*
2 *strip show;*
3 *live sex show;*
4 *stripper;*
5 *strip-tease;*
6 *internet kink-pervert;*
7 *"Porno-Dog";*
8 *phone sex;*
9 *porn/porno;*
10 *child porn;*
11 *sexy/kinky underwear;*
12 *dildo/vibrator;*
13 *inflatable female or male sex doll;*
14 *"Spanish fly," old-school roofie & chardonnay & chronic & E, all rolled into one;*
15 *Chinese balls;*
16 *sex toys, generally;*
17 *handcuffs;*
18 *"massage parlour";*
19 *donkey fucker in live sex shows;*
20 *porno comic book,*
21 *dirty book;*
22 *900-number = phone sex;*
23 *pervo-geek/nerd;*
24 *live drag show; drag review.*

YUPPIE / SNOB (& VARIATIONS) олифта

AFRIKAANS zchwah [2]
ARABIC naffāj / naffūn **
ARMENIAN hampag **
BASQUE pertsona harroputz *(m)* / pertsona harroputza *(m)* **
CANTONESE gōu dau yàhn **
CATALAN Piho/Piha de merda. [3]
CROATIAN minker *; kurčić u odijelu [4]
CZECH japi *; nadutek **
DANISH højrøvet [9]
DUTCH verwaand [9]
FARSI motakabber [6]
FINNISH hienostelija **
FRENCH Bon-chic-bon-genre [5]
GAELIC, IRISH ardnósach [6]
GERMAN amtlich propper [16]
GREEK, MOD. (ο)σνομπ / (o) snomp **
HAUSA mài hūrà hancì **
HEBREW shakhtsan **
HINDI / URDU naye fashan kā [2]
ICELANDIC uppi *
ITALIAN yuppyie *
JAPANESE ヤッピー yappī *
LATIN fastidiosus **
MALAYU sombong **
MANDARIN 势利小人 shìlì xiǎorén **
NORWEGIAN nymotens [2]
POLISH pracoholik [8]; robotnik [8]
PORTUGUESE yuppy *; esnobe **
RUSSIAN хиппеоисие / hippeoisie **
SERBIAN шик / šik [10]
SOTHO, N kgwara *
SPANISH ¡Pinchí fresa! [11]; ¡Fresa maricón! [13]
SWAHILI mwanzisha mtindo [2]
SWEDISH Jävlayuppie! [11]; Jäkla-yuppie! [12]
TAGALOG postúra *; kuátroshi [14]
TURKISH üsluba uygun *
UKRAINIAN сноб / snob **
UZBEK олифта / olifta [6]; бой-бачча / boy-bachcha [7]
VIETNAMESE nguò'i dua dòl **
WELSH crachfonheddwr / crachach *(pl.)* **
YAQUI / YEOME havele [6]
YORUBA òlajú **
ZULU isinothongana **

* *yuppie;*
** *snob;*
2 *upmarket, elegant, trendy;*
3 *shitty yuppie;*
4 *prick/dick in a suit;*
5 *trendy brand-name addled yuppie shit head;*
6 *showy, snobbish & pretentious;*
7 *spoiled brat of rich snobbish shits;*
8 *workaholic yuppie;*
9 *snooty;*
10 *chic;*
11 *Fucking yuppie!*
12 *Goddamned Yuppie!*
13 *Faggot Yuppie!*
14 *Trez-plus-un(e)-chic;*
15 *city-slicker;*
16 *cool/groovy/hip.*

ヤッピー

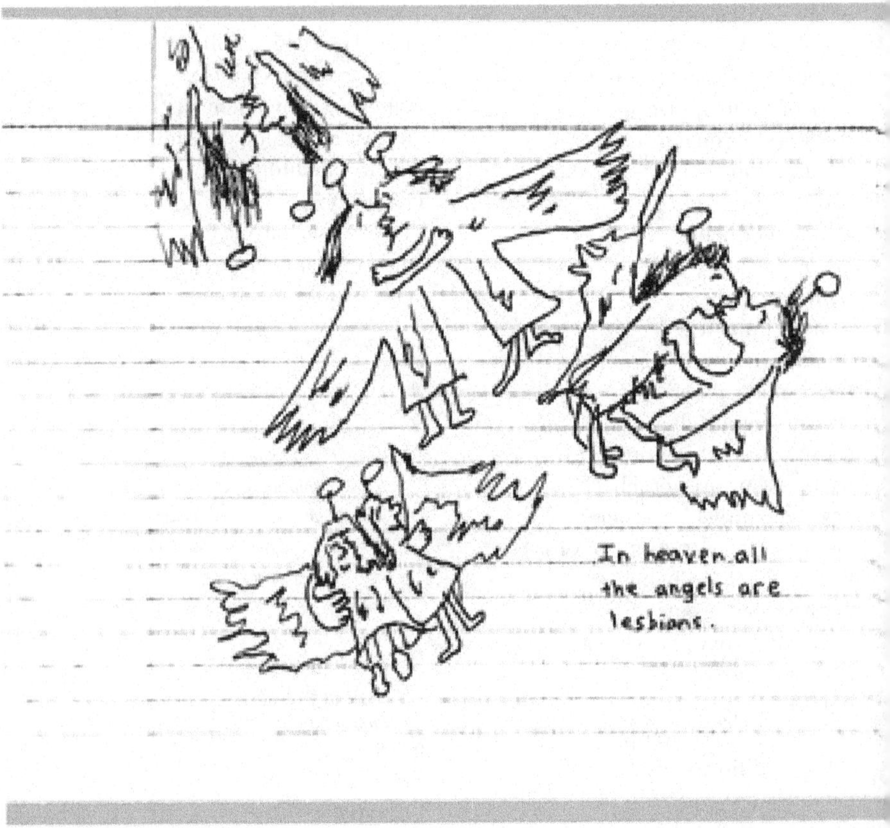
In heaven all
the angels are
lesbians.

Liz Swados

II.)

PHRASES

& a few words...

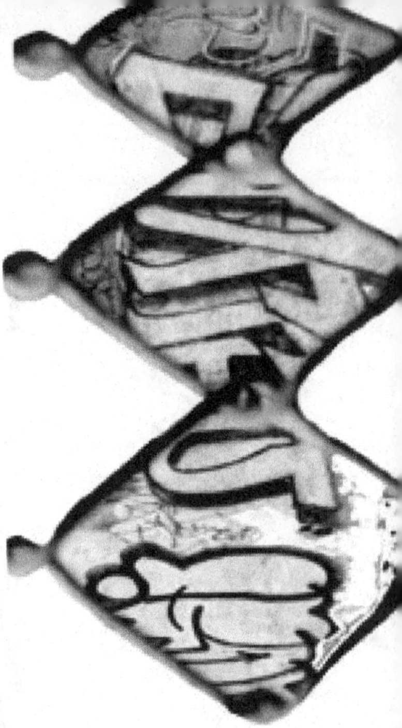

BASTARDS & S.O.B.'S, BORN, SELF-MADE, & OTHERWISE
(& VARIATIONS)

AFRIKAANS So'n helsem! [3]
AFRIKAANS Die poes! [4]
AFRIKAANS Jou bliksem! [5]
ARABIC, EGYPT. Yabn el zanya. [6]
BASQUE Sasiko! *
BASQUE Putakume! /Putasemea! [2]
BENGALI Kutar baicha haramjada botla! [7]
CANTONESE Pūk gāai fo. *
CATALAN Fill de truja! [8]
CROATIAN / SERBIAN Kurvin sine! [9];
Курвин сине! / Kurvin sine! [9]
CZECH Zmrde míenec! [10]
DANISH Horeunge. [11]
DUTCH Apenkind! [12]
DUTCH Kind van dertig homo's. [13]
FARSI Mâdar jendeh! [2]
FARSI Bachchataloq! **
FINNISH Saatanan kakarat! [14]
FRENCH T'es juste un salaud. [15]
FRENCH Fils de chienne. / Fils de putain. [2]
FRENCH Tu est fils de péde et de pute. [16]
GAELIC, IRISH Bastart! *
GAELIC, IRISH Mac an bitseach! [2]
GAELIC, SCOTS Dìolain. *
GAELIC, SCOTS Mac a' bhaobh. [2]
GERMAN Drecksack [17]
GERMAN Drecksau! / Dreckskerl! [18]
GREEK, MOD. μουλε! / Moule! *
GREEK, MOD. γε τις πυτνας! / Ge tis putnas! [9]
HEBREW Tamut mamzer. [19]
HEBREW Tamut zevel. [20]
HEBREW Ben shel meelyon kalba. [21]
HINDI / URDU Kisi´ harami ki ghalti hai´tu. [22]
HINDI / URDU Sali kuta. [23]
HUNGARIAN Rohadék! *
ICELANDIC Bastarður! **
ICELANDIC Tíkarsonur. / Horu sonur. [2]

ITALIAN Stronzo di merda! [24]

ITALIAN Fill'e bagassa! [2]

JAPANESE 野郎 Yarō. *

JAPANESE アマの息子 Ama no musuko. [2]

KANNADA Hadaragittike. [9]

KOREAN Sŏ-ch'ul. *

MACEDONIAN/SERB Копиле! / Kopile! *

MALAYU Anak haram. [25]

NORWEGIAN Drittsekk! [26]

POLISH Sukinsyn! **

PORTUGUESE O seu filho de corno! [27]

PORTUGUESE O seu bastardo gordo. [7]

ROMANIAN Nelegitim. *

ROMANIAN Fiu de cătea! / Fiu de târfa! [2]

RUSSIAN говнюк. /Govnjuk. *

RUSSIAN Сволочь... / Svóloč'... [28]

SLOVENIAN Pizdonterje. *

SPANISH Cabron! [29]

SPANISH Hijo de millónes putas! [30]

SWAHILI Yehe ni mshenzi. [31]

SWEDISH Jävla idiot! [10]

TAGALOG Nampútsa! [2]

THAI Kŏw le'ou! [31]

THAI Luog'ga'rèe. [2]

TURKISH Piç! / Rezil herif! *

UZBEK Итвачча. / Itvachcha. [2]

UZBEK Занталок. / Zantaloq. **

VIETNAMESE Con tu'-sinh. *

VIETNAMESE Thằng khốn! [32]

WELSH Uffar gwirion. [33]

YIDDISH Momzer! *

* *"Bastard!" / "Bastard.";*

** *"Bastard!" / "Son of a bitch";*

2 *Son of a bitch!" / "Son of a bitch";*

3 *"What a bastard!"*

4 *"That cunt bastard!"*

5 *"You bastard!"*

6 *"Bastard son."*

7 *BENGALI: "Fat bastard!";*
PORTUGUESE: "You fat bastard!"

8 *"Son of a sow!"*

9 *"Son of a whore!"*

10 *CZECH: "You fucking bastard!";*
SWEDISH: "Fucking idiot! / Fucking bastard!";

11 *"Bastard child / Whore child.";*

12 *"Apechild! / Monkeykid!"*
13 *"Child of thirty faggots.";*
14 *"Goddamn evil bastards!"*
15 *"You're nothing more than a bastard." Québ. dial.;*
16 *"Yr father's a faggot son of a bitch."*
17 *"Dirt-bag bastard.";*
18 *"Filthy bastard swine!"*
19 *"Die, bastard."*
20 *"Die, bastard scum."*
21 *"Son of a million bitches."*
22 *"You're a blunder-fuck of some bastard."*
23 *"Stupid bastard."*
24 *"Fucking balls-for-brains-shithead bastard!"*
25 *"Rotten bastard."*
26 *"Sack-of-shit Bastard!"*
27 *"You son of a bastard!"*
28 *"Lower than duck shit..."*
29 *"Stubborn fucking bastard!"*
30 *"Son of a million bitches!" /*
"Son of a million whores!"
31 *"He's a bastard!"*
32 *"You damn bastard."*
33 *"Silly bastard."*

BITCHES
&
STITCHES
(& VARIATIONS)

AFRIKAANS Jy is 'n teef. *
AFRIKAANS Eet kak en vrek jou teef. **
AFRIKAANS Jou Joan. [2]
ALBANIAN Ti je rrotë kurve! [3]
ARABIC Sharmuta Bikwarethā. [4]
BENGALI Tor māie khanki! [5]
BENGALI Khanki magi. [6]
BENGALI Tui goru. [7]
BOSNIAN Kurvo usrana! / Drolja usrana! [8]
BOSNIAN Debela kurvo! / Debela drolja! [9]
BOSNIAN Mama ti je kurvo! / Mama ti je drolja! [5]
CANTONESE Séi baat pòh! **
CANTONESE Gwái pòh. [10]
CATALAN Puta piha de merda! [11]
CATALAN Mal karma puta. [12]
CATALAN Mecàgum la verge puta Maria. [13]
CATALAN Mecàgum la mar puta! [14]
CROATIAN / SERBIAN Kuka mama ti je domina. [15];
Кука мама ти је домина. / Kuka mama ti je domina. [15];
CROATIAN / SERBIAN Kuka patetična. [16];
Кука патетична. / Kuka patetična. [16]
CZECH Kravo zasrana! [17]
CZECH Jdi do hajzlu, kurvo! [18]
CZECH Tahni do prdele, kurvo! [19]
CZECH Vykursh mi ho, kurvo! [20]
DANISH Sut dvaergepik, din tøjte. [21]
DANISH Æd lort og dø din tøjte. **
DANISH Hippie tøjte. [22]
DANISH Lede kælling! / Lede sæk! [23]
DANISH Forpulede tøjte. [24]
DUTCH Je moet mij niet dissen, kutwijf. / Je moet mij niet dissen, trut. / Je moet mij niet dissen, kaffer. [25]
DUTCH Eet pinguin poep trut. **
DUTCH Tering-wijf! / Tering-trut! [26]
DUTCH Je moeder is een vingerwijf. [27]
DUTCH Aso trut! / Aso kaffer! [28]
FARSI Antareh gav. [7]
FINNISH Ime mun muna lutka! [29]
FRENCH Quel grogniasse! / Quel poufiasse! / Quel greluche! / Quel garce! [30]
FRENCH Quel conasse! [31]
FRENCH Quel chienne foutue. [24]

FRENCH Tu est une salope! / Tu est une grogniasse! / Tu est une poufiasse! / Tu est une greluche! / Tu est une garce! *
FRENCH T'es juste une salope. [32]
FRENCH T'est qu'une sale conasse qui se met du portable dans le cul. [33]
FRENCH (VERLAN) "Quel tassepé!" [30]
GAELIC, IRISH Tá do mháthair bitseach meisciúl. « [34]
GAELIC, IRISH Tá do mháthair caillach. [35]
GAELIC, SCOTS Tha do mhathair misgear. [34]
GERMAN Gertrud! [36]
GERMAN Bißgurrn! [37]
GREEK, MOD. Συ γαμο τι σκιλα μανα! / Su gamo ti skila mana! [38]
GREEK, MOD. μουσική πονκ σκιλα! / Monsiki pank skila! [39]
HEBREW Lech le Aza, kalba! [40]
HEBREW Lo mafhidim kalba im zain. [41]
HINDI / URDU Sali kutti! [42]
ICELANDIC Mamma þín er belja! [7]
ITALIAN Baldracca! / Zoccola! / Bagascia! / Puttana! [43]
ITALIAN Cagna! / Vacca! [7]
ITALIAN Stronza! [44]
ITALIAN Una brutta strega. [45]
ITALIAN Porca culona! [9]
ITALIAN Porca grassona! / Baldracca grassona! / Zoccola grassona! [9]
ITALIAN Cagna pigrona! / Vacca pigrona! [46]
ITALIAN Porca zoppa! / Zoccola zoppa! [47]
ITALIAN Porca nana! / Zoccola nana! [48]
ITALIAN Porca gobba! / Zoccola gobba! [49]
JAPANESE アマ Ama! [43]
KOREAN Net shibal nyon! [50]
LATIN Vacca stulta. [7]
MACEDONIAN Стока крава! / Stoka crava! [7]
MACEDONIAN Стока путана! / Stoka putana! [55]
MACEDONIAN Ти си моја крава! / Ti si moja crava. [51]
MACEDONIAN Сачма! / Sachma! [52]
MACEDONIAN Бацими го газов кучка! / Bacimi go gazov kučka. [53]
MACEDONIAN Да ти ебам бозество кучка! / Da ti ebam bozestvo kučka! [54]
MALTESE Tiegh¯ek kelba ommok. [5]
MALTESE Inbullek fuq tiegħek kelba ommok. [56]
NORWEGIAN Din påståelige jævla hore! / Din påståelige jævla tøs! [57]
NORWEGIAN Mora di er ei tøs. [5]
NORWEGIAN Nymotens tøs! [58]
NORWEGIAN Dra til helvete hespetre! [59]
NORWEGIAN falsk tøs. [60]
NORWEGIAN Kan ikke du gå og henge deg, tøs? [61]
NORWEGIAN Pukkelrygget tøs! [49]
NORWEGIAN Sutt lut og dø tós! [62]

NORWEGIAN Tøs kronidiot! 63
POLISH Matka kurwo syfilisem cie obdazyla! 64
POLISH Zrobisz mi loda, laska? 65
POLISH Muzuł suka! 66
POLISH Żydówka suka! 67
PORTUGUESE Senta e voltea, vadia. 68
ROMANIAN Ma pis pe mata târfa! 69
RUSSIAN Кушай говно сука. / Kušay govnó suka. **
RUSSIAN Цучка дерганая! / Cučka derganaya. 70
RUSSIAN Сука буду–не забуду! / Suka budu—ne zabudu. 71
RUSSIAN Как жизнь, сучий потрох! / Kak zhizn', suchiy potrokh? 72
SLOVENIAN Praisica! 73
SPANISH ¿Te gustan las perras, no? 74
SPANISH ¡Dale a la perra madre! 75
SPANISH ¡Tu vieja es una puta del orto! 76
SPANISH ¡Tu madre es puta perra y pendeja y heroinomana y voy a llamar la programa de asistencia social! 77
SWAHILI Yehe ni jahili nakala tatu! 78
SWEDISH Jävlaslyna! / Jävlahynda! 17
TAGALOG Chichay Chákakhan! 79
THAI Teu yai bâh! 80
THAI Teu săm sòrn! 81
THAI Teu săm bit'cha! 81
TURKISH Orospu! / Cadı kadın! / Fahişe! 43
TURKISH Bad asl kuni! 23
VIETNAMESE Bá chang! 82
WELSH Mae dy fam ti yn ast salw. 83
WELSH Dos i chwarae gyda'r traffig y'r ast hyll. 84
WELSH Cer i grafu y gast! 85

* *"You're a bitch."*

** *AFRIKAANS: "Eat shit & die, bitch.";*
CANTONESE: "Die, bitch!";
DUTCH: "Eat penguin shit, bitch.";
RUSSIAN: "Eat shit, bitch";

2 *"You Joan." = bitchy bitter Joan Crawford faggot;*

3 *"You're a real bitch!"*

4 *"Certified Bitch."*

5 *BENGALI: "Yr mother's a bitch!";*
MALTESE: "Yr bitch mother!";

6 *"You rude bitch."*

7 *"Cow!";*
BENGALI: "You're a cow.";
FARSI "You annoying cow.";
ICELANDIC: "Yr mother's a cow!" / "Yr mother's a bitch!";

LATIN: "You dumb-ass/arse cow!":
MACEDONIAN: "You're my cow.";
8 "You shitty bitch!"
9 BOSNIAN: "You fat bitch!";
ITALIAN: "Fat-ass/arse bitch!"/"Fatso bitch!," respectively;
10 "Old white devil foreigner bitch."
11 "Shitty Yuppie bitch!"
12 "That bitch is bad karma."
13 "I shit on the Virgin Bitch Mary."
14 "I shit on the bitch ocean."
15 "Yr bitch mother's a dominatrix."
16 "You pathetic pitable bitch."
17 CZECH: "You fucking cow!";
SWEDISH: "Fucking bitch!"
18 "Jump into a toilet bowl, bitch!";
19 "Go up an ass/arse bitch!"
20 "Blow me, bitch!"
21 "Suck dwarf dick/cock, you bitch."
22 "Hippie bitch."
23 DANISH "You evil bitch!";
TURKISH: "Evil back-stabbing faggoty queen bitch!";
24 "Fucked-up bitch." / "What a fucked-up bitch!";
25 "You shouldn't fuck with me, bitch."
26 "T.B. bitch!"
27 "Yr mother's a clit wanking bitch."
28 "Sociopathic bitch!" / "Antisocial bitch!";
29 "Eat my cock/dick, bitch!"
30 FRENCH: "What a bitch!";
FRENCHVERLAN: "What a bitch!" / "What a whore!";
31 "What a silly bitch!"
32 "You're nothing more than a bitch," Fr. Québ. dial.;
33 "You're a crazy bitch who shoves portable/mobile phones up yr ass/arse.
34 "Yr mother's a drunken bitch."
35 "Yr mother's an old witch."
36 "Nympho bitch!"
37 "Nasty bitch!" — Bav.;
38 "I fuck yr bitch mother!"
39 "Punk rock bitch!"
40 "Go to the Gaza Strip, bitch!"
41 "You're not going to scare a bitch with a dick/cock."
42 "Stupid bitch!"
43 "Bitch!" / "Slut!" / "Whore!";
JAPANESE / TURKISH: "Bitch!";
44 "Shitty cunt-for-brains bitch!"
45 "One ugly bitch." / "One ugly witch.";

46 *"Lazy cow!"*
47 *"Crippled bitch!"*
48 *"Bitch dwarf!"*
49 *"Hunchback bitch!"*
50 *"Online bitch!" / "Online slut!" / "Online whore!";*
51 *"Stupid cow!"*
52 *"Ugly bitch!"*
53 *"Kiss my ass/arse, bitch."*
54 *"Fuck yr God, bitch!"*
55 *"Stupid bitch!" / "Stupid whore!" / "Stupid slut!";*
56 *"I piss upon yr bitch mother."*
57 *"You damn fucking stubborn bitch!";*
58 *"Trendy bitch!"*
59 *"Go to hell, you mean bitch!"*
60 *"Two-faced bitch."*
61 *"Can't you go hang yourself, bitch?"*
62 *"Suck lye & die, bitch!"*
63 *"Queen bitch of the idiot prom!"*
64 *"Yr bitch mother gave you the clap!"*
65 *"Could you do me an ice cream, you gorgeous foxy bitch?"*
= Wld you please blow me, babe?"
66 *"Moslem bitch!"*
67 *"Jewess bitch!"*
68 *"Sit & twirl, bitch," Braz.;*
69 *"I piss on yr bitch mother!"*
70 *"Deranged crazy bitch!"*
71 *"I'll be a* [good] *bitch—I won't forget." —trad. Russ. oath, equally sincere & solemn & worthless;*
72 *"How's life, bitch guts?" —trad. Russ. intimate greeting — can be insulting, but not w/ friends or lovers;*
73 *"Sow!"*
74 *"You really like the bitches, don't you." /Ch.;*
75 *"To the bitch mother with him!" = Fuck him under, let God sort him out;*
76 *"Yr mother's a fucking bitch!" —Arg.;*
77 *"Yr mother's a whoring bitch & an idiot shit-for-brains ass/arsehole & junkie & I'm calling social services!"*
78 *"She's a bitch in triplicate!"*
79 *"Bitchy nasty-tempered ugly super-bitch!" = Fucking virago looks like Chaka Khan;*
80 *"She's a crazy psycho bitch!"*
81 *THAI, 2 variants: "She's a bitch!";*
"She's a bitch!" = Bit'cha/Bitch, Eng. loan-word;
82 *"Mean old bitch!"*
83 *"Yr mum's an ugly bitch."*
84 *"Go play in the traffic, you ugly bitch."*
85 *"Fuck off, you bitch!"*

BLASHEMY...
& WAS IT
A BLAST FOR YOU
(& YOU ARE GOD *WHO*?)
(& VARIATIONS)

AFRIKAANS Naii jou Jesus. *
ALBANIAN Ta qifshä zotërin tënd turqíshte. **
ARABIC / TUNIS. Nān dēn bōk. [2]
ARABIC / TUNIS. Nān rabb bōk. [3]
CATALAN Mecàgum Déu puta. [4]
CATALAN Mecàgum Judes puta! [5]
CATALAN Mecàgum Christo puta. [6]
CATALAN Mecàgum les putas llagues de Crist! [7]
CATALAN Mecàgum putas els dotze apostols putas! [8]
CATALAN Mecàgum tots els sants putas en una bóta puta i Déu puta per tap! [9]
CATALAN Mecàgum la Santíssima Trinitat puta! [10]
CATALAN Mecàgum Déu puta i sa Mare puta. [11]
CATALAN Mecàgum el Déu puta que et va fotre! [12]
CATALAN Mecàgum el cap de Déu ver cony! [13]
CATALAN Mecàgum el cony puta de Déu! [14]
CATALAN Mecàgum el collons putas de Déu puta! [15]
CATALAN Mecàgum el Crist puta crucifiat! [16]
CATALAN Mecàgum la sang cony de Cristo! [17]
CATALAN Mecàgum el Fill puta de Déu. [18]
CATALAN Mecàgum el Fill de Déu puta. [19]
CATALAN Mecàgum el Pare Sant puta feixista! [20]
CROATIAN / SERBIAN Jebem ti Boga! [21] ;
Јебем ти Бога! / Jebem ti Boga! [21]
CROATIAN / SERB Jebo naci papu! [22] ;
Јебо наси папу! / Jebo naci papu! [22]
CROATIAN / SERB Jebem ti Isusa. * ;
Јебем ти Јсуса! / Jebem ti Isusa. *
DANISH Kors i skuret. [23]
DUTCH Ga je God neuken! [24]
FARSI Kuni mollah. [25]
FARSI Madar mollah. [26]
FINNISH Jeesuskyrpä! [27]
FINNISH Kristuksen vittu! [28]
FINNISH Vedä vittu päähän ja pakene Jeesuskyrpä. [29]
FRENCH Bondieu de merde! [30]
FRENCH J'encule Dieu! [21]
FRENCH J'encule ta scene de nativite! [31]
FRENCH Je l'encule ton bebe Jesus dans sa crèche! [32]
FRENCH J'encule le pape nazi! [22]

GAELIC, IRISH D'anam don cac. [33]
GAELIC, IRISH Do bháltaí don dia. [34]
GAELIC, IRISH Focáil an Pápa. [22]
GERMAN Jesus im Stuka! / Jessas im Stuka. [35]
GREEK, MOD Γαμο το θεο. / Gamo to theo. [21]
GREEK, MOD Γαμο τον αντιχριστο. / Gamo ton antichristo. [36]
ICELANDIC Þú fokkar ekki með hina óspjölluðu Maríu. [66]
ICELANDIC Ríddu Jesúsbarninu í jötu útstillingunni. [32]
ITALIAN Gesu e un cornuto! [37]
ITALIAN Va funcuolo porca Dio and tutte i santi! [38]
ITALIAN Va rompe il cuzzo porca di Dio. [39]
JAPANESE テメーの神社をやれ！ Temē no jinja wo yare! [40]
JAPANESE テメーの中絶された妹／弟をやれ！ Temē no chūzetsu sareta imōto / otōto no haka wo yare! [41]
JAPANESE オマエのクソっぽい新宗教をやれ！ Omae no kusoppoi shinshūkyō wo yare! [42]
JAPANESE 麻原彰晃はオマエのアホな母と寝たんやで！ Asahara Shōkō wa omae no aho na haha to netan yade! [43]
LATIN Deus Christianus tuus futuatur. [67]
LATIN Christus tuus futuatur. [68]
MACEDONIAN Да ти ебам бозество кучка! / Da ti ebam bozestvo kučka! [44]
MALAYU Celaka! / Lahanat! [45]
MALAYU Perang sabil! [46]
MALTESE Inbullek fuq liba vatikan. [47]
MALTESE Inbullek fuq alla. [48]
MALTESE Qisek dik ilsbjana il madonna. [49]
MALTESE Inbullek fuq dik ilsbjana il Madre Teresa. [50]
MALTESE Inbullek fuq dawk il minestra pufti apostli. [51]
MALTESE Inbullek fuq pufti evangelisti. [52]
POLISH Muzuł suka! [53]
POLISH Żydówka suka! [54]
ROMANIAN Ma pis pe crucea ma`tii. [55]
ROMANIAN Ma pis pe icoana matii. [56]
ROMANIAN Ma pis pe biserica matii! [57]
RUSSIAN Ёб Иерусалим́! / Ëb Ierusalím! [58]
RUSSIAN Спокойной ночи, мать вашу в три креста! / Spokonoy nochi, mat' mashu v tri kresta! [59]
SLOVENIAN Marijii na Jezus! [60]
SPANISH ¡Gracias a Dios que soy ateo! [61]
SPANISH ¡Me cago en Dios y los tres cientos-sesenta-cinco santos del año! [62]
SPANISH ¡Vámonos con el diablo a Nueva Jork para bailar el twist por todo la noche! / ¡Vámonos con el diablo a Nueva Yerjsí para bailar el twist por todo la noche! [63]
SWEDISH Din mama suger Kristus. [64]
URDU Tujh pe khuda ka qahar barse. [65]

YIDDISH Schtupp elohim! / Stup elohim! 21

* *AFRIKAANS: "Fuck yr Jesus.";*
CROATIAN / SERB: "I fuck yr Jesus";
TAGALOG: "Fuck Jesus!"

** *"Let the Turkish fuck yr Lord God."*

2 *"Damn yr father's religious faith."*

3 *"Damn yr father's God."*

4 *"I shit on God the bitch."*

5 *"I shit on bitch Judas!"*

6 *"I shit on bitch Christ."*

7 *"I shit on the bitch wounds of Christ!"*

8 *"I shit bitches on the twelve bitch apostles!"*

9 *"I shit on all the bitch saints inside a bitch's bottle & that bitch God for a cork!"*

10 *"I shit on the Holiest Bitch Trinity!"*

11 *"I shit on God the Bitch & His Bitch Mother."*

12 *"I shit on the bitch God who fucked you!"*

13 *"I shit on the Head of the True Cunt God!"*

14 *"I shit on the bitch cunt of God."*

15 *"I shit on the bitch balls/bollocks of the bitch God."*

16 *"I shit on the Crucified Christ bitch!"*

17 *"I shit on the cunt-blood of Christ!"*

18 *"I shit on the Bitch Son of God."*

19 *"I shit on the Son of the Bitch God."*

20 *"I shit on the fascist bitch Pope."*

21 *CROATIAN / SERB: "I fuck yr God!"*
FRENCH: "Fuck God!";
GREEK: "I fuck God!";
YIDDISH: "Fuck God!" = Fuck the most Holy God whose name we dare not pronounce — at least not correctly, nor probably even dare utter, according to Talmudic trad.

22 *CROATIAN / SERB; FRENCH: "Fuck the Nazi Pope.";*
GAELIC, IRISH: "Fuck the Pope." — popular 1980s Dublin graffito;

23 *"Cross in the loo." / "Cross in the toilet."*

24 *DUTCH: "Go fuck yr God!";*

25 *"Bottom faggot Mullah."*

26 *"Yr mother's a Mullah."*

27 *"Jesus-cock!" / "Jesus-dick!";*

28 *"Jesus Christ's cunt!" / "Jesus Christ's pussy!"*

29 *"Draw a cunt on yr forehead & run for Jesus-cock/Jesus-dick."*

30 *"Good God of shit!"*

31 *"Fuck yr Nativity display!"*

32 *FRENCH: "Fuck yr Baby Jesus in a chreche";*
ICELANDIC: "Fuck yr Baby Jesus in His Nativity display."

33 *"Yr soul to the shit."*

34 *"Yr cunt to God."*

35 *GERMAN: "Jesus in a Stuka!";*
2nd. entry, "Jessas im Stuka," Bav. dial.;

36 *"I fuck yr antichrist."*

37 *"Jesus is a cuckold!"*

38 *"Fuck Bitch Christ & all the saints!"*

39 *"Go bust Christ's bitch ass/arse."*

40 *"Fuck yr Shinto shrine!"*

41 *"Fuck yr aborted sister's / brother's grave!"*

42 *"Fuck yr shitty religious cult!"*

43 *"Shoko Asahara* [**Aum Shinrikyo cult leader**] *fucked yr idiot mother!"*

44 *"Fuck yr God, bitch!"*

45 *"Infidel!"*

46 *"Holy war!"*

47 *"I piss upon the Vatican."*

48 *"I piss upon God."*

49 *"You're like that lesbo-dyke Virgin Mary."*

50 *"I piss upon that lesbo-dyke Mother Teresa."*

51 *"I piss upon those minestroni faggot apostles."*

52 *"I piss upon the faggot evangelists."*

53 *"Moslem bitch!"*

54 *"Jewess bitch!"*

55 *"I piss on yr mother's cross."*

56 *"I piss on yr mother's icon."*

57 *"I piss on yr mother's church!"*

58 *"Fuck Jerusalem!"*

59 *"Good night, & fuck yr mother & three crosses, too!" = after-dinner valediction;*

60 *"Holy Virgin Mary on Jesus!"*

61 *"Thank God I'm an Atheist!" = old Spanish & Mex. prov., often attrib. to Luis Buñuel;*

62 *"I shit on God & the calendar year's 365 saints!"*

63 *"Let's go to New York/New Jersey with the devil & dance the twist all night long!"*

64 *"Yr mother sucks Christ."*

65 *"Allah damn you."*

66 *"You don't fuck with the Virgin Mary."*

67 *"Fuck yr Christian god!"*

68 *"Fuck yr Christ!"*

BUGGER BUGGERY... IS THAT YOUR COCK/DICK UP MY ASS/ARSE OR ARE YOU JUST GLAD TO SEE ME? (& VARIATIONS)

AFRIKAANS Jou boudkapper. *

AFRIKAANS: Jou dipsticktrekker. **

CATALAN Vas t'en a prendre pel cul puta. [2]

CATALAN Que et donin pel cul puta! [3]

CROATIAN / SERB Jebi si svog travestita u guzicu. [4]

Јеби си свог траветиста у гузицу. / Jebi si svog travestita u guzicu. [4]

CROATIAN / SERB Jebi se s drškom biča u guzicu, pederčino u crnoj koži. [5]

Јеби си дршкон бича у гузицу, педрчино у срној кожи. /Jebi se s drškom biča u guzicu, pederčino u crnoj koži. [5]

CROATIAN / SERB Jebi se s vibratorom od lezbača, pederčino u crnoj koži. [6]

Јеби сивибратором од лезвача, педрчино у црној кожи. / Jebi se s vibratorom od lezbača, pederčino u crnoj koži. [6]

CZECH Odpanit mi prdel. [7]

DANISH Op i røven med det. [8]

DUTCH Ik laat je vader bukken. / Ik laat je broer bukken. / Ik laat je zoon bukken. [9]

DUTCH Wil je neuken naadsoldaat? [10]

DUTCH Wil je neuken naadninja? [11]

FARSI bachchaboz [12]

FINNISH Anna persettä. [13]

FINNISH Otat kuulemma perseeseen mielelläsi. [14]

FINNISH Revi huoranpersees. [15]

FINNISH Ruskean reiän ritari. [16]

FRENCH Frappe mon cul. [17]

FRENCH J'me suis fendu le cul pour toé! [18]

GAELIC, IRISH Thuas do thóin. [8]

GAELIC, IRISH Suas do thóin le buideal briste. [19]

GAELIC, SCOTS Suas do thòin. [8]

GAELIC, SCOTS Suas do thòin le botal briste. [19]

GAELIC, SCOTS Brod thusa le postiar nan Elton John 'sa seòmar-mullaich nam pàrantan. [44]

GERMAN Du bisch dr hingerletscht Füdischläker [20]

GREEK, MOD. τουρλολιγηούρις / tourlolighoúris [21]

GREEK, MOD. Γαμισο! /Gamiso! [22]

HINDI/URDU gānd marau [23]

ICELANDIC Hoppadu uppi rassgatid a ter. [24]

ITALIAN il giochetto dei frati [25]

ITALIAN Se il cazzo dei froci avesse le ali, la tuo culo sarebbe una aviorimessa. /

Se il cazzo dei froci avesse le ali, la tuo culo sarebbe una pista di atterraggio. [26]
JAPANESE ケツの穴でやる / ketsu no ana de yaru. [22]
MARATHI pascadadvaragami [27]
NORWEGIAN Din påståelige jævla rumpeknuller! [28]
NORWEGIAN Din jævla baksetehumper! [29]
POLISH Daj dupy proszę. [30]
POLISH Chuj ci w dupe proszę. [31]
PORTUGUESE Vou surfer na sua bunda. [32]
PORTUGUESE O seu irmão te fodeu na sua bunda. / O seu pai te fodeu na sua bunda. / O seu filho te fodeu na sua bunda. [33]
PORTUGUESE O seu olho do cú é tão imenso que até um porta-aviões cabe lá dentro. [43]
ROMANIAN Sugi pula si cu curu. [34]
RUSSIAN Сто хуев в жопу не тесно? / Sto xúev v žópu, ne tésno? [35]
SLOVENIAN Okoli žep v riti! [36]
SPANISH A noche me folle a tu hermano por el culo. / A noche me folle a tu padre por el culo. / A noche me folle a tu hijo por el culo. [37]
SPANISH Vamos a buscar petróleo. [38]
SPANISH Te voy a romper el culo. [39]
TAGALOG Pakímbero mo! [40]
TAGALOG Kantot sa p'wit. [22]
WELSH Twll tin y gont hoyw! [41]
YIDDISH Tsu tillas gescheften. [42]
YIDDISH Tuchus arine. [8]

* *"You ass/arse chopper."*
** *"You dipstick puller."*
2 *"Go take it up yr bitch ass/arse."*
3 *"Fuck you up yr bitch ass/arse!"*
4 *"Fuck yr drag queen transvestite ass/arse."*
5 *"Fuck you with a whip handle, you faggot leather-boy."*
6 *"Fuck you with a dyke's dildo, you faggot leather-boy."*
7 *"Pop my ass/arse cherry." /"Deflower my ass/arse-bud.";*
8 *DANISH: "Up the ass/arse with that";*
GAELIC, IRISH / GAELIC, SCOTS: ""Up yr ass/arse.";
9 *"I'll ass/arse-fuck yr father." /*
"I'll ass/arse-fuck yr brother." /
"I'll ass/arse-fuck yr son";
10 *Do you want to fuck me, you butt-crack trooper?"*
11 *"You want to fuck me, you butt-crack ninja?"*
12 *collector of dancing toy-boys;*
13 *"Give me some ass/arse.";*
14 *"I hear you enjoy taking it up the ass/arse.";*
15 *"Rip yr slutty ass/arse open."*
16 *"Knight of the Faggot Bung Hole"*
17 *"Spank my ass/arse."*
18 *"I split my own ass/arse just for you!"*

19 *“Up your ass/arse with a broken bottle.”*
20 *“You're a motherfucking ass/arsefucker,“ Bern/Sw.;*
21 *“lusts for a bulge”;*
22 *“Fuck you up the ass/arse!”*
23 *ass/arse-fuckee, bottom;*
24 *“Climb up yr ass/arse.”*
25 *“the friar's little game”;*
26 *“If faggots' dicks/cocks had wings, yr ass/arsehole wld be the airplane hangar.”/*
“If faggots' dicks/cocks had wings, yr ass/arsehole wld be the landing strip.”;
27 *“ass/arse-fucking faggoty pederast”;*
28 *“You damn fucking obstinate/stubborn ass/arse-fucker!”*
29 *“You fucking back-seat humper!”*
30 *“Give me some ass/arse, please.”*
31 *“Dick/cock up yr ass/arse, please.”*
32 *“I'll surf up yr ass/arse,” Braz.;*
33 *“Yr brother fucked you up yr ass/arse.”/*
“Yr father fucked you up yr ass/arse.”/
“Yr son fucked you up yr ass/arse,” Braz.;
34 *“Suck my dick/cock with yr ass/arsehole.”;*
35 *“Isn't a hundred dicks/pricks/cocks up the ass/arse just a tad tight?”*
36 *“Around yr pocket and into yr ass/arse!”*
37 *“Last night I fucked yr brother's ass/arsehole.”/*
“Last night I fucked yr father's ass/arsehole.”/
“Last night I fucked yr son's ass/arsehole.”;
38 *“We're going to drill for oil,” Ch.;*
39 *“I'm going to break yr ass/arsehole”/*
“I'm going to tear yr ass/arsehole”;
40 *“You gay ass/arsefucker!”*
41 *“Up yrs, you gay cunt!”*
42 *“Shove it.”*
43 *“Yr ass/arsehole's so huge an aircraft carrier wuld fit right in.”*
44 *“You wank to an Elton John poster in yr parents' attic.”*

CELL & MOBILE PHONES & LAP-DANCING LAP-TOPS & OTHER CRIMES AGAINST A CIVIC SOCIETY (& VARIATIONS)

AFRIKAANS Fok almal op jou selfoon speed dial. *

AFRIKAANS Fok almal op jou selfoon. **

CROATIAN Mama ti se jebe sa Srbima na Internetu. [2]

CROATIAN Sestra ti se jebe sa Srbima na Internetu. [3]

CROATIAN / SERB Sin ti je rob domine na Internetu. [4]

Син ти је роб домине на Интернету. / Sin ti je rob domine na Internetu. [4]

CROATIAN / SERBIAN Jebi sve na svom brzom biranju. [5] ;

Јеби све на свом брзом бирању. / Jebi sve na svom brzom biranju. [5]

CROATIAN / SERBIAN Jebi sve na svom brzom biranju na mobitelu. * ;

Јеби све на свом брзом бирању на мобителу. / Jebi sve na svom brzom biranju na mobitelu. **

CROATIAN / SERB Mama ti je kurva na Internetu. [6]

Мама ти је курва на Интернету. / Mama ti je kurva na Internetu. [6]

CROATIAN / SERB Mama ti je drolja na Internetu. [7]

Мама ти је дролја на Интернету. / Mama ti je drolja na Internetu. [7]

CROATIAN / SERB Sestra ti je kurva na Internetu. [8]

Сестра ти је курва на Интернету. / Sestra ti je kurva na Internetu. [8]

CROATIAN / SERB Sestra ti je drolja na Internetu. [9]

Сестра ти је дролја на Интернету. / Sestra ti je drolja na Internetu. [9]

CROATIAN / SERB Baba ti je drolja na Internetu. [10]

Баба ти је дролја на Интернету. / Baba ti je drolja na Internetu. [10]

FINNISH Vitut kikille kännykkäsi pikavalinnassa! / Haistata vittu kännykkäsi pikavalinnassa! *

FINNISH Työnnä se kännykkä perseeseesi / vittuusi! [11]

FINNISH Pistä se känny värinälle ja tunge se perseeneesi! [14]

FINNISH Suljetko se vitun kännykän, vai tungenko sen hanuriisi? [15]

FRENCH Je l'encule ton portable! [11]

FRENCH T'est qu'une sale conasse qui se met du portable dans le cul. [12]

GAELIC, IRISH cacphost [21]

GAELIC, SCOTS Rach chun an diosg cruaidh nan donais! [16]

GERMAN Fick Jeden in deiner Schnellwahl! [5]

ICELANDIC Ríddu öllum á hraðvalinu í gemsanum þínum. **

ITALIAN Scopa tutti nel tuo fonino. **

JAPANESE エロ電 ero den [13]

KOREAN Net shibal nyon! *"Online bitch!" / "Online slut!" / "Online whore!";* [17]

KOREAN net ta-ta-ri *internet wank / internet wanking;* [18]

MACEDONIAN Да ти ебам све по телефон! / Da ti ebam sve po telefon. **

NORWEGIAN Et virus herpa harddisken min. [19]

RUSSIAN Ебай всех в твоей мобильник. / Ebaj vsex v tvoej mobil'nik. **

SPANISH ¡Porque no apagas tu cellular y te lo metes al culo! [20]

* *"Fuck everyone on yr mobile phone/cell phone speed dial.";*

** *"Fuck everyone on yr mobile/cell phone."*

2 *"Yr mother has internet sex with Serbs."*

3 *"Yr sister has internet sex with Serbs."*

4 *"Yr son is a dominatrix' internet slave.*

5 *"Fuck everyone on yr speed dial."*

6 *"Yr mother's an internet whore."*

7 *"Yr mother's an internet slut."*

8 *"Yr sister's an internet whore."*

9 *"Yr sister's an internet slut."*

10 *"Yr grandmother's an internet slut."*

11 *"Fuck yr portable / mobile / cell phone.";*

12 *"You're a crazy bitch who shoves portable/mobile phones up her ass/arse."*

13 *porn/sex 900 phone numbers, or just an obscene phone call;*

14 *"Why don't you set that mobile/cell phone to vibrate & shove it up yr ass/arse!"*

15 *"Will you turn off that mobile/cell phone or shall I ram it where the sun don't shine!?"*

16 *"Go to the devil's hard disk!"*

17 *"Online bitch!" / "Online slut!" / "Online whore!";*

18 *internet wank / internet wanking;*

19 *"A virus damaged my hard disk." = my brain hurts;*

20 *"Why not turn off yr cell phone & shove it up yr ass/arse!"*

21 *"shit mail" — i.e., spam mail*

CORPUS POLITIC... OR, WHAT WOULD CALIGULA SAY/DO?
(& VARIATIONS)

AFRIKAANS Naai jou Waarheid en Versoening. / Fok jou Waarheid en Versoening. *
AFRIKAANS halskette **
AFRIKAANS Soweto halskette [2]
AFRIKAANS halssnoermoord [3]
ALBANIAN Të qiftë Milosh! [4]
ALBANIAN Fashísti janë vegla të kapitalistëve! ***
CANTONESE Díu laa sīng! [5]
CANTONESE Gwái tàuh. [6]
CANTONESE Lòh baak tàuh [7]
CATALAN mocador [8]
CATALAN Mecàgum el Pare Sant puta feixista! [9]
CATALAN Si ma mare puta fos Espanya jo seria un fill de puta. [10]
CREOLE / HAITIAN Tonton Macoute [11]
CREOLE / HAITIAN Père Lebrun **
CROATIAN Mama ti je pušila kurac Srbima. [12]
CROATIAN Mama ti se jebe sa Srbima na Internetu. [13]
CROATIAN Sestra ti se jebe sa Srbima na Internetu. [14]
CROATIAN / SERB Ethno Brojalica. [15]
Етхно Бројалиса / Ethno Brojalica. [15]
CROATIAN / SERB Pička ti materina fašistička. [16]
Пичка ти материна фашистичка. / Pička ti materina fašistička. [16]
CROATIAN / SERB Jebo svoju evropsku uniju. [17]
Јебо своју европску унију. / Jebo svoju evropsku uniju. [17]
CROATIAN / SERB Jebo svoj pasoš. [18]
Јебо свој пасош. / Jebo svoj pasoš. [18]
CROATIAN / SERB Jebi si svoju vizu. [19]
Јеби си своју визу. / Jebi si svoju vizu. [19]
CROATIAN / SERB Jebem ti narodno zdravlje. [20]
Јебем ти народно здравље. /Jebem ti narodno zdravlje. [20]
CROATIAN / SERB Jebo te Hitler. [21]
Јебо те хитлер. / Jebo te Hitler. [21]
CROATIAN / SERB Jebo te Milosovič. [4]
Јебо те Милосович. / Jebo te Milosovič. [4]
CZECH Nacista! [22]
DANISH Kajakperker [23]
DANISH Skide krigsforbryder! [24]
DANISH Har du studeret hvalknep i Congo? [25]
DANISH Nørd jøde. [26]

DANISH Dum muhamedaner. / Dum muhamedansk. [27]
FRENCH Je l'encule ton premier mai! [28]
FRENCH Catho coco. [29]
FRENCH Situationiste de merde! / Connard de situationiste! [30]
FRENCH parachuter un Sénégalais [31]
FRENCH Révolution c'est l' opium des intellectuelles... [42]
GAELIC, IRISH Bidh rudaí athrú chun donachta roimh siad áthru chun donachta. [32]
GAELIC, IRISH Feiseann do mháthair leis na hOráistaigh. [33]
GAELIC, SCOTS Bidh do mhàthair a' dàireadh le Catiligich. [34]
GAELIC, SCOTS Bidh do mhàthair a' dàireadh le Pròsdanaich. [35]
GAELIC, SCOTS Bidh do mhàthair a' dàireadh le Calvinaich. [36]
GAELIC, SCOTS Bidh do mhàthair a' dàireadh le Sassanaich. [37]
GERMAN die Juden türken. / Neger klatschen / Türken klatschen / Türken klatschen [38]
GERMAN Untermensch [39]
GERMAN Arbeit macht frei. [40]
GERMAN Die Religion ist das Opium das Volkes... [41]
GERMAN Die Revolution is das Opium das Intellektuell... [42]
GERMAN Hitler hat ein Ei, und Himmler keins.... / Hitler hat ein Ei, und Goering keins... [80]
GERMAN Diene Grossmutter leckt Hitlers Ei! [81]
ITALIAN cattocommunista [29]
JAPANESE 麻原彰晃はオマエのアホな母と寝たんやで！Asahara Shōkō wa omae no aho na haha to netan yade! [43]
LATIN Quid faciat Caligula!? [82]
MACEDONIAN Нацист! / Natzist! [22]
MACEDONIAN Да ти ебам народ! / Da ti ebam narod! [44]
MALAYU Celaka! / Lahanat! [45]
MALAYU Perang sabil! [46]
MALTESE Inbullek fuq l ewropa! [47]
MANDARIN 你妈了操尝毛主席席! Nĭ māle cào cháng mao zhŭ xí! [48]
NORWEGIAN Forpulte norske hvaldreper! [49]
POLISH Muzuł suka! [50]
POLISH Żydówka suka! [51]
PORTUGUESE Micro-onda [52]
RUSSIAN чопорные сныовя. / Čópornye snyov'já. [53]
RUSSIAN Ёб глáсность! / Ëb glasnost'! [54]
RUSSIAN Ёб Иерусали́м! / Ëb Ierusalím! [55]
RUSSIAN Головорез! / Golovorez! [56]
RUSSIAN Арбуз на солнце любит зреть, Армяшка в жопу любит еть. / Arbúz na sólnce lyúbit zret', Armyáška v žopu lyúbit et´. [57]
SOTHO, N. pheta **
SPANISH ¡Pinchi gringo! [58]
SPANISH ¡Pobre Mexico! Tan lejos desde Dios y tan cerca de Estados Unidos. [59]
SPANISH "Quiero enseñar al mundo cantar en Mandarin perfecto / como Madame

Binh y Ho Chi Minh y Mao y su cuarteto." [60]
SWEDISH Jävla utlänning! [61]
SWEDISH Din mama suger norsk svan pitt. [62]
SWEDISH Jävla krigsförbrytare. [63]
TAGALOG dóble kára canúto / dóble kára kanúto [64]
TAGALOG dóble kára japók [65]
THAI lim huàa ròon ràaeng [66]
THAI farang lim huàa ròon ràaeng [67]
THAI farang kèenók [68]
THAI farang ngôh [69]
URDU Bhārtīy [70]
URDU Chinki. [71]
URDU Lal Salaam [72]
UZBEK қалб / qalb [73]
UZBEK қочоқлар / qochoqlar [74]
WELSH Twll din pop Saes! [75]
WELSH Mae dy fam yn llyfu cociau Saes. [76]
WELSH Cadwch Cymru yn lan. Danfonwch y sbwriel i Loegr! [77]
YIDDISH Schtupp Moskze. / Stup Moske. [78]
YIDDISH Shoah business [79]
ZULU umgaxo / umlengiso **

* *"Bugger yr Truth & Reconciliation!" / "Fuck yr Truth & Reconciliation!";*

** *AFRIKAANS / CREOLE, FRENCH / SOTHO, N. / ZULU: "necklace" / "necklacing" = placing a petrol-soaked rubber tire around someone's torso & setting it on fire; orig. by Rhodesian security forces in 1960s & 1970s; spread to S. Africa in mid-1980s & used by all conflicting factions through early 1990s; practice also spread to Haiti, Nigeria & Braz.;*

*** *"Fascists are nothing but Capitalist tools!"*

2 *"Soweto necklace" = see ** NOTES, above;*

3 *"necklace murder" = see ** NOTES, above;*

4 *ALBANIAN: "Let* [**Slobodan Milosevič**] *Milosh fuck you!" = Milosevič, ex-Serb pres. & war criminal; CROATIAN / SERB: "Milosevič* [ex-Serb president & war criminal] *fucked you."*

5 *"Fucking Paki!" / "Fucking Indian!";*

6 *"Ghost head." = foreign boss-man/Westerner;*

7 *"Turnip head" = Jap.*

8 *"Spanish flag" = snot rag [see Joyce's ULYSSES, ch. 1, for Irish equivalent...];*

9 *"I shit on the bitch fascist Pope."*

10 *"If my bitch mother were Spain I'd be a son of that bitch."*

11 *"Uncle Gunnysack" — Papa Doc's death-squads; later employed by Baby Doc's regime & in subsequent Haitian civil wars, circa 1957–2000; wore brownshirt drag & sunglasses & cultivated a vodun aura; used semi-automatics, but machete was prefered weapon;*

12 *"Yr mother gave Serbs blowjobs."*

13 *"Yr mother has internet sex with Serbs."*

14 *"Yr sister has internet sex with Serbs."*

15 *"Ethnic Eeny-meeny-miney-moe." = also title of poem by Croatian poet Delimir Resicki;*

16 *"Fascist motherfucker."*

17 "Fuck yr European Union."
18 "Fuck yr passport."
19 "Fuck yr visa."
20 "Fuck yr National Health."
21 "Hitler fucked you."
22 "Nazi!"
23 "Persian from Greenland"
24 "Shitty War Criminal!"
25 "Did you study whale fucking in the Congo?"
26 "Nerdy Jew."
27 "Dumb Moslem."
28 "Fuck yr May Day!"
29 "Catholic Communist";
30 "Situationist Wanker!"
31 "parachute a Senegalese" = take a dump;
32 "Things will get worse before they get worse." — Irish prov.;
33 "Yr mother fucks Orangemen."
34 "Yr mother fucks Catholics."
35 "Yr mother fucks Protestants."
36 "Yr mother fucks Calvinists."
37 "Yr mother fucks Englishmen."
38 "Beating Jews to a pulp" / "Beating niggers to a pulp" / "Beating Turks to a pulp" = Neo-nazi skinhead slang;
39 "Subhuman";
40 "Work shall make you free" = inscribed above the gates of Nazi death camps;
41 "Religion is the opiate of the people..." — Karl Marx [orig. goes on to describe religion's anodyne qualities];
42 "Revolution is the opium of the intellectual..." = pop. post-May '68 European & US graffito; found its way into Lindsay Anderson's O LUCKY MAN!;
43 "Shoko Asahara [**Aum Shinrikyo cult leader**] fucked yr idiot mother!"
44 "Fuck yr nation!"
45 "Infidel!"
46 "Holy war!"
47 "I piss upon Europe!"
48 "Yr mother fucked Chairman Mao!"
49 "Fucking Norwegian whale-killer!"
50 "Moslem bitch!"
51 "Jewess bitch!"
52 "Micro-wave" = "necklacing" variant substituting petrol-filled tin barrel for petrol-soaked rubber tire; victim's placed in tin barrel & set on fire; method used in Rio's favelas by drug dealers & vigilantes, sometimes against real journalists [**as opposed to US p.r. flaks & fuck-puppet propagandists**];
53 "Prim & proper British sons of bitches."
54 "Fuck glasnost'!"
55 "Fuck Jerusalem!"
56 "Murderous Chechen scum!"
57 "Watermelons love the sun, Armenians love being ass/arse-fucked." — Russian prov.;
58 "Fucking Yanqui Norteño Ugly American!"
59 "Pity poor Mexico! So far from God & so close to the United States." — Mex. prov.;
60 "I'd like to teach the world to sing a Mandarin perfected / like Madame Binh & Ho Chi Minh & Chairman Mao's quartet/collective!" — pop. Vencenemos Brig. Cuban work song rendered bilingually by Yanqui red diaper

volunteers, circa 1970s; also sung in var. postal annexes;

61 *"Fucking foreigner!"*

62 *"Yr mother sucks Norwegian swan dick. / Yr mother sucks Norwegian swan cock."*

63 *"Fucking war criminal."*

64 *"two-faced Yank" / "two-faced American";*

65 *"two-faced Japanese";*

66 *"Muslim extremists";*

67 *"foreign Muslim extremists";*

68 *"birdshit foreigner";*

69 *"stupid foreigner";*

70 *"Indian" / "Hindi" = Infidel;*

71 *"Chinese" = foreign Infidel;*

72 *"Red Salute" = sometimes ironic ref. to Commies;*

73 *"cheating swindling gypsy," Arab. loan word;*

74 *"displaced refugees";*

75 *"Ass/arseholes to all Englishmen!";*

76 *"Yr mother licks Englishmen's cocks/dicks.";*

77 *"Keep Wales tidy. Leave yr rubbish in England!"*

78 *"Fuck Moscow!"*

79 *Queasy intersection of remembrance & commerce grown up around W.W. II murder of 6 million Jews by Nazi 3rd. Reich. — attrib. to J. Hoberman Village Voice film critic;*

80 *"Hitler has one ball, & Himmler none..." / "Hitler has one ball, & Goering none";*

81 *"Yr grandmother licked Hitler's ball!"*

82 *"What would Caligula do?!"*

CROOKS, COOKS & LIARS (& VARIATIONS)

AFRIKAANS Jou Leonora! [3]
AFRIKAANS Jou verneuker! **
ALBANIAN Ti je dallaveraxhínj! [2]
ARABIC Ganav! [4]
ARMENIAN Toun avazag. [5]
BASQUE marketo alproja *(m)* / marketa alproja *(f)* [6]
BELARUSIAN Хлус джабані! Мусічь акуліарі начзапіы дык можа піздечь ніама ладі сзто! / Khlus džabany! Musič' akuliary načzapiu dyk moža pizdzeč' niama lady szto! [7]
BENGALI Mithyuk! *
BOSNIAN Lažeš! [8]
CANTONESE dáaitouh [9]
CATALAN Mentider! *
CROATIAN / SERBIAN beda od čovjeką [10] ;
беда од човјеką / beda od čovjeką [10]
CZECH Cíkan! [11]
DANISH Løgnhals! [12]
DUTCH Aso leugenaar! [13]
FARSI Un dorost nist. [14]
FINNISH Valehtelija! *
FRENCH J'ai été arrêté. [15]
FRENCH Les flics ne t'a pas encore trouvé? [16]
FRENCH (VERLAN) Les keufs ne t'a pas encore trouvé? [16]
GAELIC, IRISH Maistín! [17]
GERMAN Lügner! *
GREEK, MOD. Ινε ενας απατεονας. / Ine enas apateonas. [2]
HEBREW Im meram<u>e</u>h haya tippa, ata hayita kamoot! /Im meram<u>e</u>h haya tippa, ata hayita soofat! [18]
HINDI / URDU Sālā jhūthā kahī kā! [19]
HINDI / URDU Paidaishi jhōta! [20]
ICELANDIC Lygari! *
ICELANDIC Siðblindur fábjáni. [21]
ITALIAN un magrebino [22]
ITALIAN Truffatore! *(m)* / Truffatrice! *(f)* [2]
JAPANESE 病的な嘘つき byōteki na usotsuki [23]
KOREAN san-jŏk [24]
LATIN Semper timidum scelus. [25]
MACEDONIAN Ѓупста! / Gjupsta! [26]
MACEDONIAN цajкан / tzajkan [27]
MALAYU Dajal! [28]
MANDARIN 告发某人 gàofā mǒurén [29]
MARATHI Kha<u>r</u>yācē n˙khā<u>nd</u>a! [2]

MARATHI Khagrās'ā! **
NORWEGIAN Jævla løgner! 30
POLISH Kłamca! *
PORTUGUESE Bicha mentiroso. 31
PORTUGUESE Bicha mentirosa. 32
ROMANIAN Pungas! 2
RUSSIAN Пиздун! / Pizdún! 33
SLOVENIAN Okoli žep v riti! 34
SPANISH ¡Eres pinchí mentiroso! *(m)* / ¡Eres pinchí mentirosa! *(f)* 30
SPANISH Caga sala/Caga cosina/Caga bañera / Caga balcon 35
SPANISH Ladrón que roba a ladrón tiene cien años de perdón. 36
SWAHILI mteka nyara 37
SWEDISH Jävlalögnare! 30
SWEDISH Jävlamytoman! 38
TAGALOG echoséro *(m)* / echoséra *(f)* 39
THAI khót 40
TURKISH eşkiya 9
UZBEK Каззоб! / Kazzob! *
VIETNAMESE ngu'ò'i nói dô'i *
WELSH anwireddwr *
YIDDISH gonif 41
YORUBA Olóòfófó! 42
ZULU isigebengu 9

* *BENGALI / CATALAN / BENGALI /FINNISH / GERMAN / POLISH / WELSH: "Liar!"*
UZBEK: "Deceitful liar!"
** *"You swindling con artist!"*
2 *AFRIKAANS: "You're a swindler!";*
ITALIAN / MARATHI / ROMANIAN: "Swindler!";
GREEK, MOD: "He's a swindling crook."
3 *"You lying faggot!"*
4 *"Thief!"*
5 *"You're the bandit!" / "You're a bandit!";*
6 *"Despicable Spanish crook / hoodlum";*
7 *"Fuckin' liar thinks he can put on his glasses & say any fucking thing!"*
8 *"You're lying!"*
9 *crook / gangster / thug;*
10 *"bad guy" = black hat;*
11 *"Liar neck!"*
12 *"Lying gypsy!"*
13 *"Lying sociopath!"*
14 *"That's not true."*
15 *"I was busted." / "I was arrested"*
16 *"Haven't the cops busted you yet?"*
17 *"You bullying thug!"*
18 *"If swindling was a drop of water, you'd be the rainfall!" /*
"If swindling was a drop of water, you'd be the rainstorm!"

19 *"Bloody liar!"*
20 *"Liar by birth!"*
21 *"Moral idiot."*
22 *African thief, "illegal" immigrant.*
23 *pathological liar, mind-fucker;*
24 *bandit / crook;*
25 *"Crime is ever fearful."*
26 *"Gypsy!" = crook/bum;*
27 *cop;*
28 *"Father of lies!"*
29 *police informer;*
30 *NORWEGIAN / SWEDISH: "Fucking liar!";*
SPANISH: "You're a fucking liar!"
31 *"Lying bitch faggot."*
32 *Lying bitch."*
33 *"Fucking liar!"/ "Cunting liar!" / "Wimp!";*
34 *"Around yr pocket and into yr ass/arse!"*
35 *burglar shitting in your living room/kitchen/bathtub/balcony;*
36 *"A thief who robs another thief gets 100 yrs free of grief." — prov.*
37 *hi-jacker / car-jacker;*
38 *"Fucking mythomaniac!"*
39 *"Bullshit artisté" / "prankster" / "liar";*
40 *dishonest, crooked;*
41 *crook/cheat/swindler;*
42 *"Teller of tales!"*

CUNT HEAR YOU, TWAT? PRICK UP YOUR EAR
(& VARIATIONS)

AFRIKAANS Die poes! *

AFRIKAANS: Jou vader se poes. **

AFRIKAANS: Jou poesdom. [2]

AFRIKAANS: Jou simpel kont! [3]

AFRIKAANS: Jou haai poes. [4]

AFRIKAANS: Jou pielkop! / Jou trilkop! [5]

AFRIKAANS: Jou pielvel. [6]

ALBANIAN Ta henksha piçkin / piçkën. [7]

ARABIC Kuzzik zay el 'a´sal nah'l. [8]

BELARUSIAN Піжда нам! / Pižda nam! [9]

CANTONESE Sòh hāi! [10]

CATALAN El cony de deu! [11]

CROATIAN Mama ti je pušila kurac Srbima. / Baba ti je pušila kurac Srbima. / Sestra ti je pušila kurac Srbima. / Kćer ti je pušila kurac Srbima. [12]

CROATIAN Sin ti je pušio kurac Srbima. [13]

CROATIAN / SERBIAN Ako ne začepiš jebenu gubicu pozvat ću unproforce da ti patroliraju pičkom i stave na nju bodljikavu žicu. [14] ;
Ако пе зачепiш јебепу губису позват су унпрофорсе да ти патролирају пичком у ставе на њу бодљикаву жису. / Ako ne začepiš jebenu gubicu pozvat ću unproforce da ti patroliraju pičkom i stave na nju bodljikavu žicu. [14]

DANISH råbe i mosen [15]

DANISH narrefisse [16]

DANISH Nej, jeg har ikke en dildo, har du? [17]

DUTCH De kut heeft haar eigen ver/vakbond steward. [18]

FARSI Kâputam pareh shod. [19]

FINNISH Vittujen kevät! [20]

FINNISH Hevon vittu! [21]

FRENCH Si tu ne fermes pas ta putain de guele, j'appelle les forces de l'ONU pour qu'elles atrouillent autour de ta chatte cernee de fil barbele. [14]

GAELIC, IRISH Do bháltaí don diabhal. [22]

GAELIC, IRISH Do bháltaí don dia. [23]

GERMAN Querfotze, die [24]

GERMAN Blöde Fotze! [25]

GERMAN weisser Bart [26]

GERMAN Ein Schwanz in Ihrem Auge. [27]

GREEK, MOD. Ρουφα ελλινικο καυλι./Roufa elliniko kavli. [28]

GREEK, MOD. μικρι πσολί /micri psolí [29]

ICELANDIC Þú ert með lítið tippi. [29]

ICELANDIC Er þetta tippið á þér eða pókemon kall? [30]
ICELANDIC Ef þú drullar þér ekki í burtu mun ég fá friðargæsluliða S.Þ. til að vefja böllinum/píkunni á þér í gaddavír. [31]
ICELANDIC Ef þú heldur ekki saman á þér þínum hóru kuntu kjafti mun ég fá umferðalögguna til að draga píkuna á þér í burtu. [32]
ITALIAN Se il cazzo avesse le ali, la tua fica sarebbe un torre di controllo. [33]
ITALIAN Non raccontar fregne! [34]
ITALIAN Milione cazzi nel tuo occhio. [27]
JAPANESE おまんこに万歳 omanko ni banzai [35]
JAPANESE チンチンっぽい脳 chinchin-ppoi nō [36]
MACEDONIAN пичкипа клисура / pičkina klisura [37]
MALAYU Sebelum awak mati, saya nak kau tahu emak kau ada kotek! [38]
MALTESE Busli garretta ala francisa. [6]
MANDARIN 阴道 yīndào [39]
NORWEGIAN bollemus [40]
NORWEGIAN onanere [41]
PORTUGUESE ...Meu pau de lente de contato. [42]
RUSSIAN ебальник / ebál'nik [43]
RUSSIAN хуй пинам / xúj pinam. [44]
RUSSIAN Папа любит чай горячий, а мама любит хуй стоячий. / Pápa ljúbit čaj gorjačij, a máma ljúbit xuj stojáčij. [45]
SPANISH ¡Andáte a la puta concha de tu hermana! / ¡Andáte a la puta concha de tu madre!. [46]
SWEDISH Din mama suger norsk svan pitt. [47]
TAGALOG Light-sabre sa mata. [27]
WELSH Y gont! / Cer i grafu y gont! / Dos i ffwcio dy hun y gont! / Twll tin y gont! [48]
WELSH Y gont hoyw! / Cer i grafu y gont hoyw! / Dos i ffwcio dy hun y gont hoyw! / Twll tin y gont hoyw! [49]

* *"That cunt bitch! / "That cunt bastard!"*

** *"Yr father's cunt."*

2 *"You dumb twat/cunt."*

3 *"You silly cunt!"*

4 *'You shark cunt!"*

5 *"You dick head!"*

6 *AFRIKAANS: "You foreskin!";*
MALTESE: "You can French kiss my foreskin!"

7 *"I'll eat yr pussy."*

8 *"Yr pussy's honey." / "Yr cunt's honey";*

9 *"We're all cunting done for!" ;*

10 *"Stupid cunt!"*

11 *"God's cunt!"*

12 *"Yr mother gave Serbs blowjobs." / "Yr grandmother gave Serbs blowjobs." / "Yr sister gave Serbs blowjobs." / "Yr daughter gave Serbs blowjobs.";*

13 *"Yr son gave Serbs blowjobs."*

14 *"If you don't shut the fuck up now I'll send for a UN peace-keeping troop to set up patrols & border yr cunt with razor wire.";*

15 *"shout in the marsh" = giving a woman head;*

16 *"joker cunt" = tease;*

17 *"No, I don't have a dildo, do you?"*

18 *"Yr cunt/pussy has its own union steward."*

19 *"My "hood"* [condom] *ripped."*

20 *"Pussy Springs!" = Goddamn!;*

21 *"Horse's cunt!"*

22 *"Yr cunt to the devil."*

23 *"Yr cunt to God."*

24 *cunt gone sideways;*

25 *"Stupid cunt!"*

26 *"pearl necklace" = beads of cum dangling from yr chin;*

27 *GERMAN: "A prick/dick in yr eye.";*
ITALIAN: "A million dicks/pricks/cocks in yr eye."
TAGALOG: "A 'light-sabre' in yr eye."

28 *"Suck on Greek cock."*

29 *GREEK, MOD.: "micro-dick/cock";*
ICELANDIC: "You have a small prick/dick/cock."

30 *"Is that yr prick/cock or a Pokemón action figure?"*

31 *"If you don't piss off I'll have a UN peacekeepr wrap yr dick/cock in razor wire."*

32 *"If you don't shut yr whoring cunt mouth I'll have the traffic cops tow yr cunt away."*

33 *"If dicks/cocks had wings, your pussy/cunt wld be the control tower."*

34 *"Don't talk 'cunt'!"*

35 *"dick brain";*

36 *"dive headlong into pussy";*

37 *"cunt canyon";*

38 *"Before you die, I want you to know that your mother has a dick/cock!"*

39 *"way of yin" = pussy;*

40 *"bowl mouse";*

41 *"clit-wank";*

42 *"...My dick wears a contact lens." Braz.;*

43 *"cunt mouth";*

44 *"We kick prick/dick/cock."*

45 *"Father loves his hot tea, & mother loves a hot hard-on."*

46 *"Go to yr sister's whoring bitch cunt. / Go to yr mother's whoring bitch cunt," Arg.;*

47 *"Yr mother sucks Norwegian swan dick/cock."*

48 *"You cunt!" / "Fuck off, you cunt!" / "Go fuck yourself, you cunt!" / "Up yrs, you cunt!";*

49 *"You gay cunt!" / "Fuck off, you gay cunt!" / "Go fuck yourself, you gay cunt!" / "Up yrs, you gay cunt!"*

DYKES
ON
BIKES
&
QUEERS
ON
PIERS
(& VARIATIONS)

AFRIKAANS Jou beer. *

AFRIKAANS Jou manvrou. / Jou letticus. / Jou Lettie. / Jou lemon. **

AFRIKAANS Jou ouboet. [2]

CROATIAN / SERB Jesi ti promijenio spol? *(m)* [3]

Јеси ти промијенио спол? / Jesi ti promijenio spol? *(m)* [3]

CROATIAN / SERB Jesi ti promijenila spol? *(f)* [3]

Јеси ти промијенила спол? / Jesi ti promijenila spol? *(f)* [3]

CZECH Lesbička čubka. [4]

DUTCH Rot op naadninja. [5]

DUTCH Rot op naadsoldaat. [6]

DUTCH Rot op darmtoerist! [7]

FINNISH Anna persettä. [8]

FINNISH Otat kuulemma perseeseen mielelläsi. [9]

FINNISH Revi huoranpersees. [10]

FINNISH Ruskean reiän ritari. [11]

FRENCH Frappe mon cul. [12]

FRENCH J'me suis fendu le cul pour toé! [13]

GERMAN, SW. Schwudi / Schwuppel / Schwuchtlä / Schwul / Warme, der [14]

GERMAN Futlecka! [15]

GREEK, MOD. βάυρον / báyron [16]

GREEK, MOD. δουας /dóvas [17]

GREEK, MOD. καραούβο/ καραλοθβού / karaoúbo / karalouboú [18]

ITALIAN essera del'altra spondabanchina [19]

JAPANESE バラ族 bara-zoku [20]

JAPANESE ぐにゃぐにゃ gunya gunya [21]

MALAYU Sebelum awak mati, saya nak kau tahu emak kau ada kotek! [22]

MANDARIN 同志 tóngzhì [23]

MARATHI ba<u>tt</u>ebaja [24]

NORWEGIAN Din jævla baksetehumper! [25]

PORTUGUESE O seu irmão é um viado. / O seu pai é um viado. / O seu filho é um viado. [26]

RUSSIAN малшик / malšik [27]

SPANISH Marcha atrás! [28]

SPANISH El maricón se le cae el Jabon. [29]

SPANISH Anda a lavarte tu culo, maricon culiado. [30]

SWAHILI Msenge wewe! Nakala tatu! [31]

TAGALOG Pakímbero mo! [32]

TURKISH bad asl kuni [18]

UZBEK aka'si [33]
UZBEK aka singli [34]
WELSH Y gont hoyw! / Cer i grafu y gont hoyw! / Dos i ffwcio dy hun y gont hoyw! / Twll tin y gont hoyw! [35]
ZULU Ucitha isikathi sakho, nagamafeleza! [36]

* *"You bear." = butch dyke;*
** *"You butch dyke!"*
2 *"You old brother." = dyke endearment;*
3 *"Did you have a sex change operation?"*
4 *"Lesbian bitch."*
5 *"Fuck off, you butt-crack ninja."*
6 *"Fuck off, you butt-crack trooper."*
7 *"Fuck off, you faggoty bowel tourist!"*
8 *"Give me some ass/arse."*
9 *"I hear you enjoy taking it up the ass/arse."*
10 *"Rip yr slutty ass/arse open."*
11 *"Knight of the Faggot Bung Hole!"*
12 *"Spank my ass/arse."*
13 *"I split my own ass/arse just for you!"*
14 *the gay/faggot/queer;*
15 *"Bitch-blower!" = dyke;*
16 *"Byron" = swelligant gay/faggot/queer;*
17 *"rude antisocial faggot"*
18 *GREEK, MOD.: really evil & trechcerous faggot;*
TURKISH.: "evil backstabbing faggoty queen";
19 *"from the opposite riverbank" / "from the opposite quay";*
20 *"rose tribe"*
21 *limp wrist gay, faggot, queer;*
22 *"Before you die, I want you to know that yr mother has a dick/cock!"*
23 *"Comrade" = the "International Homintern" lives;*
24 *"ass/arsefucking faggoty pederast";*
25 *"You fucking back-seat humper!"*
26 *"Yr brother's a faggot." / "Yr father's a faggot." / "Yr son's a faggot," Braz.;*
27 *"Armenian gay/queer/faggot";*
28 *"Reverse gear," Arg.;*
29 *"The gay/faggot/queer drops the soap."*
30 *"Go wash yr faggoty fucked ass-/arsehole."*
31 *"You gay faggot! In triplicate!"*
32 *"You gay ass/arsefucker!"*
33 *"older brother" = said by dancing boy/bottom to pederast top;*
34 *"little brother" = said by pederast top to dancing boy/bottom;*
35 *"You gay cunt!" / "Fuck off, you gay cunt!" / "Go fuck yourself, you gay cunt!" / "Up yrs, you gay cunt!"*
36 *"Don't waste time on him, he's straight!"*

FUCK YOU TRULY, MADLY, DEEPLY (& VARIATIONS)

AFRIKAANS Naai jou Waarheid en Versoening. / Fok jou Waarheid en Versoening. *
AFRIKAANS: Fok jou en jou familie! **
ARABIC Rouh neek halak wodhas libet barabe beteezak! [2]
CANTONESE Ngóh díu néih gāu fai! [3]
CANTONESE Díu néih hìng daih! [4]
CROATIAN / SERB Jebo svoj sunčan dan. [5]
Јебо свој сунчан дан. / Jebo svoj sunčan dan. [5]
CROATIAN / SERB Jebo svoju evropsku uniju. [6]
Јебо своју еврпску унију. / Jebo svoju evropsku uniju. [6]
CROATIAN / SERB Jebo svoj pasoš. [7]
Јебо свој пасош. / Jebo svoj pasoš. [7]
CROATIAN / SERB Jebem ti narodno zdravlje. [8]
Јебем ту народно здравлје. / Jebem ti narodno zdravlje. [8]
CROATIAN / SERB Jebo te Milosovič. [9]
Јебо ту милосович. / Jebo te Milosovič. [9]
CROATIAN / SERB Jebo svoj usrani pank rock bend. [10]
Јебо свој усрани панк роск бенд. / Jebo svoj usrani pank rock bend. [10]
CROATIAN / SERB Jebo svoj usrani pank rock. [11]
Јебо свој усрани панк роск. / Jebo svoj usrani pank rock. [11]
CROATIAN / SERB Jebo svoj usrani svadbeni ciganski bend. [12]
Јебо свој усрани свадбени сигански бенд. / Jebo svoj usrani svadbeni ciganski bend. [12]
CROATIAN / SERB Jebo svoju usranu svadbenu cigansku glazbu. [13]
Јебо свој усрани свадбени сиганску глазбу. / Jebo svoju usranu svadbenu cigansku glazbu. [13]
DANISH Du kan kneppe dig selv i røven med en legoklods! [14]
DUTCH Ik laat je vader bukken. / Ik laat je broer bukken. / Ik laat je zoon bukken. [15]
FARSI Molla kundeh. [16]
FINNISH Äitisi nai poroja. [17]
FRENCH J'encule Foucault! [18]
FRENCH J'encule Baudrillard! [19]
FRENCH Je l'encule ton premier mai! [20]
GAELIC, IRISH Feisigh do nianna agus neachtanna. [21]
GAELIC, SCOTS Rach thu agus tarraing do bhanta agus mhac-brathair. / Rach thu agus tarraing do bhanta agus mhac-piuthair. [21]
GAELIC, SCOTS Bidh do mhàthair a' dàireadh le Caitiligich. [22]
GAELIC, SCOTS Bidh do mhàthair a' dàireadh le Pròsdanaich. [23]
GAELIC, SCOTS Bidh do mhàthair a' dàireadh le Chalvinaich. [24]
GAELIC, SCOTS Bidh do mhàthair a' dàireadh le Sassanaich. [25]
GERMAN Fick Jeden in deiner Schnellwahl! [26]

GERMAN I fick dei familie. **

GERMAN Fick dich ins Knie. [27]

GREEK, MOD Γαμο το θεο. / Gamo to theo. [28]

GREEK, MOD. Σου γαμο τιν μανα κε ολο σου το σοι! / Sou gamo tin mana, ke olo sou to soi! **

HINDI / URDU Behen-chut! [29]

HINDI / URDU Mā-chut! [30]

ICELANDIC Ríddu þér með Mr. Pink kallinum. [31]

ICELANDIC Ríddu öllum á hraðvalinu í gemsanum þínum. [26]

ICELANDIC Ríddu frænkum og frændum þínum. [21]

ITALIAN Va funcuolo Dio e papa e tutte i santi! [28]

JAPANESE 口でやる kuchi de yaru. [32]

JAPANESE ザッケンナヨ！ Zakkenayo! [33]

JAPANESE テメーの甥と姪をやれ！ Temē no oi to mei o yare! [21]

LATIN Deus Christianus tuus futuatur. / Christus tuus futuatur. [28]

MACEDONIAN Да ти ебам бозество кучка! / Da ti ebam bozestvo kučka! [28]

MACEDONIAN Да ти ебам све по листа телефон! / Da ti ebam sve po lista telefon. [34]

MACEDONIAN Да ти ебам све по телефон! / Da ti ebam sve po telefon. [26]

MACEDONIAN Да ти ебам народ! / Da ti ebam narod! [35]

MACEDONIAN Еби даб! / Ebi dab! [36]

MACEDONIAN Еби џунла! / Ebi jungla! [37]

MANDARIN 你妈了操尝毛主席! Nǐ māle cào cháng mao zhǔ xí! [38]

NORWEGIAN Forpulte norske hvaldreper! [39]

PORTUGUESE, BRAZ. Foda-se e morra-se. [33]

RUSSIAN Передай, ёб твою мать, водку! / Peredáj, ëb tvojú mat' sol'! [40]

RUSSIAN Передай, ёб твою мать, соль! / Peredáj, ëb tvojú mat' vódku! [41]

SPANISH ¡Chinga la purmísima hostia! [42]

SPANISH Chingado sin madre. [30]

SPANISH Chinga tu padre. / Jode tu padre. *"Fuck yr father."* [43]

SPANISH Chinga tus sobrinas y sobrinos. / Jode tus sobrinas y sobrinos. [21]

SWAHILI Nenda kutomba nakala tatu! [44]

SWEDISH Jävla evangelist! [28]

WELSH Cau dy wyneb a ffwcio dy tad! [43]

WELSH Cau dy wyneb a ffwcio dy ewythr! [45]

YIDDISH Schtupp elohim! / Stup elohim! [28]

YIDDISH Schtupp Moskze. / Stup Moskze. [46]

* *"Bugger yr Truth & Reconciliation!" /*
"Fuck yr Truth & Reconciliation!"

** *AFRIKAANS: "Fuck you & yr family!"*
GERMAN: "I fuck yr family." /Bav.;
GREEK, MOD.: "I'll fuck yr mother & yr whole family!"

2 *"Fuck yourself with a Barbi-doll!"*

3 *"I'll fuck yr lungs!"*

4 *"Fuck yr brothers!"*

5 *"Fuck yr sunshiny day."*

6 *“Fuck yr European Union.”*

7 *“Fuck yr passport.”*

8 *“Fuck yr National Health.”*

9 *“Milosevic* [ex-Serb president & war criminal] *fucked you.”*

10 *“Fuck yr shitty punk rock band.”*

11 *“Fuck yr shitty punk rock music.”*

12 *“Fuck yr shitty polka wedding band.”*

13 *“Fuck yr shitty polka wedding music.”*

14 *“You can fuck yourself up the ass/arse with a Lego brick!”*

15 *“I’ll ass/arse-fuck yr father.” /*
“I’ll ass/arse-fuck yr brother.” /
“I’ll ass/arse-fuck yr son.”

16 *“Yr mullah gets fucked up the ass/arse.”*

17 *“Yr mother fucks reindeer.”*

18 *“Fuck Foucault!”*

19 *“Fuck Baudrillard!”*

20 *“Fuck yr May Day!”*

21 *GAELIC, IRISH / ICELANDIC / JAPANESE / SPANISH: “Fuck yr nieces & nephews.”*
GAELIC, SCOTS: “Fuck yr nieces.” /
“Fuck yr nephews.”

22 *“Yr mother fucks Catholics.”*

23 *“Yr mother fucks Protestants.”*

24 *“Yr mother fucks Calvinists.”*

25 *“Yr mother fucks Englishmen.”*

26 *GERMAN: “Fuck everyone on yr speed dial!”;*
ICELANDIC: “Fuck everyone on yr mobile/cell phone direct dial”;
MACEDONIAN: “Fuck everyone on yr telephone/mobile.”

27 *“Fuck you in the knee.”*

28 *GREEK, MOD.: “I fuck God.”*
ITALIAN.: “Fuck God, Christ, the Pope & all the Saints!”;
LATIN: “Fuck yr Christian god!” / “Fuck yr Christ!”;
MACEDONIAN: “Fuck yr God, bitch!”
SWEDISH: “Fucking evangelist!”
YIDDISH: “Fuck God!” = Fuck the most Holy God whose name we dare not pronounce — at least not correctly, nor probably even dare utter, according to Talmudic trad.

29 *“Sister-fucker!”*

30 *HINDI / URDU: “Motherfucker!”*
SPANISH: “Motherless fuck!”

31 *“Fuck yourself with a Mr. Pink action figure.”*

32 *“Fuck you in the mouth.” / “Mouth-fuck you.”*

33 *JAPANESE: “Fuck off & die!”;*
PORTUGUESE: “Fuck youself & die.” /Braz.;

34 *“Fuck everyone on yr telephone list.”;*

35 *“Fuck yr nation!”*

36 *“Go fuck an oak tree!”*

37 *“Go fuck a jungle!”*

38 *“Yr mother fucked Chairman Mao!”*

39 *“Fucking Norwegian whale-killer!”*

40 *"Pass the "fuck-yr-mother" salt!"*
41 *"Pass the "fuck-yr-mother" vodka!"*
42 *"Fuck the most Holy Communion wafer!"*
43 *SPANISH: "Fuck yr father."*
WELSH: "Shut yr fucking face, father fucker!"
44 *"Go fuck yourself in triplicate!"*
45 *"Shut yr fucking face, uncle fucker!"*
46 *"Fuck Moscow!"*

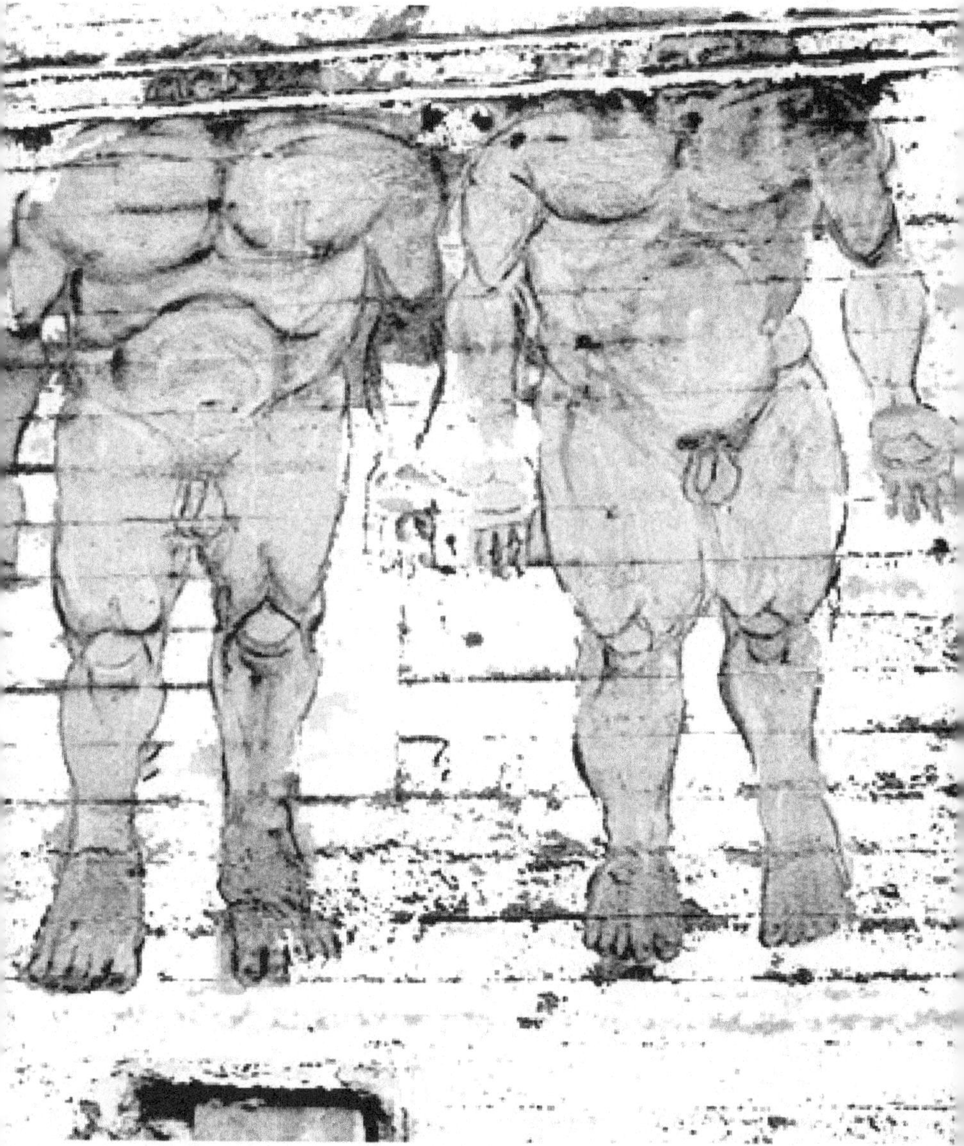

PISS ME A RIVER (& VARIATIONS)

CANTONESE Hàahng lán hōi! *
DANISH Hvem har pisset på din sukkermad? **
FINNISH Päässäsi tekee kusi patoja ja paska puroja. [2]
FRENCH C'est comme si on pissait dans un violoncelle. [3]
GREEK, MOD. Να ση κατουρισο! /Na se katouriso! [4]
ITALIAN è come pisciare controvento. [5]
ITALIAN Non troverebbe neanche l'acqua nel mare. [6]
ITALIAN Non organizzerebbe una bevuta nella birreria. [7]
MALTESE Inbullek fuq tiegh˙ek kelba ommok. [8]
MALTESE Inbullek fuq l ewropa! [9]
MALTESE Inbullek fuq liba vatikan. [10]
MALTESE Inbullek fuq alla. [11]
PORTUGUESE Mim mijo no leite da sua mãe. [12]
ROMANIAN Ma pis pe cur de idiot. [13]
ROMANIAN Ma pis pe mortii matii. [14]
ROMANIAN Ma pis pe mata si-n coliva ei. [15]
ROMANIAN Ma pis pe mormantu' lu' mata. [16]
ROMANIAN Ma pis pe mata moarta! [17]
RUSSIAN Против ветра не щи. /Prótiv vétra ne šči. [5]
RUSSIAN Щать я на него хотел. / Ščat' ja na negó xotél. [4]
SPANISH Quiero miar en la leche de tu madre. / Quiero miar en la leche de tu puta madre. [12]
THAI chèe rót gan [18]
WELSH Piso bant. *

* *"Piss off!"*
** *"Who pissed on yr sugar sandwich?"*
2 *"In yr mind's eye, dams are built from piss and rivers flow with shit."*
3 *"It was as if someone pissed into a cello."*
4 *GREEK, MOD.: "Piss on you!"*
RUSSIAN: "I myself would [definitely / probably] *piss on him."*
5 *ITALIAN: "It's like pissing against the wind";*
RUSSIAN: "Don't go pissing into the wind."
6 *"He couldn't even find water in the ocean."*
7 *"He couldn't organize a piss-up in a brewery."*
8 *"I piss upon yr bitch mother."*
9 *"I piss upon Europe!"*
10 *"I piss upon the Vatican."*
11 *"I piss upon God."*
12 *PORTUGUESE: "I piss in yr mother's milk.";*

SPANISH: "I want to piss in yr mother's milk." /
"I want to piss in yr whore mother's milk."
13 *"I piss on yr idiot ass/arse."*
14 *"I piss on yr mother's dead ancestors."*
15 *"I piss on yr mother's funeral / wake cake."*
16 *"I piss on yr mother's grave."*
17 *"I piss on yr dead mother!"*
18 *water sports, golden showers;*

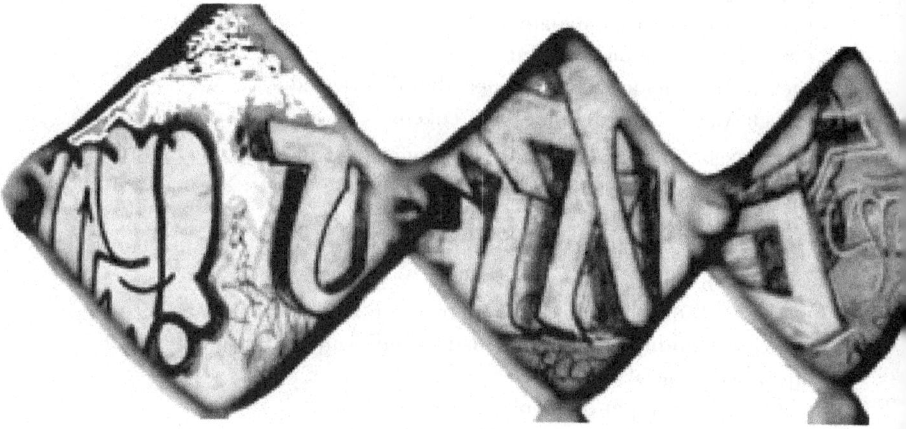

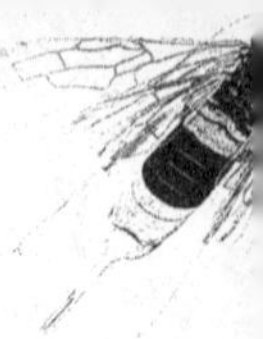

PRODUCT PLACEMENT (& VARIATIONS)

AFRIKAANS As dit die nuutste Doris Lessing / Nadine Gordimer boek is sal ek wag vir die fliek, en dit ook mis. *

ARABIC Rouh nēk halak wodhas libet barabe betēzak! **

BOSNIAN Jebo ti pokemona digimon! ***

BOSNIAN Jebo te pokemona! / Jebo te digimona! [2]

CROATIAN / SERB Jebo ti Tarzan baba! [3]; Џебо ти Тарзан баба! / Jebo ti Tarzan baba! [3]

CROATIAN / SERB Jebo te Handke. [4]; Јебо те Хандке. / Jebo te Handke. [4]

DANISH Du kan kneppe dig selv i røven med en legoklods! [5]

DANISH Knep dig selv med et lyssværd. [6]

DANISH Knep dig selv med en pokemon-figur. [7]

DUTCH aarsjedi / reetjedi [8]

FARSI Barabe arusak nanato kard. **

FARSI Pokemona nanato kard. [2]

FRENCH Va t'enculer avec un jouet Chevalier de Jedi. [9]

FRENCH Va t'enculer avec un jouet Pokemón. [7]

GAELIC, IRISH Tá sé mar Séamus Ó hÉanaí ag teacht amach ó mo thóin. [10]

GAELIC, SCOTS Bidh thu a' brodadh le postair Elton John 'sa seomar-mhullaich aig do phàrantan. [11]

GERMAN Bumsen Sie Ihe Mutter mit Pokemon Tätigkeit Abbildungen Spielwaren. [2]

ICELANDIC Ríddu þér með barbídúkku. **

ICELANDIC Ríddu þér í rassgat með hermannadúkkunni Jóa. [12]

ICELANDIC Ríddu þér með stjörnustríðshetju kalli. / Runkaðu þér með stjörnustríðs geislasverði. [6]

ICELANDIC Ríddu þér með pókemon kalli. [7]

ICELANDIC Ríddu þér með Mr. Pink kallinum. [13]

ICELANDIC Er þetta tippið á þér eða pókemon kall? [14]

ITALIAN Se questo e' il nuovo libro di Umberto Eco, aspettero' il film e saltero' anche quello. *

ITALIAN Perche' quelli che leggono Pasolini sempre si comportano come Pasolini? [15]

JAPANESE あれは坂本龍一の新しいアルバム、それともおばあちゃんのへかな？ Are wa Sakamoto Ryichi no atarashii arubamu, soretomo obchan no he ka na? [16]

JAPANESE 文学生命は最初に切腹せずには残念ですよ。Bungaku semei wa saisho ni seppuku sezu ni wa zannen desu yo. [17]

NORWEGIAN Gå å Obi-wan din pule deg i ræva. [18]

NORWEGIAN Gå å prinsesse Leia din pule deg i ræva. [19]

PORTUGUESE Vou te estuprar com um brinquedo do Pokemona. [7]

SPANISH Pinche verga de pitufo! / Pinche pito de pitufo! [20]

SPANISH Pinche verga de Pikechu! / Pinche pito de Pikechu! [21]

SPANISH Mete te un fugete de Pokeomon al culo. [2]

SPANISH Chinga te en el culo con una muñeca de Barbí. **

SPANISH Chinga te en el culo con una muñeca de G.I. Joe. [12]

SPANISH Esa vieja historia es como cuento de Borges...muerto por el culo. [22]

TAGALOG Saksak ko tong light-sabre sa wepáks mo e, puta. [6]

TAGALOG Puta Cleopatra! [23]

WELSH Ffwcio dy G.I. Joe-doli i fyny'r pen ol. [12]

WELSH Ffwcio dy Barbi-doli i fyny'r pen ol. **

* *AFRIKAANS: "If that's the latest Doris Lessing / Nadine Gordimer book, I'll wait for the movie & skip that too."; ITALIAN: "If that's the latest Umberto Eco book I'll wait for the movie & skip that too."*

** *ARABIC / ICELANDIC: "Fuck yourself with a Barbi-doll!"*
FARSI: "A Barbi-doll fucked yr mother!"
SPANISH: "Fuck you up the ass/arse with a Barbi-doll!"
WELSH: "Fuck yr Barbi-doll up the ass/arse."

*** *"Pokemón fucked Digimon!"*

2 *BOSNIAN: "Pokemón fucked you!" / "Digimon fucked you!"*
FARSI: "Pokemón fucked yr mother!"
GERMAN: "Fuck yr mother with Pokemon acton figure toys";
SPANISH: "Stick a Pokemón action figure up yr ass/arse."

3 *"Tarzan fucked yr grandmother!"*

4 *"[Peter] Handke fucked you." [playwright Handke, a German supporter of Serb extreme nationalists, became one of the most hated people in the Balkans, even more so than Milosovich by some....]*

5 *"You can fuck yourself up the ass/arse with a Lego brick!"*

6 *DANISH / ICELANDIC: "Fuck yourself with a light sabre."*
TAGALOG: "Wait till I stick this light-sabre up yr ass/arse, bitch."

7 *DANISH / ICELANDIC: "Fuck yourself with a Pokemón action figure."*
FRENCH: "Go get fucked up the ass/arse with a Pokemón toy.";
PORTUGUESE: "I'll fuck yr ass/arse with a Pokemón action figure."

8 *"ass-/arse-jedi knight" / "butt-jedi knight" = gay/queer top;*

9 *"Go get fucked up the ass/arse with a Jedi knight action figure."*

10 *"It's like Séamus Heaney emerging from my ass/arse."*

11 *"You wank to an Elton John poster in yr parents' attic."*

12 *ICELANDIC: "Fuck yourself with G.I Joe doll."; SPANISH: "Fuck you up the ass/arse with a G.I. Joe doll!"; WELSH: "Fuck yr G.I. Joe-doll up the ass/arse."*

13 *"Fuck yourself with a Mr. Pink action figure."*

14 *"Is that yr prick/dick/cock or a Pokemón action figure?"*

15 *"Why is it that people who read Pasolini always act like Pasolini?"*

16 *"Is that Ryuichi Sakamoto's new album or yr grandmother farting?"*

17 *"[On Yukio Mishima...] Too bad he didn't start his career with seppuku."*

18 *"Let Obi-wan fuck you up yr ass/arse."*

19 *"Let Princess Leia fuck you up yr ass/arse."*

20 *"Fucking smurf dick!" / "Fucking smurf prick!"*

21 *"Fucking Pikachu dick!" / "Fucking Pikachu prick!"*

22 *"That tired old bullshit's like a story by Borges, dead up the ass/arse."*

23 *"Fucking stinky Cleopatra bitch!" = That fucking bitch may look great but she [literally] stinks like a bad movie.*

graffiti grafix: l. c. bobalovna/ m. feinstein/t. warburton y bajo/GobQ

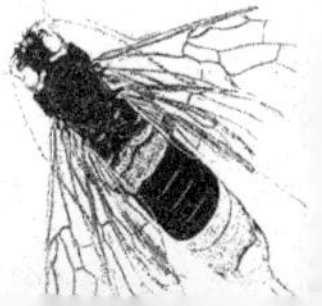

curse + berate in 69+ languages

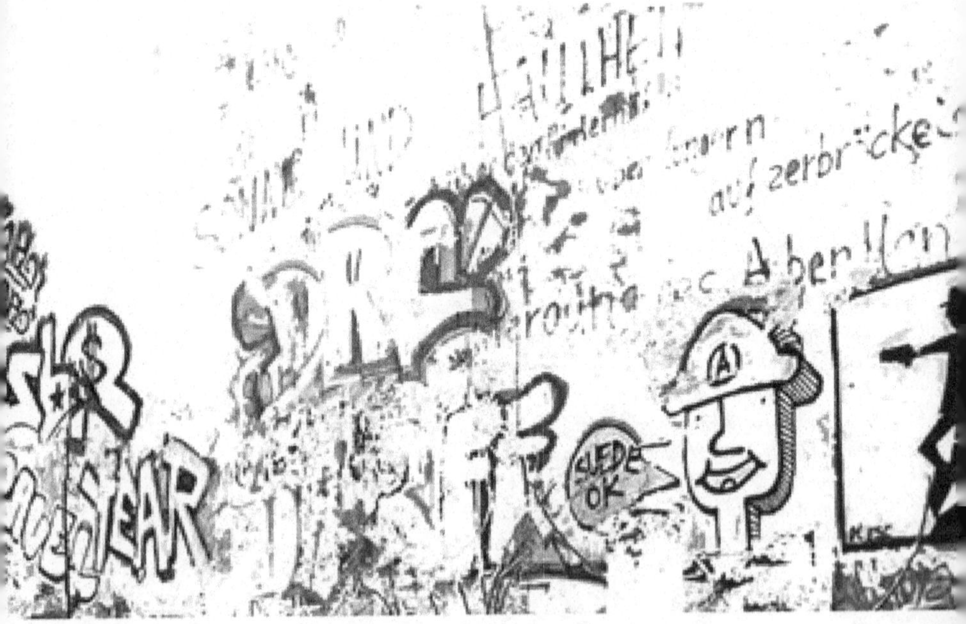

CONTRIBUTORS
&
PARTICIPANTS:

Thanks to Terry Boren (who set me upon this path, back in 1984), & to her husband James who assisted with fossicking for Native American speakers.

In addition to most of our interns listed on the title page, the following native-speakers contributed to this volume. Due to professional reasons & the vagaries of a dishonest & hypocritical society many of the names below have to use pseudonyms or initials:

Zafar A., Sarah Barrett, Boris B., Jackie B., Monica B., R.V. Branham, Julie B., M. C., Nick C., S. C., F. d'O., Channing Dodson, H.E., Edita F., Sabrina G., A. G., Jukka Heiskanen, Maurius K.,L. J., Christoph K., K. L., Rowan Leaf, G. N., M. Olson, Milosh P., "the Slow Poisoner," Stephen Raphael, F. Raphael, Mad R., I Rehorik, D. S.,P. S., P. S., Moises Salazar, M. S., N. S., George S., Luisa Valenzuela, Frigg Völundardóttir, Jensen W., & Kelly Z.

BIBLIOGRAPHY

EDITOR'S NOTE: The following dictionaries were consulted to ensure consistency in grammar & in Romanization from other alphabets. There should never be any doubt that any & all errors are the complete fault of the Bush-Cheney regime, & shall be corrected in susbsequent editions.

Standard Turkish Dictionary, Resuhi Akdikmen, Langenscheidt, NY, NY, ©1985;
Streetwise Italian Dictionary/Thesaurus, N. Albanese, G. Spani, P. Balma, E. Conti, McGraw-Hill Cos., Inc., NY, NY, ©2005;
Kurdish-English Dictionary, Aziz Amindarov, Hippocrene Books, Inc., NY, NY, ©1994;
Arabic for Travelers, Editions Berlitz, Switzerland, ©1975;
Armenian-English Dictionary, Diane Aroutunian & Susanna Aroutunian, Hippocrene Books, Inc., NY, NY, ©1993;
Basque-English Dictionary, Gorka Aulestia & Linda White, University of Nevada Press, Reno, NV, ©1992;
Hausa Dictionary, Nicholas Awde, Hippocrene Books, Inc., NY, NY, © 1996;
Serbo-Croatian, Nicholas Awde, Hippocrene Books, Inc., NY, NY, ©1996;
Bahasa Malaysia-English Pocket Dictionary, Periplus Editions, Watsonville, CA, ©1993;
Webster's New World Hebrew Dictionary, Hayim Baltsan, Wiley Publishing, Inc., Cleveland, OH, ©1992;
X-treme Latin, Henry Beard (Henricus Barbatus), Gotham Books, Penguin Group, Inc., NY, NY, ©2005;
Std. English – Serbo-Croatian Dictionary, A dictionary of Bosnian & Croatian & Serbian standards, Morton Benson, Cambridge U. Press, Cambridge UK & NY, NY, (1st. pub., © 1982) reprint © 1999;
Estonian-English Dictionary & Phrasebook, Ksenia Benyukh, Hippocrene Books, Inc., NY, NY, © 2002;
The Concise Dictionary of 26 Languages, compiled by Peter M. Bergman, Signet Classics, NY, NY, ©1968;
Zapotec-English (Isthmus) Concise Dictionary, A. Scott Britton, Hippocrene Books, Inc., NY, NY, ©2003;
Norwegian Dictionary, w./ a supplement by Kari Bra˚tveit, Routledge, London, UK & NY, NY (first pub. in Norway by J.W.Cappelens Forlag A-S,Oslo, © 1990), Routledge ed. published, © 1994;
Gayle, the language of kinks & queens: a history & dictionary of gay language in South Africa, Ken Cage w/ Moyra Evans, Jacana Media, Houghton, South Africa, © 2003;

English-Cantonese Dictionary, The Chinese University Press, Hong Kong, ©1991;
The University of Chicago English-Spanish Dictionary, Compiled by Carlos Castillo & Otto F. Bond, Washington Sq. Press, NY, NY, ©1948;
Harrap's Mini English-Khmer Dictionary, ed. by Tim Chetra & Theng Leang, ©2005;
Gujarati Dictionary & Phrasebook, Sonal Christian, Hippocrene Books, Inc., NY, NY, ©2006;
Clough's Sinhala-English Dictionary, New & Enlarged Ed., Rev. B. Clough, Wesleyan Mission Press, Kollupitiya, ©1892;
Malay-English Dictionary, A.E.Coope, Hippocrene Books, Inc., NY, NY, © 1976, rev. pbk. ed. © 1993;
Croatian-English Universal Dictionary Croatian, Langenscheidt, Berlin & Munich, ©2006;
Danish-English Practical Dictionary, Hippocrene Books, Inc., NY, NY, ©2006;
Oxford Paravia Italian-English Dictionary, edited by Tullio De Mauro (Paravia ed. © 2000), Fabrizio Cicoira — ed. & lex. supervision (OUP © 2001), Paravia Bruno Mondadori Editori & Oxford U. Press, © 2001;
Harper Collins Chinese [Mandarin] Concise Dictionary, ed. team — Marianne Davidson & Julie Keeman & Sarah Waldram, Harper-Collins, Glasgow, Great Britain, © 2005;
English Zulu Dictionary, combining the 2nd. © 1953 ed. compiled by C.M. Doke & B.W. Vilakazi & the © 1958 ed. comp. by C.M.Doke & D.McK. Malcolm & .M.A. Sikakana, Witwatersrand U. Press, Johanesberg, South Africa, (1st. comb. ed.) © 1990;
Dutch at your Fingertips, Routledge & Kegan Paul, Lexus Ltd., NY, NY, ©1987;
Dutch-English Dictionary, Berlitz Publishing Co., Ltd., Switzerland, ©1979;
Veni, Vidi, Vici, Eugene Ehrlich, Harper-Collins Publishers, Inc., NY, NY, ©1995;
Welsh-English Dictionary, H. Meurig Evans & W. O. Thomas Saphograph, NY, NY, © 1969;
First Illustrated Yoruba Dictionary, Joseph Ajayi Fashagba, Toronto, Ontario, Canada, © 1991;
Hide this French Book, Berlitz Publishing, Singapore Branch, Singapore, ©2004;
Learn Oriya in 30 Days (7th ed.), N. S. R. Ganathe, M.A., Balaji Publications, Royapettah, Chennai, ©2004;
Learn Punjabi in 30 Days (11th ed.), N. S. R. Ganathe, M.A., Balaji Publications, Royapettah, Chennai, ©2005;
An English-Persian Dictionary, Dariush Gilani, Ibex, Bethesda, MD, © 1999;
Prisma's Swedish English Dictionary (3rd ed.), Eva Gomer & Mona Morris-Nygren w/ Erik Durrant & Michael Knight & Hans Nygren Y Michael Phillips Sture Sundell & Gösta åberg, Bplförlaget Rabén Prisma, Stockholm & U. of Minessota Press, Minneapolis, © 1970, 1988, 1995;
Harper Collins German Dictionary (no ed. team or compilers listed), Harper Resource/Harper-Collins, NY, NY (1st. pub © 1990, Wm. Collins Sons & Co.) 1st. HarperResource printing © 2000;
Greek at you Fingertips, Routledge & Kegan Paul Ltd., London, UK, ©1986;
The Oxford Greek Dictionary, American Ed., Oxford University Press, NY, NY, ©2000;
Bulgarian Phrasebook, compiled by Lexus Ltd. w. Zhivko T. Gulaboff, Dorling Kindersley Pub., NY, NY. © 2000;
Nahuatl-English (Aztec) Dictionary, Fermin Herrera, Hippocrene Books, Inc., NY, NY, ©2004;
Ukrainian Practical Dictionary, Rev. Ed. w. Menu Terms, Leonid Hrabovsky, Hippocrene Books, Inc., ©1994 (1st ed., © 1991);
A Dictionary of Cantonese Slang, Christopher Hutton & Kingsley Bolton, University of Hawai'i Press, Honolulu, HI, © 2005;
Indonesian-English Pocket Dictionary, Periplus Editions, Watsonville, CA, ©1992;
Irish-English Easy Reference Dictionary, Roberts Rinehart Publishers, Niwot, CO, ©1998;
Ethiopian Amharic Phrasebook, Tilahun Kebede, Lonely Planet Publications, Oakland, CA, ©2002;
Chinese Phrasebook, ed. by J. Kleeman with V. Grundy, E. Hallett, C. Johnson, D. Watt, Larousse, Paris, ©2006;
Twi-English Dictionary, Paul A. Kotey, Hippocrene Books, Inc., NY, NY, ©1998;
International Dictionary of Obscenities, Christina Kunitskaya-Peterson, Scythian Books, Oakland, CA, ©1981;
Estonian-English Dictionary, Ksana Kyiv & Oleg Benyuch, Hippocrene Books, Inc., NY, NY, ©1994;
Italian Concise Dictionary, 2nd. Ed., Catherine E. Love & Michela Clari, Harper-Collins Publishers, NY, NY, ©2005;
Essential Scots Dictionary, ed. by Iseabail Macleod & Pauline Cairns, Edinburgh University Press, Edinburgh, ©2004;

Indonesian Dictionary & Phrasebook, Jodie Martin & Laszlo Wagner, Lonely Planet, Footscray, Vic., Australia, © 2006;
Sir Lanka [Sinhala/Sinhalese] Phrasebook, Margit Meinhold, Lonely Planet, S. Yarrah, Vic., Australia, © 1986;
Farsi-English (Persian) Dictionary, A.M. Miandji, Hippocrene Books, Inc., NY, NY, ©2003;
Norwegian Phrase Book & Dictionary, 2nd. rev. ed., Berlitz Publishing Co., Ltd., Oxford, UK, ©1990;
English-Czech Dictionary (10th. rev. ed.), Ivan Poldauf & Jan Caha & Alena Kopecká & Jiří Krámsky´, W.D. Pubs., Družstevni, Czech. Rep., Llewellyn's, Middlesex, UK, © 1998;
Ellison's Grammatical Guide & Glossary for the Goyin [incl. w. "I'm Looking For Kadak" audiocassette], Harlan Ellison, © 1980;
Portuguese at your Fingertips, Routledge & Kegan Paul, Ltd., London, UK, ©1986;
Popular Northern Sotho Dictionary, T.J. Kriel, (1st. ed. pub. by Dibukeng, Pretoria, © 1971; 2nd. ed. pub. by J.L. Van Schaik, Pretoria, © 1976) J.L. Van Schaik, Pretoria, S. Africa, 3rd. ed. 2nd. impression, © 1993;
The American Heritage Spanish Dictionary, 2nd. Ed., D. R. Pritchard, H. Schonthal, J. Pope, Berkley Books, NY, NY, ©2000;
Teach Yourself Zulu, Arnett Wilkes & Nicholias Nkosi, Hodder & Stroughton, London UK, 2003;
NTC's Vietnamese-English Dictionary, Dinh-hoa Nguyen, NTC Pub. Grp., Lincolnwood, Illinois, © 1995;
Routledge Catalan Dictionary [no editors or compilers listed], Routledge, London, UK & NY, NY (1st published in Barcelona by Bibliograph, S.A., © 1993), Routledge ed. published, © 1994;
Tagalog-English Dictionary, Carl. R. Galvez Rubino, Hippocrene Books, Inc., NY, NY, © 1998 (rev. & exp. ed. © 2002);
Yoeme-English Standard Dictionary, David L. Shaul, Hippocrene Books, Inc., NY, NY, ©1999;
NTC's Compact Finnish & English Dictionary, Sini Sovijärvi, NTC Pub. Grp., Lincolnwood, Illinois, © 1995;
Concise English-Korean Dictionary (romanized), Joan V. Underwood, Charles E. Tuttle Co., Rutland, VT & Toko, Japan, ©1954 (47th printing, ©1997);
Haitian Creole Dictionary, Charmant Theodore, Hippocrene Books, NY NY, © 1995 (3rd. printing, © 2000);
Dermo! The Real Russian Tolstoy Never Used, Edward Topol, Penguin Books USA Inc., NY, NY, ©1997;
The New College Latin & English Dictionary, John C. Traupman, Ph.D., Bantam Books, NY, NY, ©1996 (1st ed., 1995);
Byelorussian Dictionary, Alexander Ushkevich & Alexandra Zezulin, Hippocrene Books, NY NY, © 1992;
Portuguese Concise Dictionary (2nd ed.), Harper-Collins Publishers, NY, NY, ©2001 (1st ed., ©1991);
Russian Concise Dictionary (2nd ed.), Harper-Collins Publishers, NY, NY, ©2000 (1st ed., ©1994);
Romanian-English Dictionary, Marcel Schönkron, Hippocrene Books, NY, NY, ©1991;
Je Ne Sais What?, Jon Winokur, Penguin Books, NY, NY, ©1995;
Wortabet's Pocket Dictionary, John Wortabet & Harvey Porter, Librairie du Liban;
Tagalog Slang Dictionary, R. David Zoro & Rachel San Miguel, Dunwoody Press, Kensington, MD, © 1990;

(CURSE & BERATE IT IN 69 LANGUAGES QUESTIONAIRE

A LIST OF INVECTIVE & CURSES IN ___________ & ENGLISH

NAME:____________________

E-mail & snail-mail address info:_____________________________________

NOTE: Fill out this form & send to gobq @ gobshitequarterly dot com,

or to GobQ LLC, PO Box, 11346, Portland OR 97211, or request a form.

LANGUAGE(s) OF FLUENCY:

____

BODY PARTS (1 – 0)

(1 – 1) PRICK, DICK, COCK (& VARIATIONS)

(1 – 2) COCKSUCKER (& VARIATIONS)

(1 – 3) BLOWJOB (& VARIATIONS)

(1 – 4) A PRICK IN YOUR EYE (& VARIATIONS)

(1 – 5) A PRICK IN YOUR MOUTH (& VARIATIONS)

(1 – 6) KISS-ASS/ARSE, ASS/ARSE LICKER (& VARIATIONS)

(1 – 7) KISS MY ASS/ARSE, LICK MY ASS/ARSE (& VARIATIONS)

(1 – 8) DICK BRAIN, DICK HEAD, DICK FACE (& VARIATIONS)

(1 – 9) BALLS/BOLLOCKS, BALLS! (& VARIATIONS)

(1– 10) BALLS-FOR-BRAINS (& VARIATIONS)

(1 – 11) BALL-BUSTER, BALL-BREAKER (& VARIATIONS)

(1 – 12) TINY DICK (& VARIATIONS)

(1 – 13) ASS/ARSE, BUTT/ BUTTOCKS, ASS/ARSEHOLE (SPECIFY)

(1 – 14) DIRTY ASS (& VARIATIONS)

(1 – 15) ASS/ARSE-FUCKER, BUTT-FUCKER, PEDERAST (& VARIATIONS)

(1 – 16) PUSSY, CUNT (& VARIATIONS)

(1 – 17) DIRTY/BLOODY PUSSY (& VARIATIONS)

(1 – 18) HOT PUSSY, NYMPHO (& VARIATIONS)

(1 – 19) PUSSY FACE (& VARIATIONS)

(1 – 20) PUSSY BRAIN (& VARIATIONS)

(1 – 21) PUSSY BREATH (& VARIATIONS)

(1 – 22) TIT/TITTY, TITS/TITTIES, BOOB/BOOBS (& VARIATIONS)

(1 – 23) SUCK TIT/TITTY, SUCK TITS/TITTIES (& VARIATIONS)

(1 – 24) CLITORIS/CLIT (& VARIATIONS)

(1 – 25) HARD-ON (& VARIATIONS)

(1 – 26) ABORTION (& VARIATIONS)

EXCRETORY FUNCTIONS (2 – 0)

(2 – 1) SHIT / SHITTY (& VARIATIONS)

(2 –2) SHIT-HEAD (& VARIATIONS)

(2 – 3) FULL OF SHIT (& VARIATIONS)

(2 – 4) BULLSHIT, TOTAL BULLSHIT (& VARIATIONS)

(2 – 5) EAT SHIT (& VARIATIONS)

(2 – 6) SHIT ON YOU (& VARIATIONS)

(2 – 7) SHIT ON YOUR MOTHER (& VARIATIONS)

(2 – 8) I SHIT IN YOUR MOTHER'S MILK (& VARIATIONS)

(2 – 9) PISS/PISSY (& VARIATIONS)

(2 – 10) PISS HEAD (& VARIATIONS)

(2 – 11) PISS UP A ROPE, PISS OFF (& VARIATIONS)

(2 – 12) I PISS IN YOUR MOTHER'S MILK (& VARIATIONS)

(2 – 13) FART, WHO FARTED (& VARIATIONS)

(2 –14) OLD FART (& VARIATIONS)

SEXUAL FUNCTIONS (3 – 0)
(3 – 1) JERK-OFF, WANKER, SWEET HAND

(3 – 2) COCK-TEASE (& VARIATIONS)

(3 – 3) HORNY, HOT (& VARIATIONS)

(3 – 4) FUCK (SPECIFY NOUN OR VERB, PREFERABLY ONE OF EACH)

(3 – 5) FUCK YOU (& VARIATIONS)

(3 – 6) FUCK YOUR MOTHER/ FUCK YOUR SISTER (& VARIATIONS)

(3 – 7) FUCK YOUR FATHER (& VARIATIONS)

(3 – 8) FUCK YOUR BROTHER (& VARIATIONS)

(3 – 9) FUCK YOUR NIECES & NEPHEWS (& VARIATIONS)

(3 – 10) FUCK YOU UP THE ASS/ARSE (& VARIATIONS)

(3 – 10A) FUCK YOU UP THE ASS/ARSE WITH A BARBIE/KEN/ G.I. JOE DOLL, STAR WARS/ POKEMóN ACTION FIGURE, LIGHT SABRE (& VARIATIONS)

(3 – 11) FUCK YOU IN THE MOUTH (& VARIATIONS)

(3 –12) FUCK YOURSELF (& VARIATIONS)

(3 –13) FUCK ME, FUCK ME SILLY (& VARIATIONS)

(3 – 14) EAT ME (& VARIATIONS)

(3 – 15) BITE ME (& VARIATIONS)

(3 – 16) RUB PUSSY / PUSSY WANK / CLIT WANK (& VARIATIONS)

(3 – 17) EAT PUSSY (& VARIATIONS)

(3 – 18) EAT BLOODY PUSSY (& VARIATIONS)

SOCIAL+SEXUAL DEVIATIONS (4 – 0)
(4 – 1) WHORE, PROSTITUTE (& VARIATIONS)

(4 – 2) MALE PROSTITUTE / MALE WHORE / HUSTLER

(4 – 3) SLUT, NYMPHO (& VARIATIONS)

(4 – 4) DIRTY OLD MAN (& VARIATIONS)

(4 – 5) GAY / FAGGOT / QUEER / SISSY (& VARIATIONS)

(4 – 7) DOMINANT PARTNER, TOP (& VARIATIONS)

(4 – 8) SUBMISSIVE PARTNER, BOTTOM (& VARIATIONS)

(4 – 9) PEDOPHILE, CHILD MOLESTER

(4 – 10) FETISHIST, SHOE FUCKER, PURSE FUCKER (SPECIFY FETISH) (& VARIATIONS)

(4 – 11) CROSS DRESSER / DRAG QUEEN / TRANSVESTITE / TRANSEXUAL / SHE-MALE (PLEASE SPECIFY) (& VARIATIONS)

(4 – 12) S & M, BONDAGE, ROUGH TRADE, LEATHER MAN OR GIRL (& VARIATIONS)

(4 – 13) DOG FUCKER / GOAT FUCKER / SHEEP SHAGGER (SPECIFY BESTIALITY) (& VARIATIONS)

(4 –14) COPROPHILIAC, SHIT EATER (& VARIATIONS)

(4 – 14A) WATER SPORTS, GOLDEN SHOWERS (& VARIATIONS)

(4 – 15) FLASHER, EXHIBITIONIST) (& VARIATIONS)

(4 – 16) PEEPING TOM, VOYEUR (& VARIATIONS)

(4 – 17) ADULTERER, HOME WRECKER, CUCKHOLD (& VARIATIONS)

(4 – 18) CRADLE SNATCHER (& VARIATIONS)

(4 – 19) WHAM BAM THANK YOU MA'AM, PREMATURE EJACULATOR(& VARIATIONS)

(4 – 20) CRACK WHORE (& VARIATIONS)

(4 – 21) TWEAKER (SPEED FREAK) (& VARIATIONS)

(4 – 22) JUNKIE/DIRTY JUNKIE (& VARIATIONS)

(4 – 23) POT, POT-HEAD (& VARIATIONS)

(4 – 24) HUFFER, GLUE/GAS SNIFFER (& VARIATIONS)

(4 – 25) DRUNKARD / ALCOHOLIC (& VARIATIONS)

(4 – 26) VOMIT, SPEW, THROW UP, WORSHIP THE PORCELAIN BOWL, KNEEL AT THE PORCELAIN SHRINE, TECHNICOLOR YAWN, FEED THE FISH

(4 – 27) PIMP / WHOREMONGER / PLAYER (& VARIATIONS)

(4 – 28) DRUG SMUGGLER / -MULE / -COURIER (& VARIATIONS)

(4 – 29) PUNK / PUNKER (& VARIATIONS)

(4 – 30) BUM, DIRTY BUM, VAGRANT (& VARIATIONS)

(4 – 30) RAPE, RAPIST (& VARIATIONS)

MISCELLANEOUS (5 – 0)
(5 – 1) BITCH (& VARIATIONS)

(5 – 2) BASTARD (& VARIATIONS)

(5 – 4) SON OF A WHORE (& VARIATIONS)

(5 – 5) MORON, FUCKWIT (& VARIATIONS)

(5 – 6) IDIOT, RETARD (& VARIATIONS)

(5 –7) STUPID / DUMB / STUPID ASS/ARSE, DUMB ASS/ARSE (& VARIATIONS)

(5 – 9) SENILE (& VARIATIONS)

(5 – 10) MORAL IDIOT (& VARIATIONS)

(5 – 11) LIAR (& VARIATIONS)

(5 – 12) MIND FUCKER, PATHOLOGICAL LIAR (& VARIATIONS)

(5 – 13) DELUSIONAL, CRAZY, & OR FUCKED UP (& VARIATIONS)

(5 – 14) CROOK, GONIF, SHYSTER (& VARIATIONS)

(5 – 15) TIGHT ASS, PRIG, PRUDE (& VARIATIONS)

(5 – 16) INFORMER, FINK, GRASS, STOOL PIGEON (& VARIATIONS)

(5 – 17) SNOTTY, CONCEITED (& VARIATIONS)

(5 – 18) CHICKEN SHIT, SCAREDY-CAT, COWARD, WUSS (& VARIATIONS)

(5- 19) FAT ASS, LAZY, LAZY-ASS (& VARIATIONS)

(5 – 20) SLOB (& VARIATIONS)

(5-21) BIBLE BASHER, GOD FLOGGER, RELIGIOUS FANATIC (& VARIATIONS)

(5 – 22) SECTARIAN (& VARIATIONS)

(5 –23) NOSEY, BOSSY, HALL MONITOR, BULLY (& VARIATIONS)

(5 –24) BUSY BODY, GOSSIP

(5 –25) TIGHT FISTED, MEAN SPIRITED, MISERLY (& VARIATIONS)

(5 –26) GO TO HELL (& VARIATIONS)

(5 – 27) FUCK OFF (& VARIATIONS)

(5 – 28) FUCK OFF & DIE (& VARIATIONS)

(5 –29) SMART ASS, SMARTY PANTS (& VARIATIONS)

(5 – 30) GOD DAMN YOU (& VARIATIONS)

(5 - 31) (HAVE YOU) NO SHAME, SHAMELESS (& VARIATIONS)

(5 –32) LIMP DICK (& VARIATIONS)

(5 – 33) FRIGID / SNOW QUEEN (& VARIATIONS)

(5 – 34) CRIPPLE, GIMP, HUNCHBACK, DWARF, FREAK (& VARIATIONS)

(5 – 35) SPASTIC, SPAZZ (NOUN), SPAZZ OUT (VERB) / (& VARIATIONS)

(5 – 36) MOTOR MOUTH, CHATTERBOX (& VARIATIONS)

(3 – 37) SHUT THE FUCK UP (& VARIATIONS)

(5 – 38) TWO-FACED, HYPOCRITE (& VARIATIONS)

(5 – 39) FASCIST! (& VARIATIONS)

(5 – 40) PINKO COMMIE, ANARCHIST (& VARIATIONS)

(5 – 41) NIHILIST (& VARIATIONS)

(5 – 42) STRIKE-BREAKER/SCAB (& VARIATIONS)

(5 – 43) HIPPIE (& VARIATIONS)

(5 – 44) YUPPIE (& VARIATIONS)

(5 – 45) CONTROL FREAK (& VARIATIONS)

(5 – 46) SKINNY TIE, FOUR-EYES, NERD (OR NURD) (& VARIATIONS) – SPECIFY

(5 - 47) GEEK (& VARIATIONS)

(5 – 48) FOREIGNER – PLEASE SPECIFY ETHNICITY, RELIGION &/OR NATIONALITY – IF POSSIBLE (& VARIATIONS)

(5 – 49) ETHNIC CLEANSING (& VARIATIONS)

(6 – 0 & 7 – 0) SINISTER WISDOM, INCORPORATING YO MAMA
(6 – 1) SINISTER WISDOM: A short fable, folk tale, proberb, bigotry, sick joke, or curdled misanthropy from the specific country & culture. Think the Devi's Dictionary, only much fucking ruder....

YO MAMA /TU MAMA / JOU MAMA (& INFINITE VARIATIONS) (7 – 0)

curse + berate in 69+ languages

being a concise + cunting compendium + verbal pictionary + day-for-night-book + of salaams + salutations + greetings + schadenfreude + unblessings + invective + invidious comparisons + insults + sarcasms + snits + pouts + shit-fits + unkind words + anti-benedictions + obscenities, delicate + indelicate + blasphemies + verbal aggggresssssions + cris-de-coeur + merde-de-jour + esprit de l'escalier + sinister wisdoms + tantrums + thought-crimes + bigotries + dutch courage + tijuana bibles + german sense of humor + aneurysms-for-brunch + other cunt-offs + fucka-youze-allzes + sit-next-to-mezes in approx. 90 languages — give or take a dialectic or uncivil war ...

Printed in the United States
by Baker & Taylor Publisher Services